Women's Place in the Andes

Women's Place in the Andes

ENGAGING DECOLONIAL FEMINIST
ANTHROPOLOGY

Florence E. Babb

UNIVERSITY OF CALIFORNIA PRESS

University of California Press, one of the most distinguished university presses in the United States, enriches lives around the world by advancing scholarship in the humanities, social sciences, and natural sciences. Its activities are supported by the UC Press Foundation and by philanthropic contributions from individuals and institutions. For more information, visit www.ucpress.edu.

University of California Press
Oakland, California

© 2018 by Florence Babb

Library of Congress Cataloging-in-Publication Data

Names: Babb, Florence E., author.
Title: Women's place in the Andes : engaging decolonial feminist
    anthropology / Florence E. Babb.
Description: Oakland, California : University of California Press, [2018] |
    Includes bibliographical references and index. |
Identifiers: LCCN 2018000757 (print) | LCCN 2018004779 (ebook) |
    ISBN 9780520970410 (Ebook) | ISBN 9780520298163 (cloth) |
    ISBN 9780520298170 (pbk : alk. paper)
Subjects: LCSH: Women—Peru—Economic conditions. | Feminist
    anthropology—Peru.
Classification: LCC HQ1572 (ebook) | LCC HQ1572 .B335 2017 (print) |
    DDC 305.40985—dc23
LC record available at https://lccn.loc.gov/2018000757

Manufactured in the United States of America

27 26 25 24 23 22 21 20 19 18
10 9 8 7 6 5 4 3 2 1

Para mis compadres Socorro y Vicente
y para mi ahijada Magaly,
con gratitud y amor

Contents

Illustrations

Acknowledgments

Writing this book, which is based on research spanning four decades of my working life as an anthropologist, has depended on the generous support of many. While I have already thanked those who assisted me in the past in bringing out the half dozen previously published works that now serve as chapters 1–6, the all-new commentary chapters, along with my introduction and conclusion, have further indebted me to a host of individuals and organizations. I name many of them here at the risk of overlooking others, who should nonetheless know that I am deeply grateful for all the doors opened, the spirited words exchanged, and scholarly work critiqued.

I begin by acknowledging my deep debt of gratitude to the late William W. Stein, my graduate advisor, who introduced me to Peru in the mid-1970s and made it possible for me to carry out my doctoral work there. Bill, along with Liz Kennedy, another key graduate mentor, encouraged and inspired my feminist research, and Bill was instrumental in putting me in touch with Blanca Figueroa and Jeanine Anderson, whose friendship continues to this day as I make my regular trips back to Peru. Another close friend and colleague, the late Margery Wolf, was not a Latin Americanist, but her book *A Thrice-Told Tale* (Wolf 1992) helped inspire my own, with its novel use of her past writings along with commentaries to illuminate the present.

Others working in Peru have offered me their feminist insights, Andeanist knowledge, and good-humored support over the years I have worked on this most recent endeavor. Among them I count Cristina Alcalde, Maruja Barrig, Pascha Bueno-Hansen, Carmen Diana Deere, Marisol de la Cadena, Norma Fuller, Amy Cox Hall, Patricia Hammer, Billie Jean Isbell, Rowenn Kalman, Jessaca Leinaweaver, Eshe Lewis, María Emma Mannarelli, Rosario Montoya, Gonzalo Portocarrero, Jason Pribilsky, Viviana Quea, Stephanie Rousseau, Patricia Ruiz Bravo, Linda Seligmann, and Orin Starn. During my 2011–12 sabbatical, I was fortunate to be affiliated with the Instituto de Estudios Peruanos, where research director Ricardo Cuenca, researchers Carmen Yon and Francesca Uccelli, and librarian Virginia García were particularly helpful. My visits to the library at the feminist NGO Flora Tristan led me to Virginia Vargas, whose pioneering feminist activism and scholarship have been a revelation. Other venues where I found helping hands were the Catholic University and the Club Ancash, as well as the NGOs Casa de Panchita (Sofía Mauricio, coordinator) and Chirapaq (Tarcila Rivera, director). Andeanists working in and outside of Peru whose work has inspired me are my friends and colleagues at Carolina, Kathryn Burns, Rudi Colloredo-Mansfeld, Arturo Escobar, Miguel La Serna, and Raúl Necochea López. I want to mention as well the impressive work of Pamela Calla, Andrew Canessa, María Elena García, Amy Lind, June Nash, Susan Paulson, Sarah Radcliffe, Joanne Rappaport, Kay Warren, Mary Weismantel, Krista Van Vleet, and the late Elsa Chaney.

When I launched this work at the University of Florida, friends and colleagues in a Working Group on Race and Indigenous Identities in Latin America and the Caribbean, including Faye Harrison, Maya Stanfield-Mazzi, Efraín Barradas, Maria Rogal, and Leah Rosenberg, were a great sounding board. So were my colleagues Jocelyn Olcott and Cynthia Radding and graduate students at Carolina and Duke in our Working Group on Rethinking Latin American Intersectionalities as I wrapped up my writing. Since I came to Carolina four years ago, colleagues in the Institute for the Study of the Americas, including Latin Americanists Louis Pérez and Lars Schoultz, have offered vital friendship and support. In the Department of Anthropology, Tricia McAnany, Karla Slocum, Don

Nonini, Dorothy Holland, Charles Price, Glenn Hinson, Kia Caldwell, Angela Stuesse, and other members of the Race, Difference, and Power Concentration have been an inspiration.

I would not have been able to pull together and analyze all the material that has gone into this book were it not for my former and current students at the University of Florida and at the University of North Carolina at Chapel Hill. They include Dayuma Albán, Joseph Feldman, Molly Green, Diana McCarley, Jamie Lee Marks, Lucía Stavig, and Dana Williams. Dayuma, Joe, and Jamie assisted me and made travel more fun during trips to Peru, and the others helped me organize material and offered their careful reading and commentary. Along with the University of Iowa, these two universities, Florida and Carolina, have offered me generous support through the Vada Allen Yeomans and the Anthony Harrington endowed professorships, for which I am most grateful.

In thanking those in Huaraz, my deepest appreciation goes to my compadres Juana María del Socorro Sánchez Sandoval and the late Vicente Camino Minaya, along with my goddaughter Magaly Camino Sánchez, her husband, Rafael Castro Ramírez, and her siblings, Tomás Camino Sánchez, Beatriz Camino Sánchez, and Javier Camino Sánchez, for many years of familial connection and affection. Theirs has truly been my home away from home. Blanca Tarazona has been a steadfast friend since my first visit to Huaraz and, in more recent years, Gabriela Antúñez, Noemí López Domínguez, Rafael Meneses Cuadros, Jorge Recharte, Adriana Soldi, Eva Valenzuela, and Steven Wegner have been touchstones whom I have come to count on. José Antonio Salazar, minister of culture, has been an admired friend, one who honored me recently with public recognition of my four decades of contributions to anthropological research in the region. Outside Huaraz, the generous hosts at the Lazy Dog Inn, Diana Morris and Wayne Lamphier, offered a wonderful place to stay on several occasions while I was interviewing in the region. Several friends from Vicos have greatly assisted me in my ongoing research there, most especially current mayor Pablo Cilio Tadeo, and Rocio Meza Sánchez, who assisted me in Vicos and now resides in Lima. In nearby Marcará, Beatriz Rojas and Karina Costilla of the NGO Urpichallay were kind enough to share some of the work they have done with the community of Vicos and more broadly on gender complementarity and Andean cosmovision.

I give special thanks to Virginia Vargas, whom I have long admired for her far-reaching feminist vision and commitment as both a scholar and an activist in Peru, and as a global public intellectual. Gina was kind enough to write the foreword to my book even while meeting some great personal challenges—for which I can only say *mil gracias*. I am deeply indebted to her and grateful for her vote of confidence in my work.

Reed Malcolm at the University of California Press encouraged me in this project from our very first meeting, and his assistant, Zuha Khan, offered steady and friendly assistance as I assembled all the materials for my book. Bill Nelson is a talented mapmaker, and Tasha Moro offered painstaking assistance with a near-final version of the work. I could not have asked for more helpful reviewers than Cristina Alcalde and Andrew Canessa, who made this a far better book than it would have been otherwise, though neither can be held responsible for any remaining deficiencies. I also benefited from the excellent work of copyeditor Bonita Hurd, production editor Emilia Thiuri, and indexer Victoria Baker.

Finally, Victoria Rovine, life partner *extraordinaire*, has continued over many years to read all my work and sprinkle it not only with brilliant suggestions but also with motivating hearts, stars, and exclamation points. To that I add the delicious meals and excellent caregiving that I am at a loss to return in kind or to repay sufficiently in thanks. I hereby promise, Vicki, that I will rise to the occasion when your next book is in the final throes of creative activity—something you should be able to collect on soon.

·   ·   ·   ·   ·

The following published materials are interwoven into the five new sections.

Portions of the introduction were published in Spanish in *Desigualdades entrelazadas: Repensando la raza, el género y el indigenismo en el Perú andino*, in *Racismo y lenguaje*, ed. Virginia Zavala and Michele Back (Lima: Fondo Editorial PUCP, 2017). Chapter 1 is reprinted with permission of Transaction Publishers. Originally published as "Women and Men in Vicos: A Peruvian Case of Unequal Development," in *Peruvian Contexts of Change*, ed. William W. Stein, 163–210 (New Brunswick, NJ: Transaction Press, 1985). Chapter 2 is reprinted with permission of the

Review of Radical Political Economics. Originally published as "Women in the Marketplace: Petty Commerce in Peru," *Review of Radical Political Economics* 16 (1): 45–59 (1984). Chapter 3 is reprinted with permission of ABC-CLIO, LLC, Santa Barbara, CA. Originally published as "Producers and Reproducers: Andean Marketwomen in the Economy," in *Women and Change in Latin America,* ed. June Nash and Helen I. Safa, 53–64. South Hadley, MA: Bergin and Garvey, 1986). Chapter 4 is reprinted with permission of Stanford University Press. Originally published as "Market/Places as Gendered Spaces: Market/Women's Studies over Two Decades," in *Women Traders in Cross-Cultural Perspective: Mediating Identities, Marketing Wares,* ed. Linda J. Seligmann, 228–239 (Stanford, CA: Stanford University Press, 2001). Chapter 5 is reprinted with permission of *Urban Anthropology.* Originally published as "Women's Work: Engendering Economic Anthropology," *Urban Anthropology* 19 (3): 277–302 (1990). Chapter 6 is reprinted with permission of *Latin American Perspectives.* Originally published as "Theorizing Gender, Race, and Cultural Tourism in Latin America: A View from Peru and Mexico," *Latin American Perspectives* 39 (6): 36–50 (2012).

Foreword

Florence Babb's book *Women's Place in the Andes: Engaging Decolonial Feminist Anthropology* is particularly valuable, not only because of the complex reality she analyzes—Andean Peru—but also because of the historical perspective that she opens to us. This work is in many ways pioneering, recovering the paths of feminist reflection and analysis of the twentieth century and then rendering them more complex. She discards or embraces feminist genealogies in light of new theoretical reflections and epistemologies developed more fully in the twenty-first century, drawing on the decolonial thinking that feminism has contributed to so significantly.

Babb has based her work of recovery on a rich review of the arguments of decolonial theorists of today, as well as on her scholarly production on the Peruvian Andes from the 1970s to the present, in order to assess both the errors and the successes in her research. But there is more: Babb's work opens a critical, self-critical, and revelatory space, which becomes clearer and more complex as it is analyzed in relation to the advances of the present. This analysis of the past from the viewpoint of the present, as proposed by Antonio Gramsci, is one of the central contributions of her book. She makes the research and production of knowledge a living experience, a knowledge continually revisited, moving away from any absolute and immovable truth.

This is not just a theoretical exercise. Florence Babb's earlier works included in this volume illuminate the construction of feminist trajectories in Peru from their beginnings in the 1970s to the current context. And that is of singular importance: the feminist insights and contributions of this period were enormous, and yet the frames of reflection were also conditioned by the reality of the country, the exclusions and Lima-centrism, and the ethnic, racial, sexual, and generational hierarchies. During that time in Peru, one of the most important discoveries for feminism was the emergence of and alliance with the vibrant grassroots women's movement, as seen in the work of María Elena Moyano and many other activist leaders—several of whom were, like Moyano, persecuted by the terrorist group Shining Path and many times also by the so-called forces of order. Without this powerful side of the women's movement, it would not have been possible for Peruvian feminisms to develop a generative political perspective on sexuality and social class.

This was a historical moment in which feminisms developed a deep questioning of social and political organizations that unquestionably excluded women, opening the kaleidoscope to a more intersectional perspective. Feminist efforts to incorporate other key dimensions, including the ethno-racial, had been forestalled because urban Peruvians lacked the language to name a reality that was only then emerging. Even within this context, as Babb notes, there were pioneering works such as that of Marfil Francke, whose analysis of the "braid of oppression" combined class, race/ethnicity, and gender. This was an enormous proposition in a context in which class was the dominant frame of analysis and where race, sexuality, and women (gender as an analytic had not yet been conceptualized) remained invisible in the eyes of many researchers and of activists in other social movements.

Florence Babb's singular, honest, and creative reflection recovers and critiques what has developed through these past forty years as she mobilizes the development of feminist anthropological thought in relation to the development of Peruvian feminist thought. This is a great contribution.

Virginia Vargas
Lima, Peru

Peru and the Ancash region

Introduction

RETHINKING GENDER, RACE, AND
INDIGENEITY IN ANDEAN PERU

Over dinner with longtime friends during a sabbatical in Peru several
years ago, I recalled that thirty years had passed since we had all participated in the landmark Congress on Research on Women in the Andean
Region, an international gathering held at Lima's Catholic University in
1982. My three friends were residents of Peru, but for me the conference
had marked my first trip back to the country, five years after completing
my doctoral research and two years into what is sometimes called the *vio-
lencia,* the protracted period of conflict between the guerrilla movement
Sendero Luminoso (Shining Path) and national military forces.[1]

My sabbatical research in 2011–12, a reexamination of gender, race, and
indigenous identity in Andean Peru in light of past debates and more
recent feminist intellectual and political currents, had transported me
back to that earlier time. I had visited my usual field site in Huaraz, two
hundred miles north of Lima and ten thousand feet up in the Andes, but
during this yearlong affiliation with the Instituto de Estudios Peruanos, I
took up residence and carried out research in Lima for a longer period
than I had done in the past. When I was not conducting interviews across
the sprawling city, I explored Lima's libraries and research centers. In the
IEP's own library I came across a copy of the pale-blue-covered *informe*

1

final (final report) of the congress, something I had at home but had not pulled off the shelf in many years. Seeing it again after so long, I was reminded that over 120 invited participants had presented research papers on a host of subjects, from the work of women in the rural sector to their labor as migrants in the urban informal and formal sectors; their organizations and social movements; their strategies for carrying out domestic responsibilities, particularly in the popular sectors; and finally, participants' feminist research methodologies. My host at dinner that night, Jeanine Anderson, had written the final report (Anderson de Velasco 1983), and she recounted stories from the congress that were still vivid in her memory.

At that gathering three decades earlier in Lima, participants had had a clear sense of history in the making. Research on Andean women could scarcely be traced earlier than the 1970s, when feminism had begun to galvanize researchers to take women's lives seriously as subjects in themselves.[2] Moreover, this was a time of growing recognition of the transformative effect such scholarship might have on our understanding of societies more broadly within the humanities and social sciences. In a landmark moment in feminism's advance, the United Nations declared 1975 International Women's Year and convened a congress in Mexico City; at the urging of attendees, 1976–85 was named the Decade for Women. This was the era of "women and development" (Boserup 1970); and not long after the first UN conference, an academic gathering at Wellesley College (Wellesley Editorial Committee 1977) was instrumental in promoting feminist perspectives that challenged the Western development agenda, which generally had either overlooked women or expected them to carry extra burdens. Peru itself was on the map for its early feminist activism and research, and in 1983 Lima became the site of the second continental Latin American feminist *encuentro* (gathering). It was a time of passionate activity, even as the nation experienced a deepening conflict and time of fear during the confrontation between Sendero Luminoso and the military.[3]

At this historical juncture, the pioneering research on Andean women emergent in the 1970s tended toward two divergent poles: analyses that emphasized the "complementarity" of gender roles in the rural sector and suggested that a gender hierarchy was the result of externally imposed ideas and practices, whether from colonialism or contemporary urban

The author in Vicos, Peru, 2015. Photo by Dayuma Albán.

culture, and analyses that, in contrast, held that patriarchal relations were rooted in "traditional" rural communities and would be altered only with "modernization" (Babb [1976] 1985b; Isbell [1978] 1985; Bourque and Warren 1981a, 1981b). My work during this period focused on the well-known community of Vicos, a former hacienda that had been the site of a major project in applied anthropology in the 1950s and early 1960s. In many ways, the initial debates on the lives and prospects of Andean women set an agenda whose traces extend through the present, though the pace of research in Peru's rural sector slowed substantially for well over a decade as a consequence of the violence in the country.[4]

Notwithstanding the stalled pace of scholarly activity and feminist debate, a small number of researchers continued sporadic work on the Peruvian Andes (and migration to the coast) in the turbulent 1980s; while some took a symbolic approach to gender and cultural difference, relying on "Andean continuities" to account for an enduring gender complementarity, more adopted a historically grounded approach (Bunster and Chaney 1985; Silverblatt 1987; Seligmann 1989; Babb [1989] 1998). There had been too much social disruption to cling to such essentialized notions of *lo andino* (the Andean) without examining forces of change.[5] My own work, including my presentation at the 1982 congress, reflected a shift from attention to complementary gender roles in rural Peru to increasing interest in women's productive and reproductive activities as market women and household workers in commercial centers in the Andes. In many cases, both of these approaches—those embracing the complementarity and the production/reproduction frameworks—were influenced by currents in Marxist feminism, and in historical materialism more broadly, and they sought to valorize and assess women's distinct contributions as workers in the gender division of labor. In the case of urban marketers, I showed, women's work was vital to the economy even as they were frequently scapegoats for harsh economic conditions of that time.

By the mid-1990s, Peru was emerging from the internal war that had cost nearly seventy thousand lives, a loss suffered most notably in the southern Andes but throughout the nation as well. There was a gradual normalization of activity, though the deep emotional wounds of that time have been much slower to heal. As the nation sought an economic recovery, it looked not only to mining and agriculture but also to tourism as long-standing prospects for development; however, it would take another decade before many tourists were attracted once again not only to Peru's archaeological sites and the natural environment, which were perceived as safe, but also to its cultural-tourism sites and to Andean people themselves. My recent work on tourism in postconflict Latin America considered the Peruvian case as one in which memories often needed to be deeply suppressed. Indigenous women and men had a significant part to

A rural visitor to Lima's Lugar de la Memoria (memory museum), 2016. Photo by author.

play in restoring confidence in the nation's rich cultural heritage and in attracting tourist dollars. My interest during the first decade of the new millennium lay in the workings of gender and power in representations of cultural tradition as Peru began to show record economic growth and rising cultural cachet as a land of treasures, culinary delights, and diverse peoples—even as social inequalities remained deeply entrenched. Feminist and related scholarship in Peru, by this time including an increasing number of works by Peruvian researchers, had turned toward postcolonial concerns over inclusion, exclusion, and the gendered nature of citizenship participation (Ruiz Bravo 1996; de la Cadena 2000; Barrig 2001, 2007; Fuller 2004; García 2005; Mendoza 2008; Ewig 2010; Rousseau 2009; Babb 2011).

FROM GENDER COMPLEMENTARITY
TO DECOLONIAL FEMINISMS

The present volume of my selected past writings accompanied by newly written material—this introduction, three commentaries, and the conclusion—was conceived as an opportunity to revisit, from a contemporary perspective, feminist currents in Andean research from the 1970s to the present. It is not simply my conceit, as someone who undertook research on Andean Peru in the midseventies, to suggest that this is the logical starting point. Rather, that decade was fairly remarkable in Peru and much of the world for the gathering momentum of feminism as both social movement and scholarly initiative. Feminists have cast a glance at the period to see what we can glean, given our current vantage point, regarding this heady time when students, scholars, and members of communities demanded that women be better represented in texts and teaching, as well as in society (*Feminist Studies* 2008).[6] In my view, contemporary feminist politics and scholarship have returned in significant and innovative ways to issues first raised in the 1970s that are well worth discussing. In what follows I consider how the recent "decolonial turn" in scholarly and political practice can benefit from a reexamination of earlier feminist debates, just as these debates may be illuminated and critiqued with the benefit of new insights of decolonial feminisms.[7]

As I began reflecting on my own research experience in Peru spanning four decades (interspersed with periods of work in Nicaragua, Cuba, and Mexico that lent useful comparative insights), I came to realize that I was nearly alone among scholars of my generation who began working on gender questions in Andean Peru in the 1970s and sustained that interest even after forays into other research areas. I rather immodestly felt that others might benefit from my revisiting the shifting currents of feminist thought that characterized these decades. This might be a sterile exercise were it not for the many ways in which insights and conversations from the past continue to inform the present or, sometimes, provide a foil against which present formulations are constructed. What I discovered in reexamining my writings over these decades was the degree to which they represent the preoccupations of feminists seeking to make sense of gender-based and other social inequalities during the respective time periods when they were written.

Readers will judge whether these works are truly exemplary of feminist scholarship during those years, but I contend that these essays can tell us something useful about ways of understanding gender, race, and ethnicity in the Andes, and about feminist social analysis more broadly—including our omissions and blind spots. In some instances, I made interventions that were timely and original, though in other cases I was surely standing on the shoulders of those whose work inspired me, whether they addressed the Andes or other world regions. Most assuredly, readers will discover where I ran up against my personal limitations as well as the limitations of that time. The works selected for this volume were published, but in some cases in out-of-the-way places, so bringing them together here provides an opportunity to consider them in new ways. Moreover, for a younger generation coming to this material for the first time, it may be instructive to discover what feminists have been debating in recent decades and how it transformed our thinking about the Andean region and the world.

I would not be content simply to present a volume of collected essays, however; and indeed my project, in returning to Peru in recent years, has been somewhat more ambitious. My desire has been, in the five new and substantive pieces, to reopen questions and debates from the past and to stage conversations with authors and their texts, as well as with activists and ordinary Peruvians, in order to subject my earlier work to critical scrutiny. Although in my past work I sought to include the interpretations of my Peruvian research subjects and of Peruvian and other Andean writers, I have come to believe that a much fuller and richer dialogue is necessary between researchers and analysts of the global North and South—most notably, in this case, with those from Peru. Only an intercultural dialogue such as this will advance us beyond the sedimented debates of the past and the entrenched Euro-American frameworks that have continued to dominate much of feminist research and writing. Moreover, the passage of time allows for a more nuanced rethinking of earlier work, because it can be set in a fuller historical context. To that end, the chapters that follow reproduce original works with only minor editing for clarity, so that we may see them as they appeared when first published.

The rethinking that led to this book is the result of fruitful scholarly discussion and activism that has shaped my work. I can identify three closely interrelated influences that built upon one another and animated my interest in this project in feminist intellectual history. The first was the opportunity I had during my sabbatical in 2011–12 to spend five months in Peru, where I read more widely from the work of Peruvian scholars and discussed with a number of them interpretations of their work as well as my own. This enabled me to put my work into conversation with a vibrant body of literature. As a form of productive scholarly inquiry, my engagement with these scholars and their works provided the basis for what I hope will be a useful self-critique and a greater appreciation for Peru's impressive intellectual culture. In addition to this time spent largely in Lima, I made ten trips to my Andean field site in Huaraz between 2006 and 2017, when I conducted ethnographic field research to gather new material on gender, race, and cultural identity in the contemporary context. This recent work, including participant observation and interviews with rural and urban community members and provincial leaders and scholars, has also informed my current rethinking. Added to these trips to Peru during the past decade are, of course, the five research trips I made between 1977 and 1997, which were the basis for much of my earlier writing.[8]

Second, and closely related, I have been influenced by the call among a number of my colleagues for a decentering of anthropologies based in the United States and Europe and for a critical geopolitical restructuring that will recognize and engage diverse world anthropologies. Scholars have demonstrated that there are other knowledges, notably those emanating from the global South, which those of us in the global North must recognize and learn from; if we do not, we may expect to see the declining relevance of our field (Bošković 2010).[9] We need to give critical attention to how ideas travel, to engage with scholars across borders, to be mindful of how our positionality may advantage or disadvantage us, and ultimately, to challenge the current politics of knowledge. Such an approach will make our scholarship both more inclusive and more meaningful in shaping a just world. To this end, in recent years I have organized and participated in conference sessions that aim to produce the sort of dialogue that is needed if we wish to do the hard work of transforming scholarship. These sessions and my work on our professional association's Committee on World Anthropologies have contributed to the conceptualization behind this volume and position me to embrace what Ribeiro and Escobar (2006: 1) have called "the possibility of establishing new conditions and terms of conversability among anthropologists on a global level."

Third, and significantly to this project, recent discussion concerning the decolonial turn and decolonial feminisms has been highly generative in my rethinking of gender, race, and indigeneity in Andean Peru. The project, known by some interdisciplinary scholars as modernity/coloniality/decoloniality (Mignolo and Escobar 2010), draws on key insights regarding the "coloniality of power" (Quijano 2000) advanced earlier by leading political theorists of the South, including Frantz Fanon in Algeria and José Carlos Mariátegui in Peru. Given my focus here, it is worth noting that Peruvians have played an important part in the development of a decolonial theory and method. Mignolo (2010) begins with Guamán Poma de Ayala's sixteenth-century indigenous critique of colonial Spanish rule, and goes on to Mariátegui's influential writing in the 1920s on the "Indian problem," which, although collapsing race into class, revealed the structural underpinnings of poverty and the pivotal role of indigenous and laboring peoples in struggles for change. We should also include liberation theology's Gustavo Gutiérrez, who in the 1960s and 1970s reframed Christian understanding from the vantage point of the poor, and Aníbal Quijano, whose seminal work in the 1990s examined the colonial and racialized apparatus of power that continues to condition relations of class, gender, and sexuality in society. Nevertheless, we will see that decolonial feminists critique Quijano and others for naturalizing gender and failing to recognize that it is as malleable as race over the course of history and is conditioned as much by colonialism.

The *decolonial turn* (Maldonado-Torres 2011: 6) is an abbreviated way of describing an ambitious project to decolonize knowledge, to challenge Eurocentric frameworks and replace these northern interpretive frames with others emerging from diverse sites, often from the South. Sources of such reframing include the creative thought of indigenous political leaders and intellectuals who offer radically new ways of thinking about cultural difference and social inequality, and who contend that "another world is possible." Such an individual was the renowned twentieth-century Peruvian novelist, poet, and ethnologist José María Arguedas, the son of a mestizo lawyer, but who was largely raised by the Quechua-speaking indigenous women his father employed. Marisol de la Cadena (2006: 203), herself a Peruvian anthropologist who has had a major influence on refiguring received knowledge about "Indians" and mestizos, counts Arguedas among the key contributors to an anthropology "otherwise," as he resisted Eurocentric binaries in his life and his profession. Unfortunately, during his lifetime Arguedas's effort to introduce an intercultural understanding was dismissed by his modernist colleagues who had adopted universalist and hegemonic conceptual frameworks from the North. The writer-scholar truly was ahead of his time, and it was not until a hundred years after his birth that his ethnology was better conceived as presaging contemporary views on the complexity and variability of indigeneity and cultural identity.[10] Today, scholarship on Latin America is in general more attentive to the collaborative development of *otros saberes* (other knowledges), including those of indigenous and Afro-descendant peoples (Hale and Stephen 2013).

The sort of epistemic break with past (colonial) conceptual frameworks that decolonial theorists are advocating is also found in the work of some feminist theorists and activists. The potential power of this feminist orientation for reassessing scholarship on Andean women resonated for me when I heard Aymara lesbian feminist activist Julieta Paredes speak at a Latin American Studies Association conference some years ago; she was on a panel that engaged the thought of feminist philosopher María Lugones and others who have argued for decolonizing feminist scholarship and political activism. I was impressed by what I heard from the Bolivian self-described "communitarian feminist," which recalled for me the work of Aymara sociologist Silvia Rivera Cusicanqui, who might also be considered a radical decolonial (anarchist) feminist. This reorientation of radical feminist thought can be found in the "border" thinking of Gloria Anzaldúa, the antiracist theorizing of bell hooks, the postcolonial writing of Gayatri Spivak, and the transnationalism of Chandra Mohanty and Jacqui Alexander. We may find pioneering feminist contributions to decolonizing and transformative projects in the field of anthropology, including the work of Faye Harrison ([1991] 1997) and Ruth Behar and Deborah Gordon (1995).[11]

I discovered in the writings of Bolivians Julieta Paredes and María Galindo (Galindo and Paredes 1992, Paredes and Galindo n.d.) a grassroots effort to bring about an epistemological shift to recuperate a diverse community that they contend was lost with colonialist and patriarchal rule. Through street theater, urban graffiti, and writing directed to a broad social sector (including "spoken books" on DVD for those who do not read Spanish), they practice a popular feminism that is deeply radical, praising women's unsung valor and decrying men's part in undermining women, and which bears the traces of an indigenous Andean worldview, or "cosmovision." This may be contrasted with the more deeply theorized work of Lugones (2010b), which contends that our current concept of gender (and of heterosexuality) was a colonial imposition that must be challenged so that we may have a less distorted understanding of relations of race, gender, and sexuality, past and present. Aiming to bring greater precision to Quijano's notion of gender in the "coloniality of power" axis, based on European constructions of race and gender, Lugones (2010a) draws on the historical interventions of scholars, principally women of color, who have argued that, before colonization, women and men experienced much greater equilibrium; her conclusion is that gender, undertheorized by Quijano, is just as much a historical construction as race. For Paredes and Lugones, the "coloniality of gender" does not presume fully egalitarian relations in precolonial times but suggests that more complementary gender relations predated the later asymmetrical power relationships of men and women.[12]

To my surprise, I discovered the resonance of Lugones's and Paredes's positions with those of some feminists (myself included) writing on gender and race in the Andes going back to the 1970s. My commentaries in this volume address the similarities and differences in feminist theorizing and debate then and now. I ask, for example, whether the Andean complementarity perspective, which has been criticized as overessentialist and idealized, is redeemed in light of insights gained from decolonial feminisms.[13] Preconquest Andean cosmology, a principle of dualisms—night/day, sun/moon, male/female, and so on—and a gendered notion of reciprocity, has been said to account for the gender division of labor whereby women's work is more closely attached to the household and to certain aspects of agriculture such as sowing seeds, while men are more often involved in the use of the plow and in harvesting, as well as in publicly representing households in the community. This account of enduring gender relations in the Andes has been viewed by some as romanticized and as failing to explain incidences of gendered violence and of the exclusion of women from certain spheres of social life.

Could a decolonial feminist view of complementarity bring greater recognition to the significant place of women in household economies based on an ethics of interdependence and reciprocity, as well as address gendered violence and exclusion where it occurs? Or might it explain away all evidence of inequality as a legacy of a colonial past? I also question whether other feminist frameworks utilized in Andean research during the past few decades—including the production/reproduction conceptualization and the postcolonial analytic of intersecting relations of race, gender, and power—presaged a decolonial feminism, or whether they were too wedded to dualistic Eurocentric frames of knowledge to adequately challenge received ways of knowing.

I subject my own work to such questioning and, ultimately, the answers I come to are of the both/and variety rather than any singular reclaiming or disavowal of earlier positions. What I find most compelling is the new vigor that the decolonial turn brings to the discussion of past, present, and future feminist debates; it enables us to complicate and challenge overreductionist views of gender inequality in the Andes as stemming from persistent cultural "tradition" without questioning modernist assumptions—not to mention decades and even centuries of change in rural Peru. Whether it offers something new to our understanding of gender and race in Andean Peru or simply (but significantly) validates and fortifies some earlier, alternative perspectives remains to be seen. I return to the question in the final chapter of this book.

DISCOURSES OF RACE IN PERU

Three decades after the Congress on Research on Women in the Andean Region, I was back in Peru and dividing my time between Huaraz, my

A young woman from the community of Vicos, collaborating with the author in her research, interviews another Vicosina, 2012. Photo by author.

longtime research site in the north-central Andean region, and Lima, where I would carry out library research, conduct ethnographic work, and engage in the city's robust political and intellectual culture. From my vantage point at the IEP, it was impossible to overlook the vibrant and renewed interest in social inequality in Peru, largely focused on ethnicity, race, and class and only rarely bringing gender or sexuality into the discussion. One of my principal objectives in publishing this book is to bring together in conversation several important strands in the often disparate scholarship on race and gender. I reexamine my own work in light of current thinking about race, indigeneity, and gender in Peru, which has implications extending more broadly in the Andean region.

I arrived in Peru in August 2011, soon after President Ollanta Humala was installed in office, and at a time when the nation was divided in its expectations of what might lie ahead. While Humala had been elected on the promise of real change favoring the disenfranchised, more-conservative Peruvians were relieved when he selected close advisors who were inclined to shore up the status quo. Peru had seen significant economic growth in recent years, and observers in and outside the country hoped to see policy that would support that trajectory. At the same time, certain changes were introduced during Humala's early months in office, including the establishment of a new Ministry of Social Inclusion, with a feminist rural sociologist from the IEP, Carolina Trivelli, named as its first minister. The rhetoric of popular participation was broadcast widely, including on a government-sponsored TV channel devoted to the national congress's activity, with constant promotional spots announcing the new law of informed prior consent, intended to give indigenous communities the right to respond to plans for development projects that would affect them; another endless series of spots heralded the wealth of Peru's indigenous heritage and the law against life-threatening violence against women. Over the course of his first year, Humala would face the rising demands of mine workers and their allies concerned with labor conditions and the degradation of the environment, disappointing many activists who had hoped he would take a more progressive stance. While he was carried into office on a wave of popularity greater than his predecessors', Humala exhibited ambivalence toward his constituencies as he structured and restructured government posts, casting about to define his direction as president.

Since the mid-twentieth century, steady migration from the Andean region has contributed to vast population growth in cities, especially Lima, whose metropolitan area is now home to around ten million residents in a nation of more than thirty-two million.[14] Contributing to the conditions that already propelled migration—the possibility of work in the proliferating informal sector of the service economy, the desire for higher education, and the lack of adequate opportunities in the rural sector—was the violence of the 1980s and 1990s that instilled fear in many Andean communities and, indeed, throughout the nation. Where I conduct research in the Ancash region, a horrific earthquake in 1970 had earlier forced many survivors to depart from their homes for an uncertain future on the coast, and still more migrated after 1980. During my recent research in Lima, I took advantage of the IEP's close proximity to Club Ancash, founded in 1949 by well-established migrants who wished to retain their connections to their birthplace and their cultural identities as Ancashinos. My frequent visits to the social club revealed the pride mem-

Club Ancash, a regional association for migrants from Ancash living in Lima, 2012.
Photo by author.

bers had in their roots, but I also heard their lament that the older generation of migrants to Lima might be the last to retain meaningful cultural
connections to the region and to speak Quechua as well as Spanish.

Many scholars have examined migration in Peru (Matos Mar [1984]
2010), the nation's racial geographies (Orlove 1993, 1998), and the shifting meanings of being indigenous and mestizo in Peru (de la Cadena
2000; Greene 2009). More attention has begun to turn to the new urban
cultures that have emerged as a result, including youth culture and the
diverse ethnic, racial, and sexual identities found in a city as socially complex as Lima (Bracamonte Allaín 2001). While many rural-urban migrants
attempt to shed the most obvious trappings of their indigenous, or
campesino (rural peasant), identities, a growing number embrace hybrid
cultural identities as cholos, a term long used to refer to those who manifest characteristics and preferences associated with both rural and urban
Peru (Quijano 1980). A hybrid *chicha* culture (as the phenomenon

resulting from rural migration to Lima is known), expressed through dress, music, and cuisine, has proved particularly attractive among a younger population and has pervaded the popular culture as a selling point in advertising and design (Mejía Chiang 2011; Bailón and Nicoli 2010). Chicha music blasts in Lima's markets, and trendy restaurants offer a fusion of Andean and continental items on their menus. Politically edgy T-shirts celebrate cultural diversity: *cholo power, selva power* (referring to the Amazon region), and *esperanza Peru* (Peru's hope) are boldly emblazoned along with bright-pink-and-green images of proud denizens of the Andes and Amazon regions.

It is important to note the relative absence of attention to Afro-Peruvian culture, history, and identity at the national level. While the percentage of Afro-Peruvians in Peru's population, mainly located on the coast, is variously represented at anywhere from 2 to 10 percent, the popular under-representation of this demographic component of Peru's racial geography is pronounced. Afro-Peruvian music is well known, though rarely the focus of scholarly attention (Feldman 2006), while the history and cultural identities of Afro-descendant Peruvians, including those who do not recognize their heritage in Africa, has gradually begun to receive more serious attention (Cuche 1975; Golash-Boza 2011). Television programming is better known for its mockery of Afro-Peruvians than for breaking down barriers to their full inclusion in society. Discrimination and marginalization continue to be significant problems to which state and civil society are only now awakening. When Humala named the internationally acclaimed singer Susana Baca as his minister of culture, it was the first appointment of an Afro-Peruvian to so high a level in government; however, she was expected to have insufficient time for the position, given her devotion to performing and, in fact, was soon replaced. When Peruvians honored the twentieth anniversary of the death of María Elena Moyano, an urban activist slain by Sendero Luminoso in 1992, many noted her significance as an Afro-Peruvian martyr. Meanwhile, the commercial potential of Afro-Peruvian culture as a tourism draw has been discovered, for better or worse, and tours are now taken to the town of Chincha in the Ica region to the south of Lima.[15] Feminists and other social movement activists are now more careful to be inclusive of Afro-Peruvians, an encouraging sign for the future, but exclusionary practices are still highly evident.

It is fair to ask *who* exactly embraces the new hybrid identities that appear to be reclaiming formerly shunned traditions and asserting a right to be culturally different. Arguably, it is Lima youth with middle-class privilege who can risk being associated with cultural traditions of the Andean and Amazonian regions that their own parents sought to leave behind when they came to the city. Those with cash on hand may buy trendy (and not inexpensive) T-shirts, shoulder bags, and caps that announce their countercultural leanings.

One young woman I met on the *metropolitano,* Lima's bus system that speeds across the city, went so far as to display on her body a particularly striking symbol of the identity she wished to embrace. In her twenties and wearing a stylish black-and-white striped dress and fashionable shoes, and with a colorful streak in her dark hair, she sported a prominent tattoo around her neck reading "Cholo soy" (I'm cholo) in black lettering framed in a block of solid red. Opening a friendly conversation with her as we stood swaying in the crowded bus, I asked about her tattoo and why she had gotten it. She seemed surprised by my question yet pleased to talk and told me it was to reclaim her cultural heritage and express pride in being Peruvian. I asked if she was concerned about the permanence of her self-expression, and she told me confidently that she would always feel just as she does now. When I went on to inquire why she had not chosen the feminine version, "Chola soy," she replied thoughtfully that she was aiming for a more global sentiment, going beyond gender. She agreed that the meaning conveyed by *chola* would be different, commenting that it might be diminished given the force of machismo. A fledgling artist, her self-presentation seemed to be very much a product of her time, a study in the contrasts of a modern, urban hip culture and an in-your-face identity politics specific to Peru. In fact, for those in the know, "Cholo soy" refers to the song made famous by Luis A. Morales decades ago, with the refrain "Cholo soy y no me compadezcas" (I'm a cholo, and don't feel sorry for me).

Peruvian social scientists, past and present, have looked closely at persistent inequalities in the country that seem to lock Andeans in Lima in a position of second-class citizenship even as a small number climb their way to middle-class status through hard work and good fortune. Those who manage to find success, to acquire homes and property and send their children to good schools, are often resented by the older elite *blancos,* who

Young woman in a Lima shop selling trendy *cholito* T-shirts and other items, 2012.
Photo by author.

fear their own displacement from a secure place in society's top echelon.
Even progressive Limeños go to some length to explain their concern that
the recently arrived and newly rich are causing such social dislocation that
the world they knew might soon be overwhelmed by undeserving and
aggressive newcomers. This attitude contributes to the unthinking, racialized ways in which Peruvians differentiate themselves from one another, a
practice now referred to as *choleando,* one group looking down on another
and being subordinated by still another (Bruce 2007).

While I have noted the rich possibilities for deepening understanding
of the intersectional workings of discrimination by race, class, and gender,
it is striking that current scholarship on *desigualdad* (inequality) rarely
considers gender. Two edited collections that emerged from an IEP conference on the topic, as well as a coauthored book, bring out important
analyses of the contradictions of a growing and triumphalist national
economy in which the inequality gap persists (Cueto and Lerner 2011;

A Lima store offering Andean women's skirts (*polleras*) and other regional items to urban consumers, 2016. Photo by author.

Cotler and Cuenca 2011; Thorp and Paredes 2010). Systematic research findings are presented on disparities in employment opportunity, education, health care, and development, along with broad theoretical discussions of shifting currents and advances in analysis. There is attention to culture, identity, democracy, and citizenship rights, as well as to discrimination, social conflict, and social movements in the current context of Peru and the Andean region. Related to my objectives here, these works focus particular attention on the consequences of social exclusion and inequality for the indigenous population in Peru, showing how persistent exploitation via the economy, politics, and a racialized geography result in sharply distorted social relations.

Yet only rarely does gender enter in, as when Patricia Ames (2011: 34) argues for a recognition of the interlaced ways in which racism combines with other vectors of social inequality in Peru. Following earlier research, she comments perceptively that at the present time there may be less discrimination based on the color of one's skin, but that there is continued discrimination against women from the high Andes who wear *polleras* (full Andean skirts), who come from zones judged to be more indigenous. She concludes that the indigenous, the racial, and the ethnic are defined today in territorial terms, signaling the durability of social inequality even as it takes new forms. It is not at all coincidental that the Andean woman in braids and pollera is the emblematic figure in the national imagination representing the last vestiges of a "backward" and recalcitrant culture that is still on its way to extinction. In the same vein, Marisol de la Cadena (2000) contributes a nuanced discussion of the complex ways in which race and ethnicity, and often gender and sexuality, have been configured in the Cuzco region over the twentieth century, showing how earlier intellectual currents of *indigenismo*, resting on notions of cultural difference, have manifested in contemporary Peru.

With the "return of the Indian" in the Andean region (especially in Bolivia and Ecuador) as a result of a rising consciousness of race and racial discrimination accompanied by growing indigenous social movements,[16] scholarship has moved apace to consider the current salience of historical legacies of cultural and racial difference. In Peru, where there has been less activism, and where many rural Quechua-speakers prefer to call themselves campesinos rather than *indígenas* (persons of indigenous descent), a number of scholars argue that there is nonetheless sufficient evidence of cultural consciousness, not to mention discrimination based on cultural attributes, to warrant greater attention to race and cultural identity among Andean people living in rural and urban Peru (e.g., García 2005).

Some, like political scientist Martín Tanaka, examine the material basis for race and racism and posit that it can be traced to unequal conditions in Peru; in contrast to many others, Tanaka expects that racism will decline with further modernization and as disenfranchised groups resist its harsh effects.[17] Psychologist Jorge Bruce (2007: 11), a public intellectual who is a strong critic of racism, searches the national psyche and finds that Peruvians have failed to "decolonize their minds," an argument made earlier by sociologist Gonzalo Portocarrero (2009), one of the keenest observers of the damaging effects of racism in the country. Historian Nelson Manrique (1999) considers the naturalization and internalization of racism, and the mechanisms of state control that support it. By and large, Peruvian scholars examining race relations tend toward agreement with the critical assessment set out in the classic work of historian Alberto Flores Galindo (1987) and elaborated as the "coloniality of power" by Quijano (2000), but only rarely do they take gender into account in discussions of social inequality. My interest, expressed particularly in part 3 of this book, is in the significant, if ambivalent, ways in which gender, race, and cultural heritage intertwine to position Andean women as the quintessential subjects of both national pride and everyday scorn and neglect in Peru.

DISCOURSES OF GENDER IN ANDEAN PERU

Since the 1970s, feminist analysts have discussed the interconnections of gender, race, and ethnicity (and less often, sexuality) in the Andes, although not often in conversation with the work of scholars writing on *desigualdad* mentioned above. These analysts were divided between those who viewed gender inequality as rooted in indigenous peasant communities, and those who argued that indigenous gender complementarity preceded colonialism, an intervention that led to growing gender and racial inequality. The legacy of past debates is evident after decades of change in the Andean region and in theorizations of gender, race, and cultural difference. What, then, are the conceptual frameworks for examining Andean women that have had the most currency among feminists?

In Peru recently, I hunted in libraries around Lima to find as many issues as I could of *Chacarera*, a magazine published by the feminist nongovernmental organization Flora Tristan, which is devoted to matters of relevance to rural Andean women. I found striking the many articles over the years that continued to be guided by the discussions of gender complementarity that had emerged in the 1970s. It may be useful to trace the conversations and debates from that period to discover to what degree thinking continues to be linked to Andean cosmovision and the work of critical theorists like Irene Silverblatt (1987), who wrote the classic *Moon, Sun, and Witches* on Inca and colonial Peru. As Peruvian feminist writer Maruja Barrig (2006) notes, some present-day thinking (including among rural Andeans themselves) is influenced by the long-standing work of

Peruvian and international scholars who posited separate and enduring gender domains, lacking marked inequality, in the Andes based on pre-Hispanic gender ideology and division of labor. Gender complementarity, embraced by a number of northern and southern scholars, thus has offered an alternative to the dominant feminist framework of analysis originating in the North, which assumes that *different* means *unequal*.[18]

Not all have agreed with the premises of the complementarity framework, of course. Barrig (2001) contested it in her powerful extended essay *El mundo al revés*, suggesting that it was based on romantic notions of rural life that have concealed deep-seated forms of gender inequality in Andean communities. It is important to note that the idealized notions she referred to came mainly from nongovernmental organizations serving rural women, and not from rural women themselves. As I discuss in my commentary in part 1 of this book, my work on the community of Vicos was among several studies Barrig felt unwittingly contributed to such a perspective on Andean gender relations. Such differences continue to divide feminist scholars and activists, and sometimes to separate local Andean women themselves, those who describe "traditional" practices as valuable cultural heritage and those who express their serious concern about domestic violence and other obstacles to women's full citizenship rights. Suffice it to say here that it is perhaps unsurprising if we find among Peruvian women elements of both a colonialist, urban attitude regarding rural women's subordination, and a more resistant Andean view of these women's enduring strength in the face of deep inequalities.

Pioneering feminist scholars Susan Bourque and Kay Warren (1981b), coauthors of *Women of the Andes,* favored a "gender and development" approach to examining an agricultural community and a commercial town in the Central Highlands north of Lima. Their work considered women's status in relation to the gender division of labor and to opportunities for becoming more integrated in the modernizing economy and society. This early work may have overemphasized the benefits of such integration in the dependent capitalist economy, but it had the significant value of recognizing women as change agents in various contexts in Peru. In contrast, while my own archival research (Babb 1976 [1985b, 1999 Spanish edition]) on women in the community of Vicos, Peru during the mid-twentieth century was also concerned with questions of development set in a broad historical context, I argued that closer integration into the dominant national economy had generally meant increasing inequalities for women and other vulnerable groups in the community.

Beginning in the 1970s, and more notably by the 1980s, many feminists throughout the Americas and beyond were embracing a Marxist feminist framework that departed from symbolic approaches to perceived gender duality, positing instead what was later criticized as still another duality, an analytical focus on production and reproduction in society. This conceptualization enabled us to use the lens of political economy to examine the critical part played by women in reproducing not only families and households but also societies through their socially reproductive labor. Analysts from North and South, including Eleanor Leacock, Helen Safa, June Nash, Carmen Diana Deere, Heleith Saffioti, and Elizabeth Jelin, helped transform our understanding of the close intertwining of gender and class inequality and the substantial yet often unrecognized and unremunerated work of women in and beyond households. Deere and Nash, and Andean scholars like Daisy Núñez del Prado Béjar, elevated the standing of household economics in Andean studies and beyond. Along with the collaborative work of Elsa Chaney and Ximena Bunster on migrant women in domestic service and marketing in Lima, my own research extended the analysis to the productive activity of Andean market women, whose work straddled home and market (Babb [1989] 1998, 2008a Spanish edition).

While many of us during that time closely examined gender and class, race and ethnicity were frequently overlooked as salient vectors of experience and inequality or were collapsed into social class. Andeanist anthropologists Linda Seligmann (1989) and Mary Weismantel (2001) were among a small number who offered more subtle attention to Andean culture and racial politics, including the status of cholas as women "in-between." Marisol de la Cadena (1991) famously wrote that rural women living in the Cuzco area were viewed as "más indias," identifying their stigmatized racial status as well as their subordinated gender status. No writing on Andean women has been so widely cited as the article in which this proposition appeared (or the later book chapter in English translation); the work has had a great impact, reflecting a feminist view of the double or even triple jeopardy of impoverished, minoritized women. More recent work by anthropologist Cristina Alcalde (2010) examines Andean women living in Lima and the stigma they bear as *serranas* (women with origins in the highlands); she suggests that despite changes over time and place, Andean women continue to face multiple forms of discrimination, even from men of their own cultural background. Alcalde's discovery of wide-spread domestic violence among Andean migrants in Lima echoes what others have found in highland communities, posing a challenge to the notion of mutual respect accompanying gender complementarity in Andean culture (though some would argue that more egalitarian relations were corrupted by exposure to urban culture and gender norms).

Here I have emphasized anthropological contributions on Andean Peru that have taken up questions relating to gender, with some attention to race and ethnicity, but there are others who may be noted as well. Theidon (2004) and Bueno-Hansen (2015) brought much-needed attention to the gendered nature of violence and transitional justice in Peru, showing how indigenous women have often suffered most. Boesten (2010), Ewig (2010), Rousseau and Morales Hudon (2017), and Ypeij (2006) demonstrated the significance of intertwined inequalities of gender, race, and class in contexts ranging from health care and reproductive rights to the informal economic sector and indigenous social movements. My broader point remains, however, that a good deal of Andeanist work on gender has given less attention to race and ethnicity—even as we have seen that some feminist scholarship and activism has begun to turn in the direction of intersectional and decolonial practices.

DECADES OF DIALOGUE ON GENDER, RACE, AND ETHNICITY IN THE ANDES

In this schematic overview of past dialogues and debates, as well as contemporary rethinking of gender, race, and ethnicity in the Andes, I suggest that certain frameworks of analysis have continued to shape thinking, and that it will be productive to revisit them as well as engage new conceptualizations. I contend that much of the new discussion on race and social inequality in Peru has overlooked gender, and that a critical feminist perspective on both gender and race is needed to grapple with complex social realities. Based on my recent research in Peru, both in the Andes and in

Lima, I have considered whether currents of change in the region have enabled rural and urban indigenous women to gain greater leverage even when social inequality persists; I have argued that being female and Andean may have some new cultural purchase in the nation, yet these ontological conditions remain subject to still more subtle and durable forms of discrimination. This is something I take up later at greater length.

Two broad objectives underlie the long-range project that I would like to see advance: to develop a feminist anthropology of race and indigeneity that will attend to the culturally complex lived experiences of Andean women in both rural and urban contexts; and to establish stronger dialogues among Andeanists from the global South and North who have participated in rich discussions of gender, race, and ethnicity in the Andes but often in fairly circumscribed ways. Questions I would like to see addressed include whether feminist analysts (North and South) are learning from rural and indigenous women and broadening their conceptual frameworks and political activism; to what degree the gender-related concerns of indigenous peoples, both rural and urban, are currently embraced in feminist theorization; and what impact the changing currents in scholarship and in political culture may have in the everyday lives of Andean women and men. Although it is beyond the scope of this work, I certainly wish to see greater inclusion of Amazonians and Afro-Peruvians in substantive feminist discussion.

Here I want to add that, ideally, I would have given somewhat more attention in this book to the centrality of (hetero)sexuality in Andean contexts in Peru. Although I have tracked sexual politics closely in other settings, including the capital cities of Lima, Managua, and Havana, and I was on the lookout for evidence of same-sex relationships and consciousness in Andean Peru, I found little of it in my field research. I discovered fiercely independent women with strong and meaningful connections with other women, but rarely the intimate and amorous ties that would unsettle the dominant cultural expectations of heterosexuality. So, while it is productive to "queer" the pitch of such fundamental concepts as the gender division of labor, gender complementarity, and development, my research findings did not often steer me in that direction. Nonetheless, analytical frameworks that assume a singular nuclear family form or that fail to recognize the needs of women and men who, for whatever reason, fall outside the mainstream in relation to marriage and reproductive practices, must be called into question.[19]

While there is a need for more decolonial and collaborative work across intellectual and geographic borders, some laudable efforts to date in Latin American scholarship can inform our work on Andean Peru. One of the early initiatives was an anthology published in Bolivia, *Más allá del silencio*, which resulted from an international collaboration of scholars from both North and South. Edited by British anthropologist Denise Arnold (1997), the volume offers a rich array of articles assessing the value of gender analysis in the Andes and stretching the boundaries of knowledge as they do so. Some contributors counterpose Andean gender "duality" and "complementarity" with cases of independent women who do not rely on men, and others shed light on the complex ways in which society's gender representations have distinct material consequences for Andean women.

Another collaborative venture, by Canadian anthropologists Lynne Phillips and Sally Cole (2013), along with researchers Marie-Eve Carrier-Moisan and Erica Lagalisse from Ecuador and Brazil (the nations under consideration), resulted in *Contesting Publics: Feminism, Activism, Ethnography*. This work takes the familiar feminist framework of the private and public spheres in new directions, examining the experiences of women bringing private, gender-related concerns to public view as activists demanding entry into spaces of participatory democracy. They find new gender inequalities emerging at the same time that women see some movement toward social inclusion. Their concluding chapter offers a useful model for engaged collaboration as the coauthors and their colleagues share discursive space as feminist activist-scholars and public intellectuals discussing the broader implications of their work.

Anthropologists R. Aída Hernández Castillo and Andrew Canessa, feminist social analysts from Mexico and the UK respectively, brought together contributions from a wide range of activist-scholars from Mesoamerica and the Andean region. In their collection, *Género, complementariedades y exclusiones*, Hernández Castillo and Canessa (2012) map out a terrain in which they seek to build intercultural dialogue. Their theoretical formulation is at once attentive to race, cultural difference, and political struggle, and to gender and power in indigenous societies. They bring greater clarity to the tensions between feminists who stake claims for women's rights and

indigenous activists who make claims for communitarian cultural rights—
and show why issues of gender complementarity and difference remain
central to contemporary political struggle. Although the presumption that
women's rights are necessarily *individual* rights, while indigenous rights
are *collective*, is another unnecessary binary distinction, I agree with
Hernández Castillo and Canessa that what is most important is to recognize the diverse perceptions of indigenous women and men. Unfortunately,
as they note, debate has frequently stalled as the lines are drawn between,
on the one hand, those who argue that gender complementarity is a precolonial asset and that present-day notions of gender and women's rights are
the imposition and legacy of colonialism and, on the other hand, those who
maintain that respect for the idealized principle of complementarity must
not stand in the way of confronting the lived experiences of gender violence
and other manifestations of inequality. Thus, if some groups of indigenous
women embrace discourses of women's rights as a tool for confronting gender injustice, they should not be dismissed with the patronizing view that
they have given up their cultural identities and become inauthentic or
acculturated in the process. We may recall the Bolivian communitarian
feminists mentioned earlier as an example of the more complex politics of
gender and cultural identity now emerging in some parts of Latin America.

In a rich collection of writings by decolonial feminist contributors from
throughout the Latin American region, coeditors Yuderkys Espinosa Miñoso,
Diana Gómez Correal, and Karina Ochoa Muñoz (2014) map a terrain of
organic intellectual work challenging Eurocentric feminism and positing an
urgent need for an epistemic shift in how knowledge is constructed. The
volume includes not only well-known theorists and writers like Silvia Rivera
Cusicanqui and María Lugones but also other voices heard less often from
social-movement organizations presenting collective statements. The collaborators' shared project is to weave ideas together "another way" as part of
their antiracist and decolonial project. Selections were drawn from work
published over the last two decades, and in this volume they have considerable impact: they make a clear case that indigenous, Afro-descendant, and
other marginalized women will no longer remain the subjects of research but
rather will be the producers of their own new knowledge. This work is a logical step forward following the publication of an earlier anthology edited by
R. Aída Hernández Castillo and Liliana Suárez Navaz ([2008] 2011), which

offered key postcolonial feminist writings in Spanish translation (largely from English) so that Latin American feminists could more effectively participate in discussion at the transnational level. The coeditors, based in Mexico and Spain, presented essays on the often contentious politics of feminism across the North-South divide, the politics of identity, the fraught subject of the category "women" in feminist theory, and the decolonial turn in scholarship. It is a testament to the deep roots of decolonial feminism on Latin American soil that the later volume could draw exclusively on contributors from the region itself.

Several years ago, an issue of *LACES—Latin American and Caribbean Ethnic Studies*—was devoted to reconceptualizing gender, race, and indigeneity in Peru. In it, Marisol de la Cadena (2008: 341) situates the contributors' efforts to understand the epistemic moment as the state shapes social relations and as marginalized groups push back against the coloniality of power. Likewise, the Mexican journal *Desacatos: Revista de antropología social* (2009) devoted an issue to "border crossings: indigenous identities, gender, and justice" and considered such relevant matters as *interculturalidad* (interculturality), native identities and nationalism, cosmovision, and communal forms of justice. And finally, a 2013 issue of *Feminist Theory* focused on racialized bodies in Latin America and the Caribbean, fruitfully raising questions relating to differences of gender, race, and sexuality in everyday life. All of these innovative projects engage the current epistemological shift toward decolonial thought, guiding me as I revisit my own and other scholarship.

To conclude this discussion of current scholarship on gender in the Andes, let us consider a series of questions that have preoccupied me as I seek to develop a feminist decolonial anthropology of the Andes. How can a reexamination of past debates on Andean women and gender generate new knowledge that may serve in the interest of reducing gender and racial inequality? How can research on Andean women avoid the twin dangers of viewing these women as either fully subordinated in society or as iconic emblems of cultural heritage in the Andes? With race and ethnicity receiving greater attention from feminist analysts, how can we also bring sexuality into our research in more productive ways? Does the concern to develop intercultural paradigms provide a space for indigenous women and feminists (including indigenous feminists) to come together and organize effectively? How can engaged feminist researchers support the work of indigenous women, whether or not these women view gender as a key axis for change? Finally, how will scholars and activists from the North and South ensure that we are reading, citing, and critiquing each other's work in spite of our geographic distance and different languages and academic cultures? These are some of the challenges we face as we contemplate ways to decolonize scholarship and construct a more vibrant knowledge base from which to work on gender, race, and sexuality in Andean Peru.

Before mapping out what follows in this book, I would like to reflect briefly on my own "situatedness" in this text and offer a couple of cautionary remarks. As I complete four decades of ongoing research in Peru, my writing on the subject has spanned much of my life: I have gone from being a graduate student in my midtwenties undertaking fieldwork for the first time; to returning over the next decade as a married woman and mother as well as an academic; to divorcing, entering middle age, and suddenly reassessing my sexual identity; and finally, to becoming a happily-same-sex-coupled woman of a certain age who has settled into a rather more ambivalent status when traveling to Peru. I know that I am perceived differently in Lima and Huaraz, and in the rural community of Vicos, where my difference is read in various registers (or goes unnoticed). What may appear most constant for the Peruvians I have known for so long is the class and race privilege I try to wear lightly but nonetheless possess. While I grew up with many of the advantages conferred by well-educated white middle-class parents in a small town in upstate New York, I experienced some early challenges when my father died and left my mother to support three children. Even so, in recent years my US citizenship and evident ability to remain in good health, travel, and pursue opportunities that my Peruvian friends rarely find open to them have positioned me in ways I am mindful of as I make my annual visits.

Having set out some of the diverse strands of my own positioning, I am aware that my reference to "Andeans" or "Andean women" may seem at times to collapse the complexities of those I am seeking to render as fully as possible. Language limits us as we use words that have a geographic reference but which tend to obscure salient cultural, economic, linguistic, and other forms of difference and power. I caution readers that in this work I sometimes make expedient use of terms that do not do full justice to the wholeness of people's lives, yet I am hopeful that my commentaries and critical discussion will offset such limitations. It would go against my deepest desires in writing this book to reify once more the very categories we must move beyond in any effort to decolonize knowledge. I trust that readers will understand that my use of such phrasings as "Andean women" should flatten these complex lives no more than my own shorthand description as a "middle-class woman from the United States."

In another word of caution, I acknowledge that while it is the responsibility of all of us to decolonize our thinking, there has been an unfortunate tendency among northern scholars, when they are not overlooking southern scholarship, to appropriate the timely and productive ideas of the latter as their own. I seek to avoid the sort of extractive appropriation of decolonial feminisms from the South that Espinosa Miñoso, Gómez Correal, and Ochoa Muñoz (2014: 13) identify in their pivotal volume. Moreover, I aim to steer clear of any real or perceived effort on my part to use antiracist and decolonial feminisms in a self-serving way to redeem my own earlier work. Rather, I hope that these contemporary currents of feminist thought, with full attribution of their sources, can highlight new ways of understanding both the strengths and the limitations of scholarship of the past several decades. While in this volume my decolonial feminist commitment takes, by and large, the form of putting my work in conversation with that of southern interlocutors, a further step will be to more actively engage with my research "subjects" as collaborators—something I return to in the concluding chapter.

Finally, I note that the photographs accompanying this introduction, the commentary chapters, and the conclusion were all taken in recent years, and that some of them serve as a counterpoint to the discussion of earlier periods. Whenever possible I have obtained permission from individuals to use their images. Except where noted, I took all the photographs myself.

SETTING OUT THIS WORK

This book is divided into three parts, which correspond to areas of research on Andean women over the decades since the 1970s. Each part begins with a commentary that situates my work within the historical context of broad feminist debate and of scholarship on Andean Peru. Part 1 is devoted to reconsidering the Cornell-Peru Project, also known as the Vicos Project, which brought US and Peruvian anthropologists together in the 1950s in a hacienda community in the north-central Andes for one of the largest experiments in the history of applied anthropology. The project's lofty aim was to assist the indigenous peasant community in purchasing its own land and ending age-old feudal relations, while encouraging, measuring, and documenting social change. My work, based on material from the Cornell-Peru Project archives in Ithaca, New York, questioned the overwhelmingly positive accounts of the project's outcome by showing that despite good intentions, women were often overlooked in the distribution of new resources and opportunities, and that "modern" gender ideologies based on northern notions of women's place were unwittingly introduced in the community. First published in 1976, my work examining the critical underpinnings of the development project undertaken in Vicos takes up threads of feminist critique that have continued to engage many of us in debate regarding rural Andean women.

Part 2 begins with a commentary that reflects on three pieces of writing based on my long-term field research in Huaraz, Peru, focusing on market women in the economy, setting the essays in conversation with other works published from the 1980s through 2000. I show how my analysis of women's productive contribution at the local and national levels during a period of political and economic crisis was shaped by feminist discussion and debate on production and reproduction in society; by debates on the relationship of the informal and formal economic sectors; and, later in this period, by recognition of the part that culture plays in conditioning relations of gender, ethnicity, and political economy. I discuss how I was influenced by the cultural turn in feminist thought, which led me to question work—including my own—that relied heavily on economic analysis and the gender division of labor without sufficiently grappling with cultural meanings and identities. My work and that of others during this period was beginning to employ insights from postcolonial scholarship that destabilized conventional categories of analysis, questioned our own positionality, and deepened our understanding of gender, race, and class relations.

Part 3 brings together and comments on two final writings that are separated by more than two decades. Both engage comparative questions and place my work in Peru in conversation with a wide-ranging scholarship. The earlier work is a journal article from 1990 that made a case for bringing gender analysis to theory and research in economic anthropology, a subfield that was particularly resistant to, and yet stood to benefit significantly from, feminist insights. In that work, I use my research in Peru to illuminate the critical difference that attention to gender can make in such analysis. The later work, a journal article published in 2012, draws on my more recent research on tourism in Latin American nations (Babb 2011) to offer a comparative study of gender, race, and cultural tourism in Peru and Mexico. Like the earlier work, this one considers women's work and the salience of gender analysis, but it also embraces a consideration of indigenous identity and cultural representation in the fashioning of national tourism practices. I move toward a decolonial feminist reworking of the entanglements of gender and race as I ask to what extent being female and indigenous has acquired cultural capital in the marketplace of tourism, and to what degree the coloniality of power is still paramount.

In my conclusion, I go further in suggesting how decolonial feminisms may be of significant value as I pose challenging questions in relation to my own and other work on Andean women. I seek to discover how well our earlier and more recent scholarship holds up under the scrutiny afforded by decolonial analysis. Ultimately, I argue for the development of a decolonial feminist anthropology that will generate continuing debate and engaged practice in our work and our activism with Andean women wherever they reside.

PART I Gender and Rural Development

THE VICOS PROJECT

Commentary

My monograph on the applied anthropology project in the Andean community of Vicos, Peru, originally was written as a master's thesis (1976) and, once revised, was my first published work (in various incarnations, Babb 1976, 1980a, 1985b, and, in Spanish translation, 1999). Presented as the sole entry in part 1, "Women and Men in Vicos, Peru: A Case of Unequal Development" was read in its several versions by a fairly specialized group interested in the anthropology of Peru and in gender and development in Latin America, and it did not have as broad a reach as might be expected. This may be because it did not appear in a high-profile venue and because of its chilly reception by those who were closest to the project.

The work created something of a disturbance among at least a few of the Cornell-Peru Project (CPP) personnel, who nonetheless remained publicly silent regarding the gendered implications of the applied anthropology initiative. I was gratified, however, to find that feminist scholars embraced the work and found it insightful or provocative, depending on their own perspectives. What I find particularly useful at this remove from the project's history and from my own writing about it is to revisit what made my intervention challenging to some and generative to the thinking of others. Most significantly to my current endeavor, I assess here how the monograph engaged with the pioneering works in the field of gender and development, and how it participated in some of the earliest debates on Andean women. My discussion also anticipates how my work lends itself to a decolonial feminism.

I begin by setting the Vicos Project in its historical context of mid-twentieth-century anthropology and as a collaboration between scholars from the United States and Peru. Much of that story appears in my work that follows, so here I will be brief. When Cornell anthropologist Allan Holmberg took the opportunity to lease the Hacienda Vicos in 1952 and worked with a team of US and Peruvian social scientists to conduct an ambitious experiment in guided social change, it was in the context of both the Cold War and fledgling applied anthropology. Modernization theory underpinned the dominant paradigm for understanding social problems such as underdevelopment, inequality, and what was perceived to be a slow pace of change. The anthropologists who participated in the project, introducing and documenting change, worked from the assumption that once Vicosinos experienced freedom from centuries of near-feudal conditions, became involved in self-governance, and enjoyed higher levels of education and better health care, they would enter the "modern" world. First, however, these indigenous peasants would need the assistance of the project to shake free of past practices, from subservient behavior in the company of mestizos to the use of traditional forms of agriculture. To that end, the CPP encouraged new forms of sociopolitical organization and technologies for working the land.

Not surprisingly, given the time period of the CPP (1952–62) and the orientation of anthropology during those years, the main targets of change were men, and most often younger men, rather than women or the senior men who had been the traditional authorities in the community. In the planned transition of power from former hacienda owners to community members, new skills and decision making were directed to those men identified as heads of households and potential leaders in Vicos.[1] When my graduate school advisor, William Stein, suggested that the CPP archives at Cornell University might offer a treasure trove of material on issues relating to my growing interest in the area of gender and development, I made this my chosen research base for my master's degree at SUNY Buffalo.

I spent much of summer 1975 in Ithaca, New York, in the uncomfortably cool basement of Olin Library, where the archives were housed. As predicted, I found a rich source of material that enabled me to produce a critical feminist assessment of what the CPP offered to Vicosinos—and what, for a variety of reasons, it appeared to overlook. Much of the material I found most intriguing was in the form of researchers' fieldnotes recording everyday activities and events—not intended to be part of a gender analysis but often providing fairly unfiltered and candid accounts of men's and women's lives in the community during the years of the CPP. Thus, despite the greater attention to young men by the principal project personnel and the scant attention to women in the published material, the archives themselves tell another story.

Among the field researchers with notes in the archives were anthropologists from the United States and Peru who were closely connected with the project, as well as affiliates and students from US colleges carrying out summer research in Vicos. In the latter group, among those less central to the project, but who were nonetheless keen observers in the community, was, for example, Aida Milla Vázquez—wife of the principal Peruvian scholar with the CPP, Mario de Vázquez—who was carrying out a study of the socialization of children in Vicos. Milla de Vázquez offered sharply incisive commentary about the project at times, no doubt to the consternation of the CPP.[2] Another notable participant was Harvard undergraduate Richard Price, whose fieldnotes impressed me as particularly sensitive and insightful; years later, I realized that he was the same Richard Price I knew as a prominent Caribbeanist anthropologist.[3] Other student researchers whose fieldnotes were especially useful to my exploration of gender in Vicos were Norman Pava and Harold Skalka. It may have been precisely those with a lesser stake in promoting a positive image of the CPP who most freely described sensitive aspects of the planned intervention in social change.

My work that follows this commentary conveys more clearly what I learned from the archival materials. Here I turn to my work's reception as well as its engagement with feminist debates of the time—and how I regard the work in light of more recent research and decolonial feminist theory.

THE LITERATURE ON VICOS AND
THE SILENCE AROUND GENDER

In general, those who have heard of the Cornell-Peru Project believe that there has been an abundance of attention to Vicos. However, those most familiar with the CPP know that since the time of the project, most of the attention has been in the form of brief reports, popular press coverage, and numerous textbook citations of Vicos and the CPP as a model for applied anthropology. Of scholarly treatments there have been relatively few, including several unpublished doctoral dissertations, a number of journal articles, and several books, including two coedited volumes on Vicos that were published forty years apart.

Mario Vázquez (1961) wrote a concise book of fewer than sixty pages as a reference on hacienda communities in the Peruvian Andes and later published a fuller monograph (1965) on changes in schooling in Vicos from the arrival of the CPP through the mid-1960s. The key edited collection of contributions, mainly by CPP personnel (Dobyns, Doughty, and Lasswell 1971), appeared about a decade after the CPP saw the transition of power to the Vicosinos, and it was unqualified in its praise for the intervention. In stark contrast, years later William W. Stein offered an exhaustive deconstructionist excursion into the modernity project in Vicos, which appeared first in Spanish (2000) and then in English (2003). Stein, among the cohort of Cornell graduate students who studied with Allan Holmberg, had carried out doctoral research in a community not far from Vicos; he later turned his attention to Vicos through research in the Cornell archives as well as in the community. Before anthropology's epistemic crisis of representation in the 1980s, Stein had already become a strong critic of the CPP's objectives and claims, based on his reading of Marx and, later, Derrida to reinterpret the dynamics of culture and power in Vicos.[4]

One more work I want to mention here is quite distinct, authored by the "Comunidad Campesina de Vicos" (2005) with the assistance of Florencia Zapata. Over several years, Zapata worked with the Vicosinos to prepare an oral history of their community by means of wide-ranging interviews on community history, daily life, work, identity, language use, education, health, beliefs, cultural practices, and concerns for the future. Reference to the community's past relationship with the CPP, recalled particularly by elders, reveals the ambivalence and uncertainty of many about how the project shaped the course of their lives. Some expressed gratitude, but others recalled Cornell as simply another *hacendado,* or *patrón* (hacienda owner). This oral history is an invaluable contribution to what we know of the community and of the subjectivity of Vicosino men and women today.[5]

Another edited collection came out decades after the CPP had pulled up stakes in Vicos, as an assessment of fifty years of applied anthropology in Andean Peru, with Vicos as the model (Greaves, Bolton, and Zapata 2011).[6] A variety of assessments appear in this collection, from the familiar testimonials to the project's success, to a critical appraisal of the CPP as product of the US Cold War strategy and a discussion of the tensions that manifested within the community and among personnel.[7] Yet there is no editorial effort to engage these evident differences, and readers are left to draw their own conclusions. It is worth noting the two chapters that comprise the final part of the book, "Vicos Today." This follows a dozen chapters on remembering and evaluating the Vicos Project, two chapters comparing Vicos to other applied anthropology projects, and another that considers the migration alternative favored by a growing number of Peruvians. Given the past gender politics surrounding the project, it is hard to overlook the fact that these are the only chapters in the anthology by women, Billie Jean Isbell (2011) and Florencia Zapata (2011), who played key roles at Cornell University in bringing attention back to Vicos. They led initiatives to launch the "Vicos: A Virtual Tour" website;[8] host a 2006 conference at Cornell, to which a number of us who had conducted research in Vicos and several Vicosino men were invited to participate; repatriate thousands of photographs taken in Vicos; and carry out the oral history project in the community. Their contributions balance the volume with observations concerning Vicosinos in the present context and are among the few that offer even brief attention to gender.

In her chapter, Zapata quotes several passages from the oral histories she gathered just over a decade earlier that corroborate what I found in the archives regarding Vicosinos' views of the importance of both men's and women's work in the hacienda community. For example, a Vicosino man recalled that during pre-CPP times, "on the hacienda neither women nor men were idle; everyone had his or her own tasks, men as well as the

Schoolgirls playing on a tractor in Vicos, 2011. Photo by author.

women." Another man commented, "The landlord exploited us a lot. . . . Like a contractor does now, just like that, they made us work fourteen hours, all the same, men and women" (Zapata 2011: 325–26). Opinions differed over the impact of the CPP, with one man proudly stating that with Cornell's arrival, Vicos was "liberated from the patrones" (Zapata 2011: 326), and another remembering negative impacts, such as the introduction of chemical fertilizer and what he perceived as the use of Vicosino women and men as "servants" to the CPP (Zapata 2011: 328).

The brief introduction and conclusion to the collection edited by Greaves and colleagues do not do justice to the diversity of views presented or to the unresolved questions and disagreements laid out in the volume. Concerning gender and my past work specifically, I was interested to find in the introduction a passing remark in a listing of twenty "issues and queries": "The project's inclusion or exclusion of the women of Vicos has been debated (e.g., Babb 1980a). Different authors have reached different conclusions. What is a fair assessment?" (Greaves and Bolton 2011: x). Unfortunately, the question was never addressed; although my work was one of just a half dozen citations in the introduction, there was no further

Women playing soccer in Vicos, 2015. Photo by author.

discussion of gender. A useful contrast is provided in a chapter of the volume that considers the case of Kuyo Chico, another important but less-celebrated community development project in Peru that began just a few years after the Vicos Project. Jorge Flores Ochoa (2011) offers fairly extensive remarks about ways that this project drew women into literacy classes and helped them gain voting rights; he notes failures as well, including the introduction of urban cookstoves that were not suitable for women who customarily sat while cooking. Such a gender-conscious approach might have usefully informed the Vicos Project as well.

Over time, I have come to view the avoidance of the gender question in discussions of the Cornell-Peru Project as part of a broader reluctance to take seriously those critics who would decolonize the knowledge surrounding the CPP. Generally, the notion has been that the critics suffer from "intellectual hubris" and would rather issue critiques than make a positive difference through their work.[9] Yet, certainly by now there have been enough sustained critiques within anthropology coming from both northern and southern perspectives, as well as from areas that have been the recipients of even the best-intended development interventions, that anthropologists must pay heed. Efforts to decolonize knowledge and practice do not have to mean a failure to act or to support initiatives that local populations desire, and in fact these intellectual efforts frequently go hand in hand with social-movement-based activism. We need only recall the individuals discussed in this book's introduction who have called for attention to the coloniality of power, including Quijano, Mignolo, Escobar, and Lugones, to recognize the deep commitment of these scholars to a more equitable world.

My critique of gender relations in Vicos during and after the project seemed to strike a particularly sensitive nerve. After the first publication of my Vicos monograph as part of a working paper series, my advisor sent copies to a number of people, including several who had been part of the CPP. In December 1976, one former CPP member, Henry Dobyns, wrote a five-page, single-spaced letter to my advisor (which the latter passed along to me) protesting that my work had been published at all, as it was "vicious nonsense." The author fumed, "All I can say is that I wish she had experienced one week as a woman in Vicos about 1946 before she wrote this nonsense!"—to which I recall thinking, did *he* bring such experience to *his* work in Vicos? As he went on to dispute my interpretations of the gendered implications of various interventions in the community, he acknowledged that the three principals of the Cornell group, himself included, "were quite aware that the interventions of the 1950s had tended to alter male roles more than female, and we sought ways to bring enlightenment to women during the early 1960s."[10] This is particularly interesting to contemplate, as such a view never made its way into print. While my work had suggested that the CPP was simply a product of its time in judging men in Vicos to be the main actors deserving of attention and development assistance, this comment regarding the CPP's gender awareness might be seen as an invitation to hold the CPP to a still higher standard.

The letter went on to protest my use of economist Ester Boserup and other scholars to make broader points about male bias in development endeavors, apparently because CPP statements alone should offer sufficient evidence on which to base reasonable interpretation. Perhaps the fundamental disagreement was most clearly expressed on the final page of the letter: "Neither men nor women can worry the way Babb and some of those she cites do about women's role until a society has reached a certain minimal level of subsistence." This, of course, reflects a masculinist view that was widely held on both the Right and the Left of the political spectrum a few decades ago, and which feminists were successfully challenging by the 1970s. In the letter's closing, my advisor is exhorted to "ride herd on" his students who make use of the CPP archives. Fortunately for me, my advisor did not share the sentiment that I should be silenced, though I suppose that (like him) I paid a certain price for stubbornly advancing my critical, feminist work.

Thankfully, I was encouraged around this same time by the much more positive reactions of feminist anthropologists slightly senior to me, including Margo Smith and Kay Warren, among the first generation of researchers in the 1970s focusing on women in Peru, who described my work as "fascinating" and "a gem." Four days after the letter discussed above was written to my advisor, Smith sent me a letter in January 1977 praising my work and urging me to submit it to paper competitions; she commented that my conclusions "fit in well with those of Elise Boulding," an Africanist scholar who had pioneered work on gender and development. She closed her supportive letter by expressing curiosity about the reaction of the CPP to my work. Another scholar, Martha J. Hardman, told me that she found in my work direct parallels to what she had discovered as a linguistic anthropologist working on the nuances of gender and language in Peru. These and other responses from feminist anthropologists, and inclusion of my work in a review essay by well-known scholar Rayna Rapp (1979), gave me the confidence I needed to commit myself to feminist work in Latin American anthropology.

THE VICOS PROJECT AND FEMINIST DEBATES ON GENDER COMPLEMENTARITY AND INEQUALITY

In contrast to the initial response to my work in the United States, it had a quite different reception by feminist scholars in Peru, for the most part after the work was published in Spanish in 1999. While I have always desired to see my work circulate in Spanish in Peru, it has sometimes taken decades because of the logistics of translation, the cost of production, and so on. As a result, my earlier work has been considered in light of much more recent feminist theory and research. Some of my original intention and meaning has no doubt been lost in translation and with the passage of time, but I have been gratified to discover the renewed interest in my work—whether in agreement or disagreement with what I have to say. I was pleased that my work was regarded as timely enough for publication at the turn of the millennium in a collection of groundbreaking essays translated from English to Spanish on gender and development in the global South (Babb 1999). The essays were described in the preface as among the most important articles presenting new and critical perspectives and opening up feminist, intercultural debate on gender and postcolonial development.

In a few cases, I became aware of appraisals of my work on Vicos some years after they appeared. This was the case when I came across critical reflections by Maruja Barrig, one of Peru's best-known feminist writers and activists, who has written on a wide range of subjects relating to women and gender relations in Peru. Based in Lima, she is interested in, among other things, gender and development questions that are of central importance here and which I will discuss at some length. Her work *El mundo al revés,* published in Argentina (Barrig 2001), examined representations of Andean women in the historical writings on Peru, ethnographic accounts since the 1970s, and her own more recent interviews with staff members in rural NGOs working with Andean communities. Some of this work was reprised in English translation as a book chapter published in the United States in a widely circulated edited collection on gender and development (Barrig 2006).

When I met with Barrig at a bookstore café in spring 2012, she noted being significantly influenced by the work of Amartya Sen, whose theory of human development calls for a series of freedoms, including women's freedom to be the protagonists of their own lives. At the time, I was interested in talking with her about our current work, since most Peruvians are more familiar with my earlier writing on Vicos and on Huaraz market women (in Spanish translation, 2008a)—but I was also hoping to engage with her on our earlier work. In fact, when I encountered her chapter in the anthology on women and gender equity in development, I was dismayed to realize that she referenced my work written fully three decades before in a way that did not situate it historically or capture the subtleties in my argument. Nevertheless, on closer reading, I came to appreciate the way that she addressed some of the vexing questions I am raising now. Notwithstanding our somewhat different conclusions, I find much that is compelling in her work and her interpretations.

Serving as a development consultant for several international funding agencies carrying out projects in Peru's southern Andean region between 1999 and 2002, Barrig was concerned about the gender inequalities that have persisted over the years in Andean communities. In her writing, she positions herself as a veteran feminist who, like others in Lima, was long silent on the question of Andean women. However, she was aware of the academic debates over gender complementarity and of the practical difficulties that often arose when northern expectations of promoting gender equity were met by local NGO resistance to the gender concept. In her review of the historical writings of such chroniclers as Guamán Poma de Ayala and the ethnographic writings of feminist anthropologists, she challenges the interpretation of gender relations in the Andes as complementary and free of what we might now call the coloniality of power.

Among the ethnographic writings she questions are works by Irene Silverblatt, Billie Jean Isbell, and myself, finding that "this social construction [of Andean society] is not fully convincing" (Barrig 2006: 109). The ethnographic objectives, subjects, and methodologies were vastly different among the three of us, yet she finds in our work what she describes as an idealized notion of gender relations in precolonial Peru and in contemporary indigenous peasant communities. This, she contends, has contributed to the popularly held view in Peru that gender is not a particularly relevant category in Andean communities, where the family unit is fundamental and women and men have equally valued, though separate, roles in the private and public spheres. In her view, such interpretation is flawed and has contributed to failed attempts to address gender inequality in the Andean region.

If Barrig is correct and ethnographic writings on Andean worldview and cultural practices have been deployed by others to "protect" communities from interventions that would ameliorate gender inequalities in the Andes, this would be a serious charge. On the other hand, if ethnographers and NGO practitioners are correct that a certain form of gender equity has been long-standing in Andean society, most often disrupted under the influence of external, exploitative relations, then it would be crucial to revisit past interpretations in light of new knowledge—even as urgent social inequalities must be addressed.

Interestingly, and in contrast to Chandra Mohanty's ([1986] 2003) well-known criticism of northern views of "Third World women" for inappropriately applying external, essentialist concepts to their understanding of the "Other," Barrig is critiquing both Peruvian and outsider-northern views that reject northern gender analysis of Andean culture and society. It might, of course, be argued that romanticized versions of gender complementarity (as opposed to historicized accounts of gender complementarity) are the product of essentializing colonialist thought, and that this must be reckoned with in our past and present representations of Andean women. However, as I discuss later in this book, my own concern is that urban coastal currents of feminism often reveal the traces of modernist and colonialist expectations that rural women have a cultural deficit and must leave behind past practices and worldviews if they are to gain rights as Andean women.[11]

Barrig points to Silverblatt's ethnohistorical treatment of the relative harmony of women and men in precolonial Peru and the harsh gendered impact of the Spanish conquest, as well as Isbell's symbolic approach to contemporary Andean worldview and her dualist representation of gender complementarity in the southern Peruvian community of Chuschi. My early work on Vicos, however, receives the most attention as an example of an anthropological account that underscores "original harmony" and "external degradation" (her words) as leading to unequal gender relations. Still, she concedes that I qualified my conclusions to suggest the "relatively greater inequalities" for women following the introduction of CPP innovations in technology and decision making to men. In other words, she understood that I was not claiming an absence of gender inequality in the community under the former hacienda system, that I was, instead, suggesting that as the CPP assisted men in "modernizing," the unintended result was that women were left behind. Nonetheless, she disagreed with my contention that women's retention of traditional dress and use of Quechua may have resulted not only because of unequal access to resources but also as a form of cultural resistance and rejection of the culture of the dominant class. Barrig (2006: 119) found in some later ethnographic work by such scholars as Marisol de la Cadena, Penelope Harvey, Patricia Ruiz Bravo, Sarah Radcliffe, and Andrew Canessa "evidence of gender asymmetries in Andean communities" and clarity in arguing that the presence of the state and new forms of sociopolitical organization "have not produced the differences that exist between men and women but have simply exacerbated them."

Barrig's incisive assessment of ethnographic work from both North and South on Andean women and gender relations provides an opportunity to revisit past representations from the vantage point of new knowledge gained through at least two epistemic shifts: first, a shift from the universalizing tendencies in the 1970s to greater recognition of cultural and historical particularities by the 1980s, and then a shift over the last decade or two from the critical focus on inequalities to the decolonial emphasis on difference and the coloniality of power. I am confident that many of us who wrote of gender complementarity in earlier decades were also convinced of the contemporary gender inequalities that begged for attention in the Andean region. Moreover, many who theorized about gender relations in the 1970s and found ourselves in some disagreement in debates over earlier forms of egalitarianism versus universal gender asymmetry have been eager to join ranks in addressing current gender injustices, whatever their lineage.

In my own work that follows this commentary, I am in fact strongly critical of the spread of capitalist relations bringing about growing inequalities of class and gender. But I suggest here that those who are now offering penetrating decolonial analysis and questioning whether gender and other concepts developed in the North should be applied in the South are bringing still another critical perspective to the conversation—one that may help sort through the thorny issue raised by Barrig regarding a perceived tension between collective cultural rights and women's individual rights.[12] Indeed, we may discover that subjectivities are emerging to interrupt the stalled debates over the collective cultural rights of communities on the one hand and the rights of individuals within collectivities to self-determination on the other.

Those embracing decolonial feminisms include indigenous intellectuals and academics, southerners and northerners, who are building new knowledge and advocating change through participation in social movements and other forms of critical engagement. This new knowledge is understood to come from diverse sectors, including indigenous women and men, subalterns who themselves may stand in some disagreement with one another. De la Cadena (2010: 358) has discussed "indigenous cosmopolitics in the Andes," suggesting that new ways of knowing may need to include the "other-than-human," or natural beings such as mountain spirits that figure importantly in contemporary political responses to mining and other interventions in the name of modernization. While this may present a challenge to the Left as well as the Right in Andean nations, she argues persuasively that in her position as an engaged intellectual, "I hope not to be interpreted as an advocate of 'indigenous peoples' singular or pristine conditions." Instead, she is seeking "to make anthropology say something different—to open it up beyond our world, to an anthropology of worlds."[13] The conclusion to the present volume returns to the question of whether the decolonial option could mean the revindication of some earlier work, or if still different meanings and new knowledge will emerge to challenge us further.

REVISITING THE VICOS PROJECT FOUR DECADES LATER

When I wrote the original version of my work on gender relations in Vicos, I was a young graduate student who had not yet visited Peru. My research was based on a summer spent in Cornell University's archives and substantial background reading about the project and Peru. As I reread the material now, I find the writing somewhat dated (not surprisingly), but I am impressed by what I learned in so short a time, and by the careful and original work I did in assessing the (unintended) gendered impact of the CPP intervention.

Gender and development was still a new field and applied practice when I traveled to Ithaca in 1975—the same year the United Nations declared International Women's Year and launched the Decade for Women. It had taken me some time to track down my university library's copy of Ester Boserup's (1970) *Woman's Role in Economic Development*, now a classic. Although today this book is considered in the mainstream "women and development" tradition, it had far-reaching implications when it appeared and helped transform my thinking. Other influences on my research and writing at the time came from more radical socialist feminist theory, including the classic work of Juliet Mitchell (1973) on women's estate, Renate Bridenthal (1976) on the dialectics of production and reproduction in history, and Mina Davis Caulfield (1974) on imperialism and cultures of resistance. In addition, I drew on some key Marxist and postcolonial writings, including Engels's ([1884] 1972) *Origin of the Family*, Fanon's (1967) *A Dying Colonialism,* and Illich's (1972) *Deschooling Society.* Two pioneering anthologies in feminist anthropology came out as I undertook this work, *Woman, Culture and Society,* edited by Rosaldo and Lamphere (1974), and *Toward an Anthropology of Women,* edited by Rapp Reiter (1975)—it was my good fortune to discover the first just as I entered graduate school and to find the second at Cornell's bookstore as I was working in the CPP archives. All these works, along with many more on Peru and Vicos, inspired my thinking and writing, which I view as fairly synthetic, as I sought material that could shed light on the fieldnotes I was so absorbed in reading in the archives.

I see in my work on Vicos that I was drawn to the Andean paradigm of gender complementarity, but that I also sought to situate my work in a meaningful historical context. To this end, I drew on Marxist feminist theoretical insights on production and reproduction in society, leading me to examine the areas of work, family, and sexuality—a framework I developed further in my later work on Huaraz marketers, discussed in part 2 of this book. I found evidence in the archives of surprisingly egalitarian family relations, even as exploitative hacienda practices endured into the 1950s. There was abundant evidence of gender disparities in what the CPP brought to the Vicos community, whether through benign neglect or because it was felt that broader social problems needed to be ameliorated before women could expect to see improvements in their lives. While I stand by my work as offering a needed counterweight to the official and popular accounts of the development intervention, this is not to say that if I were writing today the work would look just the same.

During many of my fifteen trips to Peru from 1977 to 2017, I visited Vicos, and twice I stayed with families for short periods of interviewing and accompanying Vicosinos in their daily activities. My visits over the

Outside the church after a wedding in Vicos, 2011. Photo by author.

last decade have given me an acute sense of current problems of domestic abuse, alcoholism, and women's secondary status, even at a time when more women are taking on local leadership roles, when as many girls as boys are sent to school, and when a number of them go on for further study outside the community. As more young people leave Vicos, it may be that what we see in the community are the more traditional practices among those who remain. If I were carrying out a similar study today with the benefit of firsthand field research, I would address these contradictory tendencies, and I would also seek out more material on the cultural meanings and social inequality based on race and ethnicity to complement my political economic analysis of gender relations. Indeed, I have conducted more recent ethnographic work in Vicos with these concerns in mind, at a time when there is much national and local attention to the value of cultural heritage, patrimony, and tourism, which I discuss in part 3. Here, I note that while I was influenced in the 1970s by the feminist anthropological concern to theorize the "origins of women's oppression" in the development of class relations and the interface of peasant society and the state, since that time I have become more conscious of the profoundly racialized history of social relations, as well as the more subtle ways that sexism plays out in Andean settings.

It is worth relating an experience I had a few years ago when I visited one of the NGOs working closely with Vicos, in nearby Marcará: I had arranged to go with two of my graduate students from the University of Florida to a meeting to discuss the NGO, Urpichallay, and its perceptions of the Vicos community, including Vicos's development prospects and its foray into cultural tourism. I had indicated an interest in gender questions, but my students and I were surprised to be met by a poised young woman on the staff who was prepared to give us an elaborate presentation, complete with visuals projected on a screen, on gender complementarity in the Andes and, specifically, in Vicos. She told us about Andean cosmovision and the dualism of gender practices, explaining that the harmony in the community was based on these enduring principles. When we raised some pointed questions about how to interpret everyday practices such as women eating last in the family or walking behind their husbands, she had both practical and symbolic answers at hand. She was not as well prepared to speak about more troubling instances of domestic violence. I found it remarkable how closely she adhered to the textbook descriptions of age-old Andean gender complementarity, though this is what Barrig found among NGOs in southern Peru as well. Certainly such ideological views held by nonindigenous people are rooted deeply in notions of lo andino, and if ethnographic accounts have contributed to their enduring character, we need to be mindful of that.

In another research trip soon after, I got to know a schoolteacher who had taught in the Vicos community for over twenty years. A mestiza from Marcará, she had close ties to the children in the school and to many of their families. She told me in some confidence that she was alarmed by what she knew of domestic violence in families, where men were often shielded because women were reluctant to denounce them publicly. To publicly denounce them, women would need to travel to Huaraz and file formal complaints; I related this to the teacher, giving her contact information for several offices serving women in the region. Sadly, it appears that the force of customary practices and community ties generally keeps women from taking these steps. While my reading of the CPP archives did not offer me evidence of domestic abuse within families, and the egregious cases of gendered violence that I found were the result of Vicosinas being assaulted by men from outside Vicos—usually mestizos from nearby towns—it is quite possible that violence within the family and community was present in earlier times. However, it would be difficult to determine whether such violence in the community has increased in recent decades with greater integration in the wider society. To be sure, there has been much change in Vicos; and even with out-migration the population has tripled since the early 1950s, potentially contributing to social dislocation and violence against women.

While my work on gender relations in Vicos during a period of dramatic change continues to receive occasional reference in the United States and Peru, it may be largely receding from view, never having made a discernible impact on the thinking of others working in the community. Billie Jean Isbell (2011: 300), who directed efforts to reconsider the CPP a half century later and to encourage new collaborative relations between Cornell University and the community, noted that I was "the first person to point out that women had been excluded from the Cornell potato project." However, while the introduction of new varieties of seed potatoes to the men of the community was a telling case of the implications of leaving women out of development processes (particularly when they are key to the maintenance of biodiversity), my analysis went well beyond this single area of the CPP intervention. My broader project sought to demonstrate the shortcomings and unforeseen consequences of "gender-neutral" Western development interventions, which had wide ramifications that were felt by individuals, families, and the community. This is no doubt why it has been largely overlooked, because once the prevalence of gender disparities is recognized it is difficult to retain the same narrative of development success.[14] Yet, as Pribilsky (2009) has noted in his discussion of Vicos as a Cold War laboratory for social change, it may be the unforeseen "side effects" of the intervention that can tell us the most and which should be examined most closely.

In the proceedings of a conference held in Lima on rural women in Latin America, pioneering feminist anthropologist Jeanine Anderson (longtime resident in Peru, mentioned in the introduction), describes my work on Vicos in flattering terms as a "precioso análisis," or beautiful analysis, of the problematic way in which a rural development project can be misguided in its sense that women will be assisted by relieving them of productive activities and giving them still more (reproductive) domestic responsibility. She further links such development practice to a politics of care that requires of women ever-greater unremunerated labor to maintain family and society (Anderson 2011: 49–50). While this may not have been the conscious objective of the CPP, I believe Anderson is correct in concluding that it was the practical consequence of the interventions introduced during its tenure in the community.

Notions of gender complementarity have continued to shape the thinking of many analysts and activists, as seen for example in the pages of the Peruvian magazine *Chacarera* (mentioned earlier), published over several decades by the Lima-based feminist NGO Flora Tristan and directed toward rural women. To contrast articles representing very different perspectives offered by two contributors, we may consider an interview with prominent anthropologist Luis Millones (*Chacarera* 1997) and a piece written by feminist and public intellectual Wilfredo Ardito Vega (2005). Millones maintains that male bias and cultural bias have produced erroneous notions about Andean families and gender relations, and he argues that these are twentieth-century ideological constructions held by those unfamiliar with the important part played by Andean women. He describes Andean women as active participants in love and gender relations, rather than passive subordinates. Ardito Vega, on the other hand, contends that those who wish to recognize fundamentally different cultural practices and social norms of indigenous peasant communities, and who view interventions from outside as a Western imposition, embrace a "cultural relativism" that may stand in the way of efforts to extend women's rights to the rural sector. Both views have merit and warrant further discussion. Despite their differences, however, I believe that both authors might agree with a point made by feminist historian María Emma Mannarelli (1992: 8) in an earlier issue of *Chacarera*, that "complementarity and hierarchies are not necessarily mutually exclusive."[15]

I continue to find much food for thought in the feminist positions we held in the debates emerging in the 1970s and in the legacy of these debates today. While my work on Vicos may have been too critical of the CPP to be well received by many anthropologists who were closely identified with the project, I am gratified that it has gotten more substantive attention from critical and feminist analysts. In the conclusion to this book, I revisit the question of decolonial feminism's new insights into some of the heated debates of the past. For now, however, I leave it to readers to judge whether the work that follows, despite its limitations, illuminates past and present feminist thought on Andean women and beyond.

1 Women and Men in Vicos, Peru

A CASE OF UNEQUAL DEVELOPMENT

The following appeared as a chapter in a book edited by my graduate school advisor, William W. Stein, *Peruvian Contexts of Change* (Transaction Books, 1985). Earlier versions came out as working papers (Babb 1976, 1980a), and, much later, the work was translated into Spanish and published in Lima in a feminist series on gender and development (Babb 1999).

.   .   .   .   .

Over the decade 1952–62, the Andean community of Vicos in Peru was the location of one of the largest and best-known projects in applied anthropology in the world. It won international attention especially because of its success in guiding Vicos through a transition from feudal hacienda to autonomous community. While the abolition of the servile mode of production must be viewed as progressive for the community as a whole, this essay shows that some important changes brought about in Vicos, which were intended to assist in the transition to greater participation in the dominant capitalist economy, had very different consequences for men and women.

The Peru-Cornell Project began in Vicos in 1952 as the cooperative effort of Cornell University and the Peruvian Indian Institute. The late professor Allan R. Holmberg took the opportunity to lease the Hacienda Vicos in order to direct and study social change, and many social scientists and technical personnel worked with the project over the next ten years. My study draws heavily on unpublished field data of members of the Peru-Cornell Project, as well as the published literature on Vicos, to document the changing conditions in women's and men's lives. Vicos is not unique in Peru, for much of the country underwent similar land reform a few years later, but it is unique in the conscious way that many changes were introduced and reported by researchers. This makes Vicos particularly appropriate for a study that traces the effect of capitalist development on the fabric of human relations.

The last few years have seen a growing body of research concerning the differential effects of capitalist development on women and men, and this has aided me in taking a critical approach to the subject. Much of this essay shows that women were not integrated in the development of Vicos in the 1950s, and this is what we may expect of capitalist development. More accurately, women are and always have been integrated in society, but often in ways oppressive to them. I do not mean to idealize the past in contrasting the community under the hacienda system and after its abolition. Feudalism was oppressive to both men and women, and women, as throughout class societies, were subordinated to men. If I emphasize the strengths of the traditional Andean family under feudalism, it is not to deny that there were inequalities between women and men but to show the relatively greater inequalities that came with the historical changes in Vicos.

In this essay I first describe women's and men's lives under the hacienda system. Then I consider the changes brought about by the project in the transition to community autonomy, including the commercialization of agriculture, leadership and skill development, and improved education. The next few sections focus on how women's role has been devalued in the areas of production, socialization, and sexual relations. Next, I discuss resistance to change in the contexts of the family under the hacienda and of women after its abolition. Finally, I place the unequal effects of capitalist development on women and men in Vicos in a broader perspective.[1]

WOMEN AND MEN OF HACIENDA VICOS

From 1952 until 1957 the hacienda system remained intact in Vicos under Cornell's management, and changes were introduced in the areas of agriculture, leadership, and education. Between 1957 and 1962 the Vicosinos rented the estate themselves and attained self-government, and in 1963 Vicos was permanently expropriated and sold to the Vicosinos with a twenty-year government loan. Here the routine of life under the hacienda system is discussed, as reported by Peru-Cornell Project field-workers; the changes are considered in the next section.

Located in north-central Peru 250 miles from Lima, Vicos lies in the valley of the Santa River, the Callejón de Huaylas. In 1952, the population of Vicos was slightly less than two thousand Quechua-speaking people (it has since increased to over four thousand). Vicosinos are peasants (country people), but they have frequent contact with mestizos (townspeople) surrounding Vicos. Their relations with mestizos, who are bilingual Spanish-Quechua speakers of the Andean middle class, have often been exploitative, since the Vicosinos are part of a subordinated social class. This essay refers particularly to the relationship of Vicos to the nearest mestizo town, Marcará.

Traditionally, the Vicos estate was leased every five or ten years to the highest bidder by the Public Welfare Society of Huaraz. Heads of households were required to work three days per week for the *patrón* (lessee), and in return, their families were allotted small plots of land to farm. When Cornell took over the operation of the hacienda in 1952, there were 252 registered *colonos,* or peons (Barnett 1960: 28). Almost all were men, with the exception of several women, mainly widows and deserted wives. However, other women substituted for their husbands and sons. Barnett (1960: 30) writes that there were sometimes up to one hundred women and children in the fields, particularly before fiestas. Their work generally consisted of planting, weeding, and harvesting.

While men had the major responsibility to work in the fields, women carried out most household tasks, and this division of labor still exists.[2] Women prepare and serve food, launder clothes, tend household gardens and small animals, fetch water and firewood, and care for their children. When older children are not available to herd larger animals on the *puna* (high grasslands), women perform that task as well. And whenever they are not otherwise occupied, women busy themselves with their spinning.

In addition to these everyday activities, men and women carry out a number of occasional or specialized activities. Many men perform wage labor outside Vicos. Most men weave, and some specialize in making baskets, rope, adobes, and a number of other goods. Women card and wash wool, brew *chicha* (corn beer), and carry on most of the weekly trade in the town of Marcará, six kilometers below Vicos in the main valley. *Tintoreros*, or specialists in dying cloth blue, are found among both women and men, but in 1950 women outnumbered men seven to three among principal tintoreros (PCP: Vázquez 3/50).[3] A person of either sex may specialize as a *curandero* (curer), but here, too, women are in a majority. Women with this skill are highly respected and often sought out: "Curanderas can treat anything the doctor can, and witchcraft and related ills besides" (PCP: Blanchard 2/3/56). Although most women know how to assist in childbirth, some women, often curanderas, are skilled *parteras* (midwives). All these specializations carry prestige in Vicos, although many people believe that mestizos in Marcará are better at performing these services.

The division of labor by sex in Vicos is fairly rigid. Men's and women's tasks are clearly defined and are for the most part carried out in different spheres, the public, or social, sphere and the domestic sphere, respectively. The fieldnotes show that if a man does "women's work" he may be ridiculed (PCP: Vázquez 4/22/49). Despite the reluctance of many men to carry out tasks customarily done by women, there are exceptions. Some men regularly fetch water, wash eating utensils, prepare the bed, and perform other such jobs (PCP: Pava 6/27/52).

Women's role appears to be more flexible than men's. As already mentioned, women were required to work on the hacienda fields when no men were available, and when there was extra work to do. Women's familiarity with agricultural work makes them in some ways less dependent on men than vice versa.[4] When there are no women in a family, a man often needs to hire community women to produce goods or perform household tasks that men are not trained to do.

It is probably best to regard sex roles in Vicos as interdependent or complementary (Stein 1975a), for unattached adults of both sexes have difficulties in providing for themselves. Most Vicosinos without spouses are elderly, and most of the elderly are women; William Mangin (1954: II-3) counted forty-two men and eighty-six women over sixty in 1952. The problems of these Vicosinos in supplying themselves with food are increased, and unless they are lucky enough to be cared for by their children, they may be reduced to begging from neighbors (PCP: Pava 2/17/52). A number of cases of elderly widows in the fieldnotes indicate their insecure and impoverished condition.[5]

The importance of the male-female unit in community life is revealed in Vicosinos' attitudes toward marriage. As Richard Price (1965: 319) writes, the marriage ceremony "marks the entrance of a Vicosino couple into the adult world." A man can become a *varayoq* (traditional official) or sponsor a fiesta or work party only if he has a wife. Women occasionally sponsor fiestas and work parties, and they, too, are usually married, although a widow may organize a work party (PCP: Barnett 12/17/53). In general, women are cosponsors with their husbands.

Whether or not a wife acts as cosponsor of a fiesta or work party with her husband, it is a joint effort. Daisy Irene Núñez del Prado Béjar (1975a: 395), who did fieldwork in southern Peru, points out that there are two requirements for an *ayni* (reciprocal labor party): the male sponsor must fulfill his obligations in the labor exchange and his wife must provide food of good quality. This means organizing a work group of her own, and both her own status and her husband's will increase if she manages well and is a good cook. It is largely through a couple's success in organizing fiestas and labor exchanges that the husband, as the formal representative of the family, derives political power. The wife's cooperation is essential for his advancement, since she controls the household's economic distribution— that is, the means for gaining political power (Núñez del Prado Béjar 1975b: 626–27).

Women in Vicos hold considerable power in the family. It is clear that their collaboration is required in all important matters concerning the family, and their opinions are sought before any major decisions are announced by their husbands. For example, when Cornell introduced new seed potatoes, many of those men who agreed to try planting them indicated that their wives encouraged them to do so (PCP: Vázquez 4/27/54). One man who was thinking of sharecropping with the hacienda's new seeds reported that some Vicosinos were afraid since it was not the custom, but that his wife was encouraging him: "In married life it is good to talk everything over. If she said it would be bad, I wouldn't sow" (PCP: Barnett 1/5/54). Women also seem to have been influential in the community's decision to rent Vicos (PCP: Vázquez 4/23/56, 4/25/56). In one case, when a man neglected to consult his wife before accepting an office, she was very angry since it would mean that they would be unable to pay their share of rent for the hacienda (PCP: Vázquez 10/5/56).

Men in Vicos generally own more land and animals than women do, but women's role in the household gives them considerable economic control over the family property. Property in Vicos is theoretically passed down from parents to sons and daughters equally. However, sons appear to be the preferred inheritors—Mario Vázquez (1952: 44) writes that sons and unmarried daughters inherit *chacras* (fields)—and sometimes, when there are no male heirs, other male relatives claim chacras (PCP: Pava 8/17/52). Under the hacienda system, land and homes belong to the estate, but they are held by families for generations. Cattle are the only valuable property that can be sold, and they constitute the measure of wealth in Vicos (Vázquez 1965: 414). Land, animals, and other property are cared for without regard to ownership, but along the lines of the sexual division of labor. However, all goods are individually owned. The fieldnotes offer conflicting views on the control of buying and selling of property. One view states that the owner has control over his or her property (PCP: Pava 5/17/52), while another states that, regardless of ownership, women control small property and men control cattle and other large property (PCP: Vázquez 4/28/49). Most likely there is flexibility. When one man was asked if husbands and wives could sell each other's property without permission, he said that it was possible, but that if there was love between them they would not (PCP: Pava 2/17/53). Nevertheless, women's central role in the household and in marketing gives them greater leverage than men over the family economy.

The family in Vicos is not only a good economic arrangement but also a close-knit social group. Men and women express love and respect for one another and great affection for their children. This closeness is not displayed publicly, where those of different sex and age do not so readily mix, but at home: as one Vicosino said, "We do everything together." While all agree that the man is "head of the house," this appears to reflect his role as public representative for the family rather than his position in the household. When pressed, one man added that while he was "head" of work in the fields, the women in the households were "heads" of the kitchen and the animals (PCP: Pava 2/17/53).

A number of men and women in Vicos were asked what is expected of a wife or a husband, and nearly all responded that it is most important that they be good workers. Those few who do not meet their family obligations are criticized; they are not "real men" or "good women." Love between spouses is considered important and fidelity is generally expected, although men have a little more leeway. In their sexual activity, women and men seem to be equal participants, neither sex playing a dominant or submissive role (PCP: Pava 2/17/53). The only exception to the general pattern of mutual respect of the sexes appears to be when there is drinking, especially by young men after fiestas. At such times men may become sexually aggressive, but their intoxication sometimes enables women to overpower them, as several cases in the fieldnotes show (Vázquez 1952). The contrast between private and public sex is part of the cultural convention that women act as subordinates in the public sphere.

In traditional Vicos, women were not fully equal with men. The publicly held view that women were "worth less" was expressed to fieldworkers by both sexes. However, women's public status was less important than their position in the household, where they had something very near equality with men. The complementarity of women's and men's roles derived from the recognition of the equal importance of their activities. As I will show, women's position in Vicos is deteriorating as a result of the devaluation of the household sphere of activity.

SOCIAL CHANGE, 1952–63

When the Peru-Cornell Project came to Vicos, there were several focal areas in which the organizers planned to introduce change. Improvements in agriculture and skills, development of community leadership, and better schooling were the major goals. Men were the targets of modernization, and women were affected only indirectly in ways that have been largely ignored in the Vicos literature. Although some consequences of development in Vicos have had adverse effects on women, this does not reflect the intentions of the project, whose members clearly desired to improve the lives of all Vicosinos. However, the male bias of Western social science and community development programs is clear in the Vicos Project.

One of the first agricultural innovations Cornell introduced in Vicos was a new type of seed potato. A recent blight made this timely, and it was hoped that production would increase sufficiently to make potatoes commercially profitable for the community. Since men made up the majority of peons and performed most work on both the hacienda and their own fields, it is not surprising that agricultural items were introduced to them and not to their wives. What was not realized, however, was the degree to which decision making was traditionally a family affair. The weight of women's opinions in the decision to plant new seed potatoes was discussed in the previous section. Women do not necessarily reach agreement with men once they are included in the decision-making process; I take up women's opposition to changes unfavorable to them later in the chapter.

One student doing fieldwork in Vicos recognized the importance of women's influence (from a male point of view). He makes the following comments about one couple:

> Manuel seemed to be a rather assertive sort of person. In addition, he is a fairly important person in the community. His wife seems to be a very shy, sweet, retiring person. Yet Paul Doughty [director of student researchers] says that she runs the family and that Manuel is just a "yes man." The retiring character of the women in public among Vicosinos may be misleading in terms of decision making and authority (as is true among gringos). A study should definitely be made of the influence of the women on their husbands, whether officers in the community or not, as far as decision making and attitudes are concerned. The project may be able to reach a more amiable rapport with the community by convincing the women of its beneficence— with the weight of their opinions then being a push for the men. (PCP: Skalka 6/30/61)

Since modern farming techniques were taught to men but not to women, this increased the importance of men's labor for the hacienda, while women's traditional methods and tools kept their production as occasional peons and household gardeners at the same low level. With the introduction of cash crops for cultivation by modern methods, men earned incomes that could be invested in the improvement of their production, while women's traditional production suffered a relative decline.[6]

As a result of reforms in the hacienda system, women lost some of the few "rights" they had as workers, exploitative as the system may have been. In its effort to end abuses, the project eliminated the positions of household servants and unremunerated peons. Three of nine positions (not including *mayorales,* or "field bosses") had been reserved for women under the traditional system, and these were abolished. The hacienda *huarmi,* or hacienda woman, served as cook for the administrative staff and received *temple* (the peon bonus) as well as two weeks' rest at the end of her service. The *cuchi mítzej,* or pig herder, was a widow selected to care for the hacienda's pig herd for two weeks, without compensation. The *mítaj* was a single woman working as a servant or assistant to the cook for one week, without compensation (Stein 1975b: 87). These last two positions were the only unremunerated tasks peons performed. Despite the exploitative nature of the services women carried out, these institutionalized positions with the hacienda may have given them a degree of leverage with the patróns that was lost when Cornell took over operations. The privileges that peons had formerly won from patróns were seen as rights; the project's replacement of the paternalistic practice of granting privileges with improved, but stricter, working conditions was considered by many Vicosinos to usher in a new type of abuse. It should be noted that women were not offered new positions when their old ones were abolished.

Under the traditional hacienda system, women and children served as registered peons when adult males were not available. The project, too, permitted their participation, but the fieldnotes suggest that women and children may have been discouraged from working for the hacienda. One woman who desired work with the hacienda thought she would not be accepted because she was a woman; she was permitted to register as a laborer, but only on the condition that her brother carry out the work (PCP: Vázquez 1954). And researcher Norman Pava (PCP: 1/23/53) reported that "the hacienda often did not accept the children."

Another deprivation women experienced during the project's tenure was loss of their gleaning rights. Traditionally, patróns permitted women and children to gather potatoes left by the men during the harvests. Assessing the change in Vicos up to 1964, Doughty (1971: 111) writes,

"Gone, however, are the hordes of gleaners who scavenged the Patron's fields and the degrading experience this constituted. . . . [This change has] taken place without prompting from Project personnel." That this change was in the interests of the Vicosinos and motivated by them is contradicted in the following passage from the fieldnotes written during the project's period as operator: "Perhaps because the patrón [overseer] was observing, the *mayorales* were very active in defending the hacienda from the women and children. As guardians, they seemed to have no sympathy for the marauders; they shouted at them, swore, lashed out with their whips, lashing women on the legs to keep them back" (PCP: Pava 1/24/54).[7] Women were also carefully guarded when they worked as sorters, as they sometimes hid potatoes in their skirts. Pava describes the expert maneuvers of one young woman as she hid a large potato (PCP: 1/22/52), and the collaboration of men and women in pilfering potatoes (PCP: 1/31/52).

Women's declining activity in the fields meant not only a less important role in agriculture but also fewer opportunities to join with other women and men in the public sphere. Aside from fiestas, working for the hacienda and gleaning during harvests were the only occasions they had to take part in large social gatherings. William Blanchard (PCP: 5/8/53), then field director, observed a lunch break on the hacienda field: "[The work] kept on until 1:00, at which time the people moved off to eat their lunch. Enrique Luna [*mayordomo* employed by the project] said that the women are much friendlier than the men. He said that they all gather together in a circle and even share their food. The men, on the other hand, tend to stay apart in groups, and do not ever share food with one another."

Describing gleaning as a social event that draws women and children from miles around, Pava (PCP: 1950) recorded one woman's experience: "Gleaning was a time for women to gossip and visit in the chacra with other women, and for kids to play. Carolina seemed to like to go to glean; she often went even when there were plenty of potatoes in the house."

A number of new skills were introduced to the Vicos community outside the area of agriculture, and here too it was primarily men who were affected. Attention was focused on teaching masonry, carpentry, and other skills to men, who became specialists in building construction and were contracted by authorities in and outside of Vicos. Dobyns (1971: 160) compares the number of artisans in different specialties in 1951 and 1963. The majority of skills listed are those of men. The largest percentage increases in artisans (with the exception of midwives, whose number increased, unaccountably, by 1,000 percent, from three to thirty women) were among those income-producing specialties whose skills had been taught to men. These new occupations included mason, flavored-ice dealer, carpenter, firewood dealer, iceman, charcoal maker, and vendor (these increased between 129 percent and 266 percent).[8]

What is striking about Dobyns's figures is that the one specialty which was introduced to women, that of seamstress, increased only slightly during the years of the project. Included with tailors, their number increased only from 12 to 14 individuals. Until 1960, one wealthy Vicos man owned the only sewing machine in the community, and he and several mestiza seamstresses from Marcará were often contracted to make Vicos women's dresses. In the early 1960s a number of Vicosinos, mostly women (toward whom the classes were directed), learned to sew from a bilingual mestizo instructor. By 1963, 167 women had enrolled and more machines were acquired. This skill freed women from the choice between the time-consuming task of making clothes by hand—Mangin (1954: I-3) writes that it is, along with agriculture and giving fiestas, one of the most time-consuming activities—or depending on and paying for the service of mestizo seamstresses. In making this instruction available, the project did Vicosinos a real service. The classes were also a chance for women to socialize and receive academic instruction. Dobyns (1971: 146) writes that 27 women learned to read Spanish during sewing classes (undoubtedly on a very limited basis).

However, in directing the teaching of sewing to women as a homemaking skill, the project may have caused women to become more entrenched in the production of household utilities for direct consumption and, thus, separated from commodity production. Very few (as indicated in the figures above) manufactured clothing for sale outside the family, nor were women encouraged to do so. In speaking of the efforts of many community development programs to make housewives more efficient, Boserup (1970: 221) points out that this sometimes covers up the lack of effort to improve women's production outside this role. Rather than bringing them into the labor market, this training may be offered to women "as a sort of compensation for the refusal to give them jobs in the modern sector and as a deliberate method of reducing the number competing with men for employment in the modern sector." This may not have been the purpose of sewing instruction in Vicos, but as a token improvement in the women's sphere it seems to have had this effect.[9]

Under the hacienda system, traditional authority was held by seventeen varayoq of nine different statuses in the political-religious hierarchy headed by the *alcalde* (mayor). According to Clifford Barnett (1960: 63) their power had been in decline since the turn of the century, and by midcentury their only functions other than religious ones were as lackeys of the patrón (renter). In its planned transfer of power from patrón to Vicosinos, the Peru-Cornell Project developed leadership among younger, better-educated men who were "more committed to the goals of modernization" (Holmberg 1971: 47). Power was transferred from project personnel to mayorales (as a transitional expedient—these men were old and respected, but less tradition-oriented than the varayoq) and then to the leaders culti-vated among the young men, ten of whom were elected as delegates in 1957. These men were frequently literate army veterans, *licenciados*, who had had experience on the coast. The transfer of power from old to young men was seen as a temporary move, the expectation being that all Vicosinos would become literate and "change-oriented" in the future (Dobyns 1971: 155). Although it may have been hoped that all men would one day be potential leaders, certainly women were never viewed in this perspective.

During the project's tenure as operator, all peons assembled for weekly meetings known as *mandos*, where they received their pay and work assignments and participated in decision making. The mando was the major source of information and communication for Vicosinos. It was composed almost entirely of men; most women who attended were recorded as representatives of their absent husbands or sons. The follow-ing report in the fieldnotes concerning a woman who appeared with her husband before the mayorales to defend their land, which was to be dis-possessed, illustrates the male-dominated character of these meetings:

> The subject was apparently settled, and the mayorales about to start dis-cussing something else, when Mendoza's wife (she looks much older than Mendoza), who had been lurking in the doorway, sprang into the room and screeched a diatribe against Sánchez and Leyva. She declared them lazy *pin-gas paradas* (erect penises) who stood up and screwed other people. If Sánchez wished to dispose of her chacra, she said, he would first have to kiss

her *chucha* [vagina], and the only way a pinga like him could get near her chucha was if she were dead. At this point, Sánchez interrupted her, demanded that she leave, and said he refused to be talked to in such a way. He said it was not proper for her to be addressing the mayorales anyway since the affair concerned her husband and not her. She refused to leave, but stood there yapping away harshly. Mario Vázquez [project staff member] asked her husband to eject her, but Mendoza did not move. Vázquez then told Tadeo to eject her, but he did not move from his seat either. Vázquez then got up from his seat and approached her and put out his hands as if to push her, upon which she sat down on the floor and refused to move, talking all the while. Vázquez pushed against her with his shins until, still declaiming, she got up from the floor and Vázquez and Enrique Luna walked her to the door and out the gate. She remained outside the gate for a minute or so, shouting through it . (PCP: Pava 8/19/52)

Excluded from the formal channels of communication, women resorted to desperate appeals to the patrón and mayorales. Such behavior was formerly typical of all Vicosinos, but reforms in the hacienda system gave men more voice in decision making and greater dignity in the community.

The third area of planned change in which the sexes were differentially affected, education, has been discussed by Stein (1975a). In contrast to development in the areas of agriculture, skills, and leadership, educational development should, in theory, have benefited male and female alike. However, Stein points out that parallel situations are forming in the economic and educational contexts—the gap is widening between those who have more and those who have less. Although a school had existed in Vicos since 1940, it had made no peasant literate by the time of the project. In 1953, a nuclear school was established. After ten years, 18 percent of Vicosinos over seven years old had attended school, and 17 percent of them were Spanish speakers (Stein 1975a: 6). Despite this progress, Stein (1975a: 13) writes, "the gap between the best educated boys and the best educated girls has increased appreciably since 1950[,] when almost everybody lacked access to schooling and ignorance was equally characteristic of both sexes. The increasing inequality seems to have accented the devaluation of the female."

Vicosinos give a number of reasons why it is not so important for girls to attend school. Some typical responses from the fieldnotes are: "It's not the custom"; and "Women belong in the house. They should work there, cooking and cleaning. They don't need to read or write for that" (PCP: Egoavil Escobar 4/8/59). For boys, on the other hand, schooling is important, as one woman, whose husband was not educated, explained to a fieldworker: "Boys, yes, they must learn Spanish so that they are not like my husband, who didn't know anything and suffered a lot in the army; also, it will serve them when they have to go to work in other places" (PCP: Milla de Vázquez 1/13/58).

Another reason why girls may not attend school is that it violates the strict separation of the sexes in public, which is maintained from childhood on. The discomfort of both sexes, but especially girls, was observed: "The boys talk among themselves and the girls whisper among themselves. Children of the opposite sex are never seen talking together in the dining area or in other places at school. On the contrary, the general attitude is one of fighting and repulsion between them. . . . The children always resist sitting next to someone of the opposite sex. . . . The little girls try to turn a little as though wanting to move away from the boys with whom they share tables" (PCP: Milla de Vázquez 10/28/58).

Although 82 girls were enrolled in school in Vicos in 1971 (there were 296 boys), they were concentrated in the first three grades, while some boys continued through fifth grade and several went on to secondary school in Carhuaz. The resistance of mothers to sending girls to school, and the resistance of girls themselves, may be explained by their perception of the social consequences of schooling. Stein (1975a: 41) writes, "By educating themselves out of the campesina category, they not only run the risk of losing the security of their role in productive labor but they face the danger of losing the sexual complementation of the rural family in order to gain the economic dependence, restriction of freedom, and sexual impoverishment which appear to mark the female role in the Peruvian bourgeois family."

The interrelatedness of the three aspects of social change discussed above and their consequences is clear. As men become more skilled and produce commercial crops for the market, their ties with the national economy grow. Similarly, as Vicosino leaders are recognized and become involved in politics at the district level, they widen their contacts with the larger society. And as all Vicosino men are now encouraged to participate in military service and more men perform wage labor outside Vicos, the differential between the outside contact of men and of women is increasing. This makes education, especially knowledge of Spanish, more important for men, who have use for it. Women's exclusion from wider participation may then be justified on the basis of their being unfit. Thus, while men become modern and active in an ever-widening sphere, women continue their traditional ways in a sphere that is rapidly shrinking.

The growing division between the domestic and public spheres in which women and men move in Vicos has meant the lowering of women's status. The traditional separation of the two spheres was quite strong in the community. While the sexes were near equals in the household, women assumed the culturally sanctioned subordinate role in public. Women's role has been described as having a dual character (Stein 1975a), one that is assertive in the home and submissive outside it. Two important activities that took on a different character in the domestic and public spheres were cooking and eating. In the household, cooking for the family and for work parties was "women's work," and although in a few households women ate apart from men, most often families ate together (PCP: Milla de Vázquez 9/30/57).[10] When food was prepared outside the home for special occasions, however, men took over the cooking; and when eating publicly, the sexes were usually segregated (PCP: Nelson 7/9/61).

Traditionally, when activities of importance took place in the public sphere, men, as the families' public representatives, performed them. With the changes set in motion by the Peru-Cornell Project, many more activities in the public sphere have been taken over by men. The development of agricultural enterprise and leadership by men has been contrasted with women's waning participation in social production and decision making. Further, although men are not directly involved, the school's emerging role in the socialization of children is moving this function from the household to the public domain.

I maintain that when work becomes socialized and profitable, it is very often taken over by men. Encouraged by outside influence, this is occurring in Vicos. For example, when the project eliminated the unpaid female work in the hacienda house, staff did not introduce a paid female position but instead created the job of "houseboy" (a job frowned on by Vicosinos since it was not "man's work"; PCP: Pava 8/11/52). When a cook was needed for the Vicos school, a man was hired, despite the fact that he did not know how to cook and had to be taught by a woman (PCP: "Diario de Francisco Colonia" 6/1/63). Similarly, cattle raising for commercial dairying, although short-lived, transferred the care of cattle from women, the traditional herders and milkers, to men.

The converse of the above point, that when work is domesticated it becomes the task of women, is also illustrated in Vicos. Traditionally, nearly all men sewed, and some sewed for profit; skilled tailors and weavers earned incomes in the community. Sewing machines, brought to women in their homes, turned an income-producing skill into a homemaking skill.

The growing gap between the social and domestic spheres—and the increasing identification of men with the first and women with the second—came about with the abolition of the hacienda system and other social changes brought about in the community. Under the hacienda, the household was the more important sphere of men's and women's activities, since the patrón had control over the social sphere. With the removal of the patrón, and as other changes were effected, Vicos men gained control over the social sphere, which is now the locus of many former functions of the domestic sphere, as well as new functions—all adding up to an increasingly important role for men in the community and a devalued role for women in the home.

WOMEN'S CONDITION

Inequality is affecting several different aspects of women's condition and can be traced to related social change in Vicos. Here I use Juliet Mitchell's (1973) framework of analysis. Like Engels (1972: 71–72), Mitchell recognizes that women's condition is based not only on their role in production but also on their role in reproduction (or the production of the family). She develops the concept of reproduction to include patterns of childbearing, the socialization of children, and sexuality. While childbearing has not undergone any obvious change in Vicos, the other two elements are, along with production, important loci of changes that affect women in the Vicos community.

These elements of women's experience are interrelated, but for analytical purposes it is useful to consider them separately. Furthermore, as

Mitchell points out, each element has reached a different stage at any given place and time. Taking a position similar to Mitchell's in order to examine the situation of rural women of Latin America, Lourdes Arizpe (1975b) has emphasized these same aspects of women's condition as crucial to our understanding.

Production

The effects of the control and commercialization of agriculture by Vicos men on the status of women's labor have already been described. We saw that as the Vicosinos gained control of their land, men's productivity increased, while women's participation in the fields appears to have declined and they were redefined as homemakers.[11] The introduction of sewing machines was useful to women, but other time-consuming tasks, such as grinding corn, were still performed in the traditional ways. Whatever the absolute change in their productive activities, it is certain that women's labor would be valued less since women would lack the new skills that men acquired.

An emphasis was placed by project personnel on cash value for labor as an indication of personal worth and dignity.[12] Unremunerated work for the hacienda was abolished, and wages were raised from their nominal level. Forced public labor for the district was also ended. Most significantly, Vicosinos reaped the rewards of their own production: "Even during the initial five-year experimental intervention, Vicosinos began to sell garden produce for cash. Ever since then, buying and selling commodities for cash has been the Vicos norm. Cash has been the means of escape from the traditional Indian subservience and interpersonal dependence that characterizes the manorial system. In the Andes, social subservience has long involved personal service. The serf or peasant with cash need no longer pay with personal service for services rendered" (Dobyns 1974: 208).

A number of enterprises besides agricultural work for the cooperative became important income-producing activities for some Vicos men during the 1960s. Some became involved in a forestation program, others began dairying, and several took over the management of the Chancos Hotel on property adjacent to Vicos. In comparison, women's work has seen little change in Vicos, as it is still geared to production for family use rather than for exchange in the cash economy.[13] When men participate in social labor and women are excluded from it, women are denied what Karen Sacks (1974) calls "social adulthood." Like Boserup, Sacks suggests that this is often useful to ruling classes in controlling laborers, whether it is deliberate or not. Once divisions are created between the sexes, differences between women and men are translated into a system of differential worth.[14]

When cash becomes a social necessity, as it is in any capitalist economy, and men are the ones who earn it, women become economically dependent on men. The contrast between women's traditional leading role in the control of the Andean economy (Núñez del Prado Béjar 1975a) and their emerging dependent role in Vicos is striking. This is illustrated by the concerns of a number of Vicos women who worried about paying their family's share of rent when the hacienda was abolished. One woman expressed the fears of others: "Asked if she was in favor of the plan to rent Vicos, she answered yes. She added, 'But we women, how will we get money to pay the rent?' [She says her husband will earn the money when he returns from military service.] 'If everyone accepts the plan to rent, we can't be the only ones not to accept it.' Once again she asked, 'How will we get the money?'" (PCP: Vázquez 4/23/56).

Socialization of Children

Women's role in the socialization of children is being challenged by the school in Vicos, which is slowly growing in importance. This is significant not only because it is another area in which women's role is being devalued but also because the school's effect as socializer is to divide the family and the community (Stein 1975a: 2).

In Vicos both women and men have traditionally taken great interest in their children, and both mothers and fathers act as disciplinarians and givers of affection. However, in Vicos as almost everywhere, mothers are the primary socializers of children. They are more closely linked with the household and oversee the rearing of their children, while their husbands work in the fields. Mothers and their children are in close contact until daughters marry and until sons begin to perform men's work with their fathers at the age of ten or twelve.

Children are given important responsibilities very early. When they reach the age of three or four they perform chores (Doughty 1971: 97), and at five or six they herd sheep and goats (Price 1961: 2). Since their work is necessary to the household, children are important and respected members of the family as an economic and social unit. Children are valued, and large families of many sons and daughters are desired. Family ties are strong, and children generally remain loyal to their parents, especially their mothers, into their old age.

One of the ways in which mothers socialize their children is to train them to fear and distrust mestizos. Beliefs about the evildoings of mestizos are widely held by peasants in the Peruvian highlands, and these stem from their experiences as a subordinated class. Doughty (1971: 95) describes the fears of Vicosinos: "Covertly, the Vicosino response to every threatening and humiliating interaction with Mestizos (and all outsiders) was one of fear and great mistrust. Mestizos were often thought to be *pishtakos*, human ogres who murdered Indians in order to make use of their bodily fat and organs as grease. As bogy-men in childhood tales and as domineering and abusive figures in real life, Mestizos were feared more than hated, and therefore shunned."

Passive resistance and feigned ignorance were the means by which Vicosinos learned to protect themselves in their relations with mestizos. Doughty (1971: 95–96) continues: "If contact were unavoidable, however, a kind of passive non-cooperation would be adopted in the interaction situation. If the Mestizo wanted him to work, the Vicosino would have to be instructed repeatedly as to his chores. 'Dimwittedness' was the sanctioned mental state; lack of initiative and brightness its manifestation in behavior."

Although ties of *compadrazgo* (ritual kinship) linked some Vicosinos to mestizos of Marcará in a patrón-client relationship, their unequal social class relationship was maintained. The most important patrón-client relationship in Vicos was that in which the cultural broker was the patrón himself. Despite his paternalistic role, he was mistrusted and feared. When project personnel took over the role of patrón, they were no exception, and a number of them were feared as pishtakos (PCP: Pava 7/5/52).

Women especially fear mestizos, partly because they have less contact with them (Barnett 1960: 76), but certainly because of the nature of that contact as well. Mestizos are feared as rapists for good reason (as is discussed later), and women are wise to steer clear of them.

Women's attitudes toward mestizos are inculcated by mothers from the time their children are infants (Vázquez 1952: 31, translated in Stein 1961: 228). Although children are taught to show deference to mestizos (Barnett 1960: 76), mothers also instill a certain pride in their children in stressing the differences between the classes. As Stein (1961: 228) writes of Hualcan, so for Vicos: "Indians on the whole feel no great impulse to become mestizos." Mestizos are considered lazy and weak because they do not like to work with their hands. Vázquez (PCP: 3/28/50) wrote in his fieldnotes: "The Vicosino considers himself to be perfect in manners and a great critic of the activities of others."

It is important to consider how the increasing influence of the school in the community may be affecting women's role as socializers. Although still only a minority of Vicos children attend school, the presence of the school and better-educated Vicosinos affects everyone to some degree. Although the school has been in Vicos only a short time, the changes that are occurring as it acquires a more important role in socialization may be shown to work to the disadvantage of women.

Stein (1975a: 2) writes that differential access to schooling in Vicos is resulting in "inequalities in the relations between men and women, parents and children, people who have more schooling and those who have less, and people who participate more advantageously in the Peruvian national market and polity in contrast with others who are disadvantaged." Not only are women the largest group to suffer the consequences of unequal access to schooling, but they must also feel most acutely the effects of "the intrusion of 'national' (i.e., dominant-class) ideology into the rural community" (Stein 1975a: 2). After all, their educated children are becoming like the people their mothers warned them against.

At the present time few students in Vicos make it beyond the first two grades, and most are schooled into subservience.[15] Some teachers in the Vicos school degraded their students to the point of using them as servants. Moreover, it is not only the young and educated who are instructed in their own inferiority, for their parents learn the message of the school through their children.[16]

Of those few who make it to secondary schools in Carhuaz and Caraz, Doughty (1971: 109) writes, "School-acquired knowledge is also precipitating some significant changes within the family, where the children now possess skills which few adults mastered. . . . Consequently, the 'learned child' *(leído)* is often placed upon a pedestal, consulted by his parents, and given special tasks and responsibility." While the education of leídos has freed them from dependence on mestizo intermediaries (Alberti and Cotler 1972: 82), they have become the intermediaries, with all that implies, for their own parents.

As the role of the school as socialization agent continues to increase in importance, and as it both teaches peasants about their own inferiority and permits a few to assume privileged positions in the community, women's role as socializers of children is seriously threatened. As leídos spread the dominant class ideology in Vicos, the solidarity of the family and the community that mothers encouraged in their children can only be undermined.

Sexuality

Like Mitchell, Gayle Rubin (1975) takes up where Engels left off, examining the relations of sexuality. She defines a "sex-gender system" whereby in every society "the biological raw material of human sex and procreation is shaped by human, social intervention and satisfied in a conventional manner" (Rubin (1975: 165). Such a view of the social determination of sexuality is useful in describing the changing conventions of sex and gender in Vicos.

The strong separation of men's and women's activities in Vicos means that male/female gender definitions are strongly marked. From an early age, children understand the different roles of the sexes and the cultural convention that men are "worth more." One father expressed pride in his young son who had made the proper gender adjustment: "Smiling, Juan tells me that his four-year-old son Alejandro already wants to handle the *chuzo* (hand pick) and makes a big distinction between boys and girls. The former can work in place of their fathers, but the latter only serve in the kitchen" (PCP: Milla de Vázquez 9/4/58). Despite the publicly held view that men are the more aggressive sex, the traditional relations of men and women are more balanced than this would suggest. This is apparent in Price's (1965: 314–15) account of courtship behavior, which is initiated by either sex:

> Vicos courtship features considerable sexual freedom, often violent horse-play, and quiet exchanges of presents. Courtship most often occurs during fiestas, visits to the market, certain agricultural activities, or while herding

sheep on the mountain slopes. Significantly, these situations all permit max-
imum freedom from parental or family observation. . . . The extensive teas-
ing, horseplay, and mock battles between the sexes which mark this period
of the life cycle, furthermore, are more than a passing phase, for throughout
their active life husband and wife continue to pummel, pinch, and wrestle
with each other in much the same way they did as late adolescents.

Sexual freedom is enjoyed until marriage, after which it is expected
that spouses will be loyal to each other. Husbands may have more freedom
than wives, but they do not frequently exercise it. When they do, they are
treated to the epithet *mancebado,* a man who has sexual relations with
two or more women (PCP: Vázquez 4/28/49). One married man who had
a relationship with another woman decided to break it off because he
feared he might lose status and be dishonored: "During the present year
he is thinking of abstaining from his visits, because he is *campo mayor* [a
fiesta sponsor], and if he commits adultery during his term he will lose his
authority. Besides, there is a belief that when his term expires they would
throw it in his face that he did not behave as he should have—that is to say,
honorably."

To a certain extent, a double standard is built into the marriage system
in Vicos. During *watanaki,* the first stage of a Vicosino marriage, it is primarily the woman and not the man who is on trial. Since residence during
watanaki is usually patrilocal, the work relationship of the woman and her
prospective mother-in-law is important. Separation during this period is
often due to the dissatisfaction of the man's family with the potential
daughter-in-law or her relatives. Less often it is the woman or members of
her family who initiate the separation (Price 1965). When one Vicosino
was asked whether there was a difference between watanaki and marriage, he responded, "The man doesn't have to keep the woman in watanaki; it's different. The woman has to do the same as if she were married"
(PCP: Pava 2/17/53).

Judging by interviews with Vicos men during the early 1950s, men and
women seem to be near equals in their sexual relationships. The men
questioned agreed that women should be active participants in sex. When
asked whether a woman had to have sexual relations with her husband if
she did not want to, the typical answer was: "If she doesn't want to she
doesn't have to, but she always wants to" (PCP: Pava 2/17/53). There

seems to be the feeling in Vicos that if one sex can be said to enjoy sex more than the other, it is women. It is unfortunate that we do not have a woman's opinion on this matter, but here is a man's: "Women should be given the penis until they are full. If not, they act as if they hadn't eaten in a week. Women should not lack food or penis. This way, they love us more" (PCP: Milla de Vázquez 9/23/55).

Although Vicosinos seem to have fairly easygoing sex lives, both women and men are shy and embarrassed when sexual matters are discussed publicly. When a project member teased a Vicosino about going to see his girlfriend, the latter insisted, "But I'm going to visit my sister." Pava (PCP: 7/20/52) comments, "Miguel Coleto appears very embarrassed when Vázquez pokes fun at him about his girlfriend. Coleto says, "I don't know any woman. I'm still a boy." He stoutly denies ever having had sexual intercourse, and when Vázquez jests with him about this, insisting that he must have had intercourse, Coleto says, 'No, no, señor,' and he hangs his head blushing."

Studying the project fieldnotes, one is struck by the absence of machismo among Vicos men, as noted by Price (1961: 3).[17] Being *muy hombre* (a real man) does not mean being virile or controlling women but, rather, taking responsibility, effectively carrying out obligations, and being a generous host. When one man complained that "men were more macho in the old days" (PCP: Barnett 3/16/54), he meant that they "had more life in them" (referring to leaders of Vicos protests; see Barnett 1960). Another man said that if he had a child, he would name his brother-in-law as his godfather "because he's a real man; because whenever he goes to his house to visit him, he doesn't let him leave without treating him to something to eat" (PCP: Milla de Vázquez 1/21/58). When Pava (PCP: 3/31/53) asked a Vicosino whether a man could go with several women in succession, he answered, "It's dishonorable. . . . I haven't changed women. I'm a man of integrity."

The positive aspects of sexual relations in Vicos should not be taken to mean that women have experienced no oppression in that regard. For example, the double standard mentioned above in relation to watanaki seems to be paralleled in attitudes toward the sexual behavior of young men and women, at least as recently as the 1960s. Price (1961: 31) writes that "parents are far more concerned with the conduct of their daughters than with that of their sons."

Most material in the fieldnotes supports the view that sex is mutually agreed upon by men and women, and that when a man initiates sex at a fiesta or on the puna, he waits to see whether the woman laughs or throws rocks at him, the signals for acquiescence and refusal. However, one description of sexual relations before marriage raises serious questions about this: "Sexual intercourse is generally a mock rape with the girl offering great physical resistance and the man truly overpowering her" (Price 1961: 10). This would suggest that men take advantage of their superior strength and that some "mock rapes" are real ones. Whether this is a recent phenomenon influenced by outside contact or a long-standing occurrence cannot be ascertained from the material at hand. It is known that the *first* reported rape by a Vicosino was committed after the hacienda was expropriated (Stein, personal communication). Significantly, the man was one of the Vicosinos with the widest experience outside the community.

Vicosinas have long been familiar with the danger of rape in their contact with mestizos, and particularly with one notorious mestizo who for years violently assaulted women (PCP: Pava 11/29/51). As Vicos men expand their sphere of movement and bring the dominant male attitudes to their community, women may increasingly suffer such violence as was associated with the men of the class that oppresses them, at the hands of their own men.

Like rape, prostitution has traditionally been known to occur with outsiders. Although there is some suggestion in the fieldnotes that a few Vicos men gave gifts of money to Vicosinas with whom they had liaisons, the circumstances surrounding this are uncertain. Men's experience with prostitutes generally came from periods spent away from Vicos, especially in the army. Women of Vicos knew sexual exploitation under the traditional hacienda system, since they were abused by their mestizo patrons when they worked in the manor house. But it appears that women who had varied sexual backgrounds, including one woman who was known to have been a prostitute on the coast (PCP: Vázquez 9/29/61), were treated no differently from other women in Vicos. Although the economic necessity for prostitution does not seem imminent, we may speculate as to whether men's increasing contact with sex as a commodity outside the community might eventually introduce a demand for prostitutes in Vicos.

It may be expected that as the dominant class ideology gains hold in Vicos, the image of women as submissive and men as their aggressors will alter traditional sexual relations. Stein (1975a: 41) notes that this is in fact occurring as machismo "intrudes itself into Vicos through the school and other relationships with members of higher social strata." As he points out, Vicosinos certainly perceive the greater sexual inequality in the larger society. Men seem to have already adopted mestizo attitudes toward more modern townswomen whom they scorn (PCP: Barnett 1/11/54), and these attitudes may soon be directed to Vicosinas. The ways in which Vicos women are resisting the intrusion of machismo into their community is discussed in the next section.

RESISTANCE TO CHANGE

> In structural terms, the closest thing to the condition of
> women is the condition of others who are or were also
> outside commodity production, serfs and peasants.
>
> Margaret Benston, 1971

The similar situation of women and peasants in relation to the larger society is supported by similar myths about both groups: that they are by nature passive, dependent, and resistant to change. The myths have been perpetuated because they veil the oppression of women and peasants and make it appear that the oppressed are themselves responsible for their condition.[18]

Holmberg (1967) described the "culture of repression" under the traditional hacienda system in Vicos. Men and women alike were subordinated to the patrón, directing their work to his prosperity and their own survival. The cooperation of male and female family members was crucial in what Mariarosa Dalla Costa (1972: 70) calls the "unity of unfreedom." What Lise Vogel (1973: 30) writes about feudalism in general would seem to pertain to the Vicos case: "Although women were certainly oppressed in the feudal family, their labor had a recognized place and function within the terms of feudalism. A division of labor according to sex was built into the feudal relations of production, and women's labor within the family was socially meaningful."

It makes sense to shift the focus from women to the family in considering Vicos under the hacienda system. It has been shown that before the hacienda was abolished, all family members regardless of sex and age were valued workers for the household, which was the center of production. In their relations with mestizos, Vicos families were forced into a dependent role, but they refused to submit fully to the system. Here, the family's resistance under the hacienda system is viewed as a positive response to oppressive conditions, and its resistance to change is seen as a response to unsatisfactory, or partial, change.

Family solidarity manifested itself in Vicos in a number of ways under the traditional and reformed hacienda systems. First, through pretended slowness and through active sabotaging of hacienda work, peasants refused to cooperate with the patrón. Barnett (1960: 32) compared their two work schedules, for the hacienda and for their families: during a seven-hour day in the hacienda field, peons actually worked about five and a half hours after their many breaks were subtracted, while in their own fields breaks were infrequent and the workday longer. Although production increased significantly while Cornell University was operator, the real advance in productivity occurred after the Vicosinos took control of the estate. Furthermore, gleaning and other forms of cooperation in which husbands and wives stole from the hacienda continued under the "reformed" hacienda system. These examples indicate that Vicosinos resisted—that is, withheld their fullest efforts—until after significant structural change had taken place within the community. (They must still resist in their contacts outside Vicos where inequalities persist.)

In Vicos under the hacienda system, there is evidence of families' attempts to prevent inequalities from growing, thus creating community solidarity. For example, neighbors discouraged those families that sold the surplus from their chacras by comparing such activity to prostitution. One man was so criticized that he finally invited others to harvest his field, though he later sold some of his surplus (PCP: Blanchard 11/23/53). Furthermore, Vicosinos expressed resentment over the inequalities in the amounts of land held, although they did not feel redistribution was in order. When Barnett (PCP: 2/8/54) asked a couple if the land should be redivided, the husband said, "'No, it isn't necessary, we have enough.' However, his wife said at this point: 'But some people have a tremendous amount and they ask for more when they really have more than they say. Those people have enough chacras. Some don't and can't manage at all, while others want more than anybody else.'" The couple agreed that it would be a good idea to abolish the hacienda system.

Another woman complained that she was rich until her cows all died, after which she lived in poverty and had to borrow money from wealthier Vicosinos (PCP: Barnett 1/7/54). A Vicosino who was richer than his relatives defended himself, arguing that he was no wealthier than others: "Poor and rich are the same here. I'm neither very rich nor very poor." However, he explained that the oldest families in Vicos had the most land, and he was able to name some "rich" Vicosinos (PCP: Barnett 1/14/54). The attempt to discourage others from growing wealthy and to play down one's own wealth may be seen as a means of leveling social differences in the community. This is also accomplished when the wealthy are pressured to sponsor fiestas and to spend money as officials.

Vicosinos have resisted the development of individual community leaders. When Cornell created leaders and specialists in Vicos, resistance was expressed through the peasants' strong preference for the appointment of outsiders to those positions. The following example from the fieldnotes illustrates Vicosinos' attempts to prevent a privileged group from forming. During a meeting of mayorales, "Vázquez asked what they would think of Andrés Reyes as a teacher. They all, some more emphatically than others, rejected the idea of Andrés—better, they said, bring someone from Carhuaz. They said that Andrés might tell people that he had taught them, that they had become proficient because of him. And this, it seems, is a bad thing" (PCP: Blanchard 2/16/54).

Full-scale protest movements in Vicos, encouraged with help from outside the community, have been described for this century by Barnett (1960), and for the last quarter of the nineteenth century by Stein (1976). Protests did not end with the abolition of the hacienda system. In both 1961 and 1971, Vicosinos successfully demanded changes in the school's personnel (Stein 1975a: 39); and in 1964, Vicosinos forcefully expelled a group of Peace Corps volunteers from the community during a controversy surrounding the Chancos Hotel.

Protests and resistance are clearly not a thing of the past in Vicos. However, there is no longer the strong sense of family solidarity that united men and women, young and old, against similarly experienced inequalities. Now that a number of influential men lead Vicos, and all men have a greater measure of freedom, divisions have been created between the sexes. This has had a definite effect on the family in Vicos.

The optimism of some project personnel in regard to change in the family is puzzling. Holmberg (1971: 44) expressed hope that the project would have a "modernizing effect on the more dependent variables," including the family and kinship. He concluded that this goal had been met, noting that while the project did not intervene directly in the family unit, the latter was affected indirectly (Holmberg 1971: 56). Apparently, what this means is that the increased power of men in the community was followed by the increased authority of the father in the family. Barnett (1960: 81) writes that the hacienda system undermined the authority of the father in the family. The North Americans' expectation of paternal authority seems to have distorted their view of peasant families. The hacienda certainly kept men in a state of dependence in the social sphere, but the relatively egalitarian relations of the sexes in the home is characteristic of rural Peru, of both autonomous communities and haciendas.

When the hacienda system was abolished, so was the "culture of repression." However, what Caulfield (1974) calls the "culture of resistance," the family's way of opposing the dominant class, also broke down as the family became a weaker unit. The growing sexual inequality in Vicos explains why women, rather than all Vicosinos, are now "resistant to change."

The submission and pretended ignorance, which formerly characterized both sexes in the public sphere, now primarily characterizes women. Their generally reserved behavior is accentuated by their lack of knowledge of Spanish, or sometimes feigned ignorance of the language, which is in wider use by men. The close correlation of dress style with language use in Peru may explain in part why Quechua-speaking Vicosinas retain the traditional dress, while Spanish-speaking men are adopting mestizo dress. Perhaps more important, both language and dress are key indicators of social class in Peru, and women's resistance to speaking Spanish and to wearing mestizo dress may be viewed as a refusal to accept the dominant-class culture. This is also suggested by women's rejection of the mestizo form of greeting introduced by the project staff (PCP: Vázquez 6/54).

The strongest form of women's resistance is probably their resistance to schooling (Stein 1975a). School is the one vehicle for self-advancement over which they have some control; in preventing their children from educating themselves out of their social class, mothers' efforts to keep their children out of school may be regarded as attempts to preserve family unity.

By now it is plain that women's resistance to change can be attributed to the adverse effect social change has had on them—increasing sexual inequality. Considering the project's lack of attention to women's situation in Vicos, the following comment is remarkable: "Women have not moved apace with the men in these developments. Few girls have been sent to school although their numbers gradually increase each year. More valuable insofar as the women are concerned has been the opportunity to learn the operation of sewing machines, a much admired skill in Vicos for both sexes. Girls who have this knowledge are considered as being potentially better homemakers than the others" (Doughty 1971: 109). This brings us back to the myths propagated about peasants and women that allow for their exploitation: If Vicos women are conservative homemakers, their subordination is their own problem.

As pointed out in the foregoing, Vicos is not unique; and to understand the changes that took place there, we must place the community in a broader social framework.[19] Here, I outline some suggestions about how we might approach the problems posed by the Vicos case. This essay has discussed some central aspects of community change in Vicos and some key areas of women's condition that were affected. Although I have utilized a historical perspective, the separation of social factors for analysis can yield a static view of society if it is not rooted in an understanding of social transformation. Thus the changes in human relations in Vicos cannot be understood apart from the community's transformation from a dominant feudal mode to a dominant capitalist mode of production.

While theoretical work on the transition from feudalism to capitalism is advancing, there is as yet very little analysis of the role of women in this social process. However, Deere's (1977) pioneering work in this area for Cajamarca, Peru, is an important beginning. Her view of the development of capitalism as an uneven process that both improves and deteriorates women's socioeconomic condition is illustrated by the historical transition in Cajamarca, but it holds for Vicos too. Just as Deere shows for Cajamarca, this essay shows for Vicos that the transition from feudal hacienda system to capitalism can mean improved economic conditions in an absolute sense for both men and women, while the status of women and women's work deteriorates. My study has attempted a close examination of the changing conditions of women's and men's lives in Vicos, but ultimately such an analysis should be linked directly to the changing requirements of capital accumulation in Peru.

As changing modes of production are examined, it is important to consider the broad context of underdevelopment in which the transitions occur.[20] The relation of Peru, a dependent capitalist country, to the world economy is reproduced at the national level, where internal colonialism characterizes the relation of the coast to the Andean area. Relations of dependency can be traced to the local level in the Andes, where peasants are dominated by mestizos, as in the case of Vicos and Marcará. Finally, women may be viewed as the last link in the chain of dependency, since their dependence on men is increasing with the spread of capitalist relations.

Carpio (1975) has taken this view of the position of women in rural Peruvian society. Her work emphasizes that while peasant women are marginalized at the end of the chain of dependency, their oppression must be understood as an imperative of the capitalist economy, and their work as essential to its maintenance. She points out, as this essay has for the Vicos case, that women's economic role is masked by the nature of their integration in society—as subordinated members of the rural subsociety. While this situation is clearly in evidence for Vicos, it should be further investigated to see how dependency relations at the local level articulate with dependency relations at the national and international levels.

This study has shown that women's position in Vicos has degenerated as ties to the dominant capitalist economy grow stronger. This is the result of the devaluation of women's contribution to family production, a devaluation that capitalist economic development promotes, and of the spread of the ideology of the dominant class, which dictates the sexual inferiority of women. The Vicos data suggest that women are not likely to cease resisting such "development" until all inequalities, sexual and social, are eliminated.

The wealth of research material from Vicos offers an unusual opportunity to study the unequal effects of capitalist development on women and men. In this essay I have attempted to document the changing fabric of life in Vicos and to point toward some explanations for the growing inequalities in the community. With the development of scholarship on women and men in the transition from feudalism to capitalism, and on the changing relations of dependency that are engendered, it should shed more light on the questions this study raises about Vicos.

PART II Gender and the Urban
Informal Economy

Commentary

The scholarship on women in Peru includes vastly different
analyses regarding women's position. While some writers
view rural Peru as nearly egalitarian in gender relations and
see inequalities as intruding from the "modern" cities,
others view traditional Andean culture as the source of
machismo, which is only slowly disappearing in the more
enlightened cities. These disparate interpretations of
women's changing condition may be traced in part to an
underlying disagreement as to whether capitalist
development is "good" or "bad" for women.

Babb, *Between Field and Cooking Pot*

The three selections of my writing that appear in part 2 of this book span
the period 1984–2001, years that saw considerable growth in the field of
gender and women's studies. In the 1970s, feminism had charted distinct
theoretical directions ranging from liberal to radical and Marxist, each
calling for research and activist priorities that would advance its objectives and address strategic needs. While liberal feminists called for wom-
en's equality as a democratic principle, radical feminists demanded an end
to patriarchal relations, and Marxist feminists decried the gendered
effects of capitalism and imperialism around the globe. By the 1980s, in
Latin America as elsewhere, there were emergent women's movements
and popular feminisms on the one hand and self-identified, often middle-
class, feminists of various political stripes on the other. Frameworks of
analysis that had already emerged were further refined, among them a
good number that embraced Western dualisms such as private/public, tra-
ditional/modern, informal/formal, and production/reproduction—all of

which influenced my thinking and that of many others in both the global North and the global South as a result of the geopolitics of knowledge and its circulation. During this period, writers paid increased attention to race and ethnicity, as well as to gender as a social relation rather than a fixed category.

In what follows, I trace some of these currents in feminist thought and politics during that period as a backdrop for discussing my work from that time that I present here. The chapters in this section were based on my doctoral research on Andean market women of Huaraz, Peru, and my return visits, which continued for a decade (1977–87) before I turned my attention elsewhere during the worst period of violence in Peru (I undertook a decade of research in Nicaragua before my return to Peru in 1997). The writings that comprise part 2 utilized such concepts as informal and formal sectors of the economy, and productive and reproductive labor, yet I was an early critic of the binary nature of these concepts. I aligned myself with others who directed attention to the limitations of Western logics such as these and sought to shine a light on articulating modes of production and exchange in society, as well as on overlapping forms of women's work that defied easy categorization as "traditional," "reproductive," "private," or "domestic." Thus, I will consider feminist and other debates of the period that showed the inadequacy of any reductive reading of "women's experience"—which failed to account for multiple and intersecting forms of participation in society and of intertwined inequalities by gender, race, class, and sexuality.

Beginning in the early 1980s, Latin America and the Caribbean saw the emergence of new strands of academic and activist feminism. I remember vividly the uproar in Peru over the Miss Universe pageant that was held in Lima in 1982.[1] Not only was there a furor over the commodification of women's bodies, but many were highly critical of the nation pouring resources into such an event at a time when political conflict was intense and economic hardship was widespread. That same year, I attended along with several hundred others the Congress on Research on Women in the Andean Region mentioned in the introduction to this book. That event offered a host of panels on women's work in the rural and urban areas, gender and family relations, and political mobilization, with an emphasis on economically marginalized sectors. The concern with women and development was everywhere evident, as was the increasing use of the

The Plaza de Armas (main square) in Huaraz, 2015. Photo by author.

production/reproduction analytic embraced by Marxist feminists to account for both the paid and unpaid work of women inside and outside the household.[2] As theorized, this framework brought together gender and class analysis and showed that the two were closely interconnected in women's double day, as their work outside the household often mirrored social reproduction at home—and both served patriarchy and capitalism.

A year later, Lima hosted the second continental Feminist Encuentro, which brought together women from throughout Latin America and the Caribbean. There, productive discussion was nevertheless accompanied by tension between popular grassroots women's organizations and feminists who wished to push the assembly to decry sexism, call for the inclusion of lesbian issues, demand reproductive rights, and so on.[3] By this time, we were distinguishing between *movimientos de mujeres* (women's movements) and *movimientos feministas* (feminist movements). Maxine

Molyneux's formulation of "practical and strategic gender interests" (1986) characterized such tensions among those who, in the Peruvian case, prioritized women's struggles for the right to land on which to live (e.g., Lima's squatter settlements); adequate nutrition for their children (e.g., *vaso de leche* program); and organized communal kitchens (*comedores populares*) on the one side and, on the other, those who organized for women's reproductive rights and an end to domestic violence. By later in the 1980s, more feminists were critiquing the sort of binary thinking behind the divisions drawn between practical and strategic interests and between productive and reproductive labor (as well as the domestic and public spheres). Yet persistent tensions revealed the potent differences among women based on their social class, ethnicity, and educational background.

By the late 1980s, feminists had come to understand the importance of adopting an intersectional approach to understanding the complex relationship among gender, class, sexuality, and, significantly, race. US-based women of color are most often credited with formulating the core principles of intersectionality (Crenshaw 1989; Mohanty 2013), yet we can find precursors to this feminist approach in Latin America as well. Peruvian feminist Marfil Francke (1990) had written several years earlier of the *trenza de la dominación* (braid of domination), an artful way of describing interwoven forms of inequality.[4] In Peru at that time, *racial inequality* often referred to differences of culture and power between Quechua- and Aymara-speaking rural indigenous campesinos in the Andes, and Spanish-speaking mestizos and whites on the urban coast. (More recently there has been greater attention to Afro-Peruvians and those indigenous Peruvians in the Amazon region.) Thus the eighties saw a shift in Peru toward a greater recognition of social difference and intertwined inequalities—particularly salient against the backdrop of that period's violence marked by racial geography.[5] This is not to say that racial frictions no longer beset the nation; these often developed even among feminists.

With the transition to the 1990s, Peru continued to contend with the conflict between Sendero Luminoso and the military, and the authoritarian government of President Alberto Fujimori. What became of feminist politics during that fraught time? By the close of the decade and Fujimori's resignation in disgrace, it had become clear that his efforts to show support for women had masked an egregious population-control (so-called poverty alleviation) program of forced sterilization targeting rural indigenous women. Stéphanie Rousseau (2009), Christina Ewig (2010), and Lucía Stavig (2017) have written about this period and contended that feminists generally overlooked the widespread practice because it was far removed from the urban coast—and moreover, they may have perceived that to protest the practice of forced sterilization in Andean Peru could have jeopardized their own struggles for reproductive rights. Indeed, the production/reproduction framework took on new meaning as poor working women's bodies became the site of increased injustice. Rural Andean women were already victims in the national conflict, and they were now finding their personal life options narrowed still further. Ewig and others employed Nancy Fraser's (1997) key theoretical distinction between the politics of (economic) redistribution and the politics of (cultural) recognition to account for the racism and sexism faced by Andean women. This formulation extends the production/reproduction analytic to bring attention to culture, race, and identity formation—and the right to have rights—which were often missing from Marxist feminist/materialist accounts.

The transnational feminism that arose in the 1990s seemed at one and the same time to champion the rights of the multiply disenfranchised and most marginalized and to turn attention away from local initiatives to broader levels of organizing activity. We might question whether the far-reaching ambition of feminists to join forces across the globe—and to organize a social movement to bring together civil society organizations and NGOs—was also inadvertently neglecting rural poor, indigenous, and Afro-descendant women. I suggest that the political and intellectual work since the 1990s has laid important groundwork for a more inclusive feminism that is still under construction. Notably, there was a growing recognition of the undervalued role of women in performing care work, at home and in the wider economy, and of the body and body politics as a critical domain for feminist activism.

Thus we came to understand the body blows of neoliberalism and how women were, under the terms of structural adjustment, expected to shoulder the needs of families and communities, to feed and nurture when incomes were diminished and state services rolled back. This needed attention sprang from the same concerns advanced by feminists who earlier called for attention to both production and reproduction in society.

What was new was a clear recognition of biopolitics and the emotional work required to sustain economy and society. That is, feminists went beyond a more economistic materialist feminism and addressed the need for recognition as well as redistribution.

MARKET WOMEN AT THE NEXUS OF PUBLIC/PRIVATE, PRODUCTION/REPRODUCTION, FORMAL/INFORMAL

Soon after completing my master's thesis and publishing my work on gender relations in Vicos, Peru, I was thrust headlong into my dissertation research. My advisor, Bill Stein, offered me the opportunity to carry out a brief period of ethnohistorical research with him in Peru and then stay on to do my doctoral work—the only difficulty was that it was just my third year of graduate school and I had not even taken my qualifying exams. The timing was unusual, but I could hardly pass up the chance to have a bit of funding and move forward in my studies. To that end, I sought a topic that would bring together my enthusiasm for examining gender questions in the Andes and my commitment to critical perspectives in development studies. Market women, who are emblematic of daily life in highland Peru, struck me as particularly fertile ground for considering women's work that appears to have much in common with (reproductive) household labor, yet is conducted in the (productive) wider economy and public sphere more commonly associated with men. My earlier work on Vicos had made me keenly aware that "traditional" women's activities may also reveal transgressive elements, since these women enact processes of resistance and change. Having read Marx and Engels, as well as Marxian anthropologists like Maurice Godelier, Claude Meillassoux, and Eleanor Leacock, I was eager to discover how women's social reproduction both in their work at home and in the market might politicize them during a period of economic austerity in Peru.

The doctoral work I carried out in the provincial city of Huaraz in the Callejón de Huaylas, an intermontane valley that had attracted many anthropologists over the years, would result not only in my dissertation (1981) but also, after several return visits, my first book, *Between Field and Cooking Pot: The Political Economy of Marketwomen in Peru* ([1989]

Mercado Central (Central Market) in Huaraz, 2011. Photo by author.

1998). In addition, I published a number of articles and book chapters, including those that comprise part 2 of this volume. On returning home from my dissertation research, however, I faced the immediate and challenging prospect of finding the most suitable theoretical framework to support my findings. I remained fully convinced of the necessity of feminist analysis of gender to reveal the often-overlooked areas of women's meaningful participation in economy and society, and of Marxist analysis to shed light on the class inequalities underlying modes of production and exchange in Peru. Yet I was discovering a lively debate emerging over urban economies in the Third World (today, I refer to the global South), variously termed the informal sector, the service or tertiary economy, or petty commodity production and exchange, which yielded important insights illuminating my ethnographic material.

The discussion over proliferating informal-sector activity in so many cities around the globe—ranging from the activity of undocumented street vendors to that of unofficial taxi drivers—had gotten traction in the early 1970s (Hart 1973), and by the end of the decade the terminology *informal* and *formal economy* had become well established among social scientists. But more critical analysts, often Marxists, were among those who argued that these binary categories were insufficient to account for these deeply intertwined and interdependent sectors in underdeveloped economies. Contributors to a special issue of the journal *World Development* (1978) and to a volume edited by Bromley and Gerry (1979) favored instead the Marxian notion of petty commodity production, which I, too, embraced in my work in order to shed light on the role of marketplace trade in the full cycle of production and exchange in the city of Huaraz. These debates inspired my thinking about these women working as small-scale and informal market sellers who underwrote the formal economy by providing cheap and ubiquitous labor, which kept prices down at a time of rampant inflation and widespread hardship. Just as women's housework subsidized the economy by keeping down their families' costs of living and stretching family earnings, so did the work of market women hold down food prices and make goods readily available to consumers who themselves were often struggling to make ends meet.[6]

Through working with Huaraz market women (and a fair number of men), I found that marketers not only participated in the exchange of goods for sale but often added significantly to their value on the market. Hardly ones to sit idly, many of them peeled vegetables for sale, packaged dry goods, knitted items from sheep's wool or alpaca yarn, or produced meals for sale to other sellers and the public. Even if they were not transforming the goods they offered for sale, they kept busy with the sales process itself, greeting customers, responding to their requests, maintaining good relations with clients and market neighbors—all necessary to remaining in business and satisfying the needs of consumers. Among the principal arguments in my book and related writings was, first, that small-scale retailers played a vital part in the wider economy that should not be overlooked and, indeed, could not be eliminated through government initiatives to bring goods directly from "field to cooking pot." Furthermore, I argued that the fact that women—often a subordinated gender—made up the majority of market sellers and street vendors should not diminish these traders' significance as contributors to the local and national econo-

Along the Plaza de Armas in Huaraz, a woman passes by announcements of producers' markets, 2014. Photo by author.

mies. Early research on market women in various parts of the world frequently emphasized their folkloric quality, "local color," and practice of gossiping as they sold goods; but since the 1980s, scholarship has considered more seriously their participation as valuable workers and strategic partners in household economies. This is true whether they work as informal street traders or as concealed wage laborers who serve as outworkers for formal businesses.

ONGOING DEBATES OVER WOMEN'S PLACE IN THE ANDES (AND OVER MY OWN WORK)

The point I have made regarding the perceived value of market women's work continued to be debated among feminist anthropologists and others concerned with the position of indigenous women in the Andean economy and society. In her much cited essay "'Women Are More Indian': Ethnicity and Gender in a Community near Cuzco," Marisol de la Cadena (English version, 1995: 329) began by challenging "the received wisdom about Andean principles of complementarity and subordination" for its failure to account for "the conflictive nature of gender relations and hierarchy" in the community where she carried out research. While she named some of the prominent scholars who in the 1970s addressed Andean gender complementarity in symbolic terms (notably, Olivia Harris and Billie Jean Isbell), she cited two materialist feminist works of the following decade as exemplary of those with whom she disagreed, Silverblatt (1987) and Babb ([1989] 1998). She disagreed with Silverblatt's reading of the ethnohistorical evidence for women's higher standing in pre-Inca and precolonial Peru; and she departed from the view presented in my book on Huaraz market women based on her assessment from her own research that women's work, even if important to the household and economy, was not held in the same esteem as men's work. Indeed, she went so far as to emphasize that women's work in and outside the home was not considered real "work."

In the same volume on historical and anthropological approaches to markets and ethnicity in the Andes where de la Cadena's work appeared, Olivia Harris's concluding chapter offered, with some irony, a different view of the relation between gender and ethnicity. She commented that, "increasingly[,] it is women who are the bearers of Indian identity in areas of high migration, and also women—the distinctive *cholas* with their marketing and trading activities—who are the prototypical mestizos" (1995: 372). She explained this apparent paradox by reference to these women's participation in consumer markets. Men, she found, had weaker connections to the market economy, and as a result their ethnic identity tended to be less firmly established as either indigenous *or* mestizo.

This is precisely what I had found earlier in my research among Huaraz marketers, that women's active role in commerce often gave them greater exposure to the public sphere than was afforded to the men in their families. This is not at all to say that they did not experience discrimination and inequality in the places where they lived and worked, but I discovered that in more cases than not their work was recognized as having value to both family and society, and they often expressed fierce pride in their work. There may, of course, have been regional or interpretive differences behind my conclusions and those of de la Cadena and Harris, and surely masculinist perceptions of women's low social value must be taken into serious account (though not conflated with social perceptions more broadly).[7] In many ways, these debates over the relative standing of Andean women and men that continued through the 1980s and 1990s had much in common with earlier debates over gender complementarity and gender inequality, as they stem from fundamental epistemological differences about what we take to be credible sources of knowledge. What we may all agree on, however, is the need for more scholarly attention to what is now called intersectionality, or the complex and intertwined inequalities of gender, race, and class in the Andes.

Relevant to my work, contributors to Larson and Harris (1995) were as interested in ethnic difference and identity as in class identity, and a few embraced gender identity as well. For these scholars, the cultural and political were as central as the economic in shaping both past and present, marking a turn from Marxian and other approaches that tended to dwell on the socioeconomic and to underestimate the force of cultural meanings and practices. Thus market relations interfaced with ethnicity and gender, shaping and being shaped by both in the process. The coeditors and their collaborators challenged the long-standing dualism in accounts of the Andean economy and society: traditional and modern, indigenous and mestizo, rural and urban, nonmarket and market, communal and individual. Implicit in such binaries are modernist assumptions about the higher value placed on the latter over the former. Yet these assumptions reflect northern biases. As Harris (1995: 369) states regarding the less well-known indigenous perspective: "They [indigenous] even feel sorry for these people [mestizos] who have little or no land, who are afraid of real work, and who depend on others to produce food for them. Mestizos from this Indian perspective are individuals who have lost their identity." This view was indeed behind the sentiment I often heard expressed by market women selling in Huaraz, that the urban population would not survive without the hard work of marketers (many of them from the rural sector), who are essential in bringing food and other vital goods to the city's markets.

Although my earlier work (on both Vicos and Huaraz) has sometimes been painted with a broad brush and described as falling into the category of critical feminism that idealizes gender relations in Andean Peru, my writing on Huaraz market women was explicit in stating that while women provide valuable services in marketing and occasionally experience a degree of empowerment, their work "is typically precarious, generates low incomes, and requires low levels of skill—making women a second-class category of workers" (Babb [1989] 1998: 65). This ambivalence I sought to show was appreciated by some scholars of Andean markets. For example, Lynn Sikkink (2001: 212) observed that, "as Babb points out in the case of the urban Huaraz market women she studied in Peru, a 'combination of a sense of potential power and a recognition of relative powerlessness' confronts women vendors even in their roles as permanent marketers (1989: 40)." Likewise, Cecilie Ødegaard (2010: 131) discovered in my work the complex way in which reproduction and production are conjoined in women's marketing activities:

> About traders in the Andes, Babb (1989) has made the important argument that they do not operate within what can simply be considered a "reproductive" sphere or by selling small-scale food products, since trading at these markets for a long time has also involved mass-production. Criticizing the widespread view of market women's labour as strictly distributive in nature, she stresses for instance how many kinds of food processing take place in the market that would readily be interpreted as productive if done in a factory (for example, by breaking down bulk quantities of food products into portions, and making small ready-to-cook packages).

While much of my writing sought to challenge existing frameworks based on Western binaries, I privileged discussion of what was novel in my work: my argument that, even given its limitations, market work often positioned women to become active and visible in the public, "productive" sphere through their trading and union activities. Relatedly, I emphasized that these women were often more open to change than their rather conservative husbands, who spent more time devoted to agricultural activities. This flew in the face of "common knowledge" about "traditional" Andean women and their timidity in public.[8]

Linda Seligmann (1989) was instrumental in identifying the ambivalent and often ambiguous status of chola marketers as "women in between" the social categories of rural/urban, indigenous/mestizo. Her influential journal article has become a touchstone for its clarity on the challenging question of how to understand cholas not simply as folkloric figures found in Peruvian towns and cities, with their full skirts and aprons, their cardigans and fedoras, but as protagonists in their own lives. Some years later, Seligmann's *Peruvian Street Lives* (2004) brought her insights to bear in a rich ethnography of Cuzco's market women.

Seligmann's edited collection *Women Traders in Cross-cultural Perspective: Mediating Identities, Marketing Wares* (2001) signaled a cultural turn in studies of market women. The volume's contributors considered, in fairly equal measure, questions of meaning and cultural identity and of materiality and economic inequality. This contribution to studies of market women coincided with my work in finding considerable value in the labor performed by women and in their activism around the issues that sellers face on the job. As Seligmann (2004: 56) wrote, "Babb (1998: 137–43) also found that men and women valued each other's work, that women valued men's work more highly, and that men recognized that women worked harder because they had a 'double day,' caring for children and working outside the home." She (2004: 221) also praised my "pioneering" work for documenting "the struggles vendors face in organizing politically and overcoming ambivalence about their class identities."

Around this time, Mary Weismantel's *Cholas and Pishtacos* (2001) appeared and made a formidable impact with its penetrating treatment of the two iconic figures of its title, one female and indigenous, and the other identified in Andean legend as white and male bogeymen. While her broad and commanding sweep of representations and meanings in the region embraced far more than market women, she nonetheless provided greater depth to our knowledge of the power of sex and race in the stories that are told about these mythic chola market women. In her discussion, Weismantel plumbed the existing literature and offered new interpretations of works such as my own. I was intrigued to read her keen observations on my book's opening vignette, which featured a description of the sights, sounds, and smells that greet visitors to the Huaraz markets. I had contrasted these colorful visions of Andean life with the harsher "realities" of poverty and inequality experienced by the majority, with the intention of undermining my own arrival trope, but Weismantel made the incisive comment that the sensorial understanding one gains in the market can be a source of critical experiential knowledge and should not be dismissed as

The author with a marketer and longtime friend in Mercado Central, Huaraz, 2011.
Photo by author.

irrelevant or misleading. Elsewhere, in discussing Andean women's dress, she noted my description of their use of pants beneath their full skirts; where I had seen a response to the chill air in the Andes, she found traces of transvestic performance with more than a hint of masculinity in cholas' appearance and demeanor. Since the time when I wrote my first book, and inspired by the work of others like Seligmann and Weismantel, I have become more attentive to the subtleties of cultural practices and their meanings, and I have brought race and sexuality more fully into my work.

The arc of my scholarship on Andean marketers, as seen in the chapters that follow, reveals a gradual turn from the more strictly political economic and gender-related toward a culturally inflected approach to the experience of market women. In my contribution to Seligmann's 2001 anthology (here, chapter 4), I surveyed the shifting ground in my own work and that of other contributors to the volume, as well as in anthropological research and writing more generally. I found that I brought new insights to my past work and discovered more layers of meaning once I was better attuned to cultural difference and power as these play out in the marketplace and the wider society. I was aided in my rethinking by scholarly contributions of the 1990s, notably including the anthology *Cultures of Politics, Politics of Culture,* coedited by Sonia Alvarez, Evelina Dagnino, and Arturo Escobar (1998), which brought the cultural on a par with the political in framing Latin American social movements. My work in Nicaragua throughout the nineties was much influenced by such work and led me to make gender and cultural politics central to my analysis of developments in the post-Sandinista neoliberal era. When I returned to Peru in 1997 after a decade's absence, and in subsequent revisits, I likewise had a much greater interest in understanding the profound part that culture plays in all aspects of political economy, national development, and identity formation.

LOST AND FOUND IN TRANSLATION

Like my work on Vicos—which came out in Spanish more than two decades after its first appearance as a published working paper—*Between Field and Cooking Pot* was published in Spanish translation in Peru almost twenty years after its release in the United States, as *Entre la chacra y la olla: Cultura, economía política y las vendedoras de mercado en el Perú* (Babb 2008a). Some years passed before I had the resources available to cover the cost of translation and to subsidize publication in Peru. I was pleased to see the book finally reach Spanish-speaking readers, especially Peruvians, and I wondered what reception it might have so long after its original publication in English. Although I was unable to travel to Peru at the time it was released in Lima, when I returned three years later I was honored to have a book presentation in Huaraz. I invited some of the marketers who had given so much to my project and with whom I had enduring ties of friendship. Unfortunately, most were elderly by that time and could not make it into town for the evening event. Instead, the occasion drew primarily the city's intellectual and political elite, as well as young professionals, including several I invited from the local Quechua-language course I was taking.

The book presentation, held on September 15, 2011, was hosted by the regional office of the Ministry of Culture, then the National Institute of Culture. The small auditorium adorned with flowers filled slowly, and as is customary for book presentations in Peru, the evening began with commentaries by local figures—literary, scholarly, public officials—before I was invited to speak about my book. The ministry's director was the first and offered gracious remarks, even if she had only a limited familiarity with my book. I had made sure that copies of the Spanish translation were distributed widely in Huaraz, but those who drew conclusions based on the book title and cover image likely assumed that its main contribution was to understandings of local food and folklore; the broader argument was not well known. More remarks were made by another employee of the ministry and by a Huaraz public school teacher with whom I had become friends.

The featured commentator, Noemí López Dominguez, was from the Huaraz teachers college; she was someone I had interviewed several times and who was passionate about cultural heritage, from the local to the international level. She was one of the most outspoken people I had met in Huaraz and had a strong commitment to retaining cultural knowledge and indigenous tradition, often chiding the younger generation for disrespecting what they viewed as consigned to the past. Her presentation offered an appreciation of my book, and based on her reading of it, she addressed the valor of the region's market women and the hard work they perform. She remarked that, indeed, "the best economists are women," meaning that the best money-managers are women. She then assured the audience that to say so is not feminist; here she pointed to the central part played by market women in the economy yet attempted to deflect any impression that she should be considered a feminist (which some might logically have concluded about her). Later, I sought clarification from a friend about another comment Noemí made regarding my foreign status as a researcher. I believe that she was somewhat bemused by the *gringa* anthropologist who kept coming back over the years, and that she revealed a trace of national pride in my evident and unflagging interest. At the same time, given her political savviness, she might well have been questioning why a foreigner rather than a Peruvian scholar had written such a book.

For my part, with the help of a young Huaracina (now a professional photographer), Eva Valenzuela, who had worked with me as a field and technical assistant, I showed images of the local markets and sellers as I read from the prefaces of the two editions of my book. In the Spanish edition, I had written the following account with a more local readership in mind:

> When I visited the Huaraz markets in 2007, I still found familiar faces, but many more were new to me. Several people commented to me about the gap that already existed between those sellers with sufficient resources to buy a stall in the modern market—that was constructed recently downtown—and many other sellers who went looking for space on the street to sell their goods. One older woman told me she had been selling in the street since 1973, and when I said I was from the United States, she laughingly exclaimed [with a pun and expletive], "Ah, de los Estados Jodidos!" [Oh, from the Fucking States!] When she realized that I had understood her word play, she immediately made a friendly gesture and offered me a *pepino* [cucumber] from a small pile she was selling. Afterward, when I bought some fruit, she hugged me affectionately. This brief encounter captured the ambivalence expressed to me in Huaraz by many sellers, those conditioned by life circumstances to be suspicious of strangers, yet willing to embrace the world around them. I still respond with surprise and gratitude to these acts of friendship and shows of affection offered in a time of economic uncertainty and globalization. (Babb 2008a: 12–13, my translation from the Spanish)

This woman's commingled bravado and kindness reminded me of another street vendor I had known who was by turns rebellious and nurturing, one whose life story I had documented years before (Babb [1989] 1998: 144–48). Elderly and toothless save for one front tooth, the woman who called herself my *abuelita* (grandmother), and whom I referred to in my book as "Carolina," had told me that her ideas came from her life. She had borne thirteen children, but at the age of seventy-four she had only one daughter who had survived a lifetime of harsh conditions. As the market union's secretary of the press and propaganda (mainly charged with herding sellers to meetings and keeping them there), Carolina was known for being feisty and outspoken. As I wrote back then, Carolina's views revealed "a combination of revolutionary and religious fervor" (Babb [1989] 1998: 147) as she pledged her faith that "the Virgin" would help her through the difficult period that marketers were experiencing. I was greatly moved when, returning to Peru in the early 1980s, another street vendor gave me a letter Carolina had prepared for me before she passed away (she herself had not learned to write), promising she would always remember me and offering her best wishes for my family. I still have her letter, dated April 1983.

Between Field and Cooking Pot called for more research to explore "the relationship of women's work and status to pressing issues of national development" at a time when women in Peru and elsewhere were "participating in the urban informal sector in ever larger numbers" (Babb [1989] 1998: 65). Today I would frame the issue somewhat differently in order to more fully encompass the noneconomic as well as the economic, race and sexuality as much as gender. I would also seek to decolonize the received knowledge concerning Andean women so that discussion of gender complementarity, the gender division of labor, and gendered meanings would not fall back so squarely on Western, dualistic systems of thought. Nonetheless, a key question remains today: how are rural and urban market women and street vendors, national emblems of cultural patrimony, contending with the ever-expanding informal sector as the main source of their livelihoods and identities?

The three selections in part 2 draw on related research findings (thus some overlapping material), yet each is addressed to a different audience and takes up a different scholarly concern. They range from a piece in the *Review of Radical Political Economics* (1984b) that defined my subject in Marxist feminist terms and argued that marketers' work was productive in the Marxian sense; my chapter "Producers and Reproducers" in June Nash and Helen Safa's edited collection *Women and Change in Latin America* (1986) that deepened my critical feminist discussion of dualistic notions of women's work in relation to my research; and finally, my chapter in Seligmann's *Women Traders in Cross-cultural Perspective* (2001) reassessing my work and that of others on marketers in light of the scholarly turn from political economy to cultural politics, signaling my stronger engagement with the commingling of gender, race, and power. The first two selections were published just a few years apart in the mideighties, while the third appeared more than a decade later, after my return to Peru in 1997, and revealed a substantial shift in my thinking about the position of market women in the Peruvian Andes and elsewhere.

2 Women in the Marketplace

PETTY COMMERCE IN PERU

First published in 1984 in the journal *Review of Radical Political Economics,* this article was part of a special issue, "Political Economy of Women."

·   ·   ·   ·   ·

In cities throughout Latin America and other areas of the Third World, an increasing number of women are entering the impoverished tertiary sector. The forms of employment they find there, notably in domestic service and petty commerce, are well known, but research is only beginning to consider some of the difficult problems of conceptualizing these women and the work they do within the broader socioeconomic framework. My aim in this essay is to explore several critical problems in the conceptualization of women workers in one area of the tertiary sector, that of petty commerce. I begin with a discussion of some existing research; then I consider the results of my own research on market women undertaken in 1977, and followed up in 1982, in the Andean city of Huaraz in north-central Peru. I examine three principal problem areas: first, how women in petty commerce are situated in urban, underdeveloped economies, and specifically, how their class position may be defined; second, the nature of women's work in petty commerce, particularly concerning its productive and reproductive character; and third, whether women in this marginalized economic sector are likely to develop a political consciousness and mobilize around issues affecting them.

Studies of Third World women in market commerce have provided rich ethnographic descriptions more often than thoroughgoing analyses of marketers' work within the wider political economy.[1] Several writers (e.g., Boserup 1970; Mintz 1971; Buechler 1976) have taken a somewhat more expansive approach, discussing the participation of market women within the framework of developments at the national or cross-national level. Yet only a few researchers (e.g., Arizpe 1975a: 77; Chaney 1976; Hansen 1980a) have analyzed the position of women in urban marketing as a consequence of increasing marginalization of the poor in the tertiary sector of Third World cities. Their work on women in petty commerce under the conditions of dependent capitalism points to the necessity of examining both social class and sex if we are to comprehend the proliferation of women in this economic sector. Further analysis must address the double exploitation of market women, as marginalized workers and as women.

THE CONCEPTUAL PROBLEMS

Petty Commerce and Class Analysis

Notwithstanding some auspicious developments in studies of market women, the questions raised at the beginning of this essay remain, to a large extent, unexplored by researchers. Many who study marketing agree, for example, that a class analysis is essential, and yet few have attempted to locate the precise position of petty marketers in the class structures in which they are found. Instead, the social groupings to which they belong are described by an array of vague terms. Sometimes they are simply defined by their most obvious characteristics and referred to as the "urban poor" or the "marginal poor." Other times they are identified by their occupational sector, as the "tertiary sector," "traditional sector," or "informal sector," or by their precarious employment experience in that sector as "casual workers," "underemployed," and so on. Still another way of defining this segment of Third World populations has been to emphasize their exclusion from the major social classes, suggesting a residual category with such terms as "subclass," "underclass" and "subproletariat." While these last have the advantage of calling attention to the subordinate structural position of workers in petty commerce, the terms do not help us to clarify the concrete features of this group in relationship to capitalist society as a whole.[2]

In order to pursue this problem further we may consider some recent work which, though it does not focus squarely on women, has made significant advances toward situating petty production and commerce within the context of dependent capitalism. In the last few years, the concept of petty, or simple, commodity production has been employed to describe the subordinate form of production that has persisted within the dominant capitalist mode in some underdeveloped areas. The concept was originally formulated by Marx (1967: 761–62) to describe a transitional stage characterized by an incomplete separation of labor from the means of production and by independent petty commodity producers engaging in the exchange of their goods to provision their households and maintain the conditions of their existence.[3] Researchers such as Gerry (1978), Moser (1978, 1980) and Scott (1979) have found a petty commodity production concept particularly useful in shedding light on the expansion of small-scale production and commerce in a number of Third World cities. They attribute the flourishing of this sector to the distorted development process of dependent capitalism: in this process only a small portion of the population finds employment in the capital-intensive industrial sector, leaving many to seek work in the marginalized sector of small-scale manufacture and trade.

In the view taken here, petty commerce, whether carried out by producer-sellers or by professional traders who complete the process of bringing goods to consumers, is understood as an essential aspect of the marginalized petty production process. Workers in petty commerce are distinguished from the working class by their self-employed status and from the petty bourgeoisie by their impoverished condition and their general inability to accumulate capital.

The petty commodity model goes a long way toward explaining the distinct features of self-employed traders in the expanding tertiary sector in many areas of the Third World. However, in some underdeveloped areas the spread of capitalist relations has undermined the autonomy of small producers and traders, a process similar to that in the advanced capitalist countries. Scott (1979), illustrating with the example of Lima, has called attention to the various subordinated forms that "self-employment" actually takes among the urban poor. She demonstrates that what may appear at first to be self-employment is often a disguised form of wage labor. Calling for a closer examination of the social relations of production, she shows that in the case of Lima such arrangements as outwork, piecework wages, and commission-selling are common in petty production and commerce.

The transition from self-employment in petty commodity production and trade to capitalist relations of production tends increasingly to occur as the former ceases to serve the interests of capital. It is necessary to examine cases of petty commerce most carefully in order to recognize persistence and change in the employment structures within which marketers operate. What we discover will help clarify what now appears to be the ambiguous class status of many small marketers, as independent sellers operating in the petty commodity form of production or as incipient commercial proletarians.

Women in Petty Commerce: Production and Reproduction

Following the lead of research on women in the advanced capitalist countries, studies of Third World women have emphasized family roles, household labor, and women's entry into the wage labor force. While these are important areas to investigate in the Third World, women's position in the growing tertiary sector has received little critical notice. African studies have paid attention to women's traditional importance in marketing, but the emphasis has only rarely been on the contemporary structure of underdevelopment (e.g., Remy 1975). Latin American studies have produced significant analyses of women in domestic service, but only a few studies of women in petty manufacture and trade have emerged.

To the extent that researchers have focused on women in the commercial and service sectors in the underdeveloped nations, they have often likened women's work in these sectors to housework, and they have viewed the women themselves as housewives whose economic roles extend to the labor force. The nature of work in these areas is indeed frequently similar or even identical in content to the work women perform in their homes. In the Third World, housecleaning, laundering, sewing, and food preparation are all services that may be purchased on the market in urban centers. Jelin (1980: 139) discusses the work of independent female petty producers of merchandise (e.g., crafts, clothing, and food) in Salvador, Brazil, as commercialized housework. In a similar way, Arizpe (1977: 36) describes the way in which poor women in Mexico City "press the system for payment of their domestic services" by taking their goods and services out of the home and selling them on the market as street sellers and domestic servants. This view of women's paid work as an extension of their unpaid work at home is expressed by a number of others who have undertaken research in the Third World (e.g., Vasques de Miranda 1977: 274; Nash and Safa 1976: 106).

The two forms of work have much in common, and this lies in their reproductive function in the economy and society.[4] Just as housework is essential to the well-being and survival of the family, the distributive trades and service occupations maintain and nourish society. As collective caretakers, women in these occupations look after the needs of the people they serve on a daily basis. Over the longer term they ensure the continuation of society from one generation to the next. Housewives through their subsistence work, and marketers and servants through the sale of their products and their services, feed, clothe, and shelter society. It is because of the vast amount of caretaking work these women do that their husbands and children are enabled to go off to work or school each day. Such a division of labor in the family, whereby women carry out "reproductive" work and free men for "productive" work, naturally serves the interest of the capitalist society.

Schmink (1977: 157), writing about the labor-force participation of Latin American women in commerce and the services, expresses this point well:

> Many service occupations are in some sense reproductive functions which secure the maintenance of the capitalist system: they are functions which in earlier stages of historical development may have been performed within the walls of a firm or household but which become separate entities through the increasing division of labor in the work force. It is precisely these less visible

aspects of production which are least understood in terms of their relation to the productive process and to the class structure. And it is to these ambiguous little niches that a large proportion of women in the labor force fall.

I noted the ambiguity of the socioeconomic position of marketers in the last section. Another ambiguous aspect of their situation is the apparent reproductive/productive dichotomy implied in the sexual division of labor.

A number of writers have noted that in areas where capitalism has not penetrated fully, the separation of reproductive and productive roles is weak (Benería and Sen 1981: 292; Deere and León de Leal 1981: 360). Moreover, as Mackintosh (1981: 10) has pointed out, the concepts in question are not really of the same order, since reproduction subsumes many productive activities. In our study of marketers, it is important to look beneath surface appearances and examine both the reproductive and the productive aspects of these women's work. That is, rather than viewing women's work in the labor force as a simple reflection of their domestic or reproductive work, we need to examine "inter-locking productive and reproductive processes" (Bujra 1982: 20). As a step in this direction, let us focus briefly on the question of women's productive activity as marketers.

We may ask whether market women's work can indeed be regarded as productive—that is, as contributing directly to the accumulation of capital. The political and intellectual debates over what forms of work are productive and what forms unproductive have been wide-ranging, and I do not wish to belabor an academic point.[5] I consider the question only as it concerns women in the tertiary sector, in an effort to shed light on the labor process and social relations of production characteristic of marketers. Some writers have argued that women's work in this sector should not be regarded as productive in the technical sense, since it "is often not directly connected to the production process" (Schmink 1977: 168). In this view, petty traders, office workers, domestic servants, and other women in the services generally create no new value and do not contribute to the growth of capital, although their work may be socially necessary. Others go further and agree with Arizpe (1977: 34), whose study of Mexican street sellers was mentioned earlier, that women in petty commerce "tend to offer an unnecessary service and to create their own demand." In contrast, my view is that such work is often both necessary and productive.

Several researchers have called attention to the productive aspect of commercial and service occupations in underdeveloped economies. Jelin (1977: 131), in her study of domestic servants in Latin America, maintains that "it seems unjustified to equate 'industrial' with productive and 'service' with unproductive employment." And Vasques de Miranda (1977: 268) describes the commerce in goods in which Brazilian women participate as a "productive activity." Unfortunately, the authors do not develop the point, leaving this to future writers.

My research suggests that women in petty commerce may be regarded as productive in the strict sense. Marketers can be understood as carrying the production process into the marketplace, where they create, transform, and distribute products. There is often no sharp line between work that produces goods and work that circulates them, and marketers are generally involved in both activities. In my analysis, distributive activity itself is understood to contribute value to goods and, so, to constitute productive work. In the case study I discuss next, I explore the specific ways that Peruvian marketers contribute to capital accumulation.

Women in Petty Commerce: Political Consciousness

The recent discussion concerning productive and unproductive labor was in large part generated by a desire to discover the political potential of various groups of workers in society. The view has generally been that only productive workers are in a position to develop a critical awareness and seek to change their situation in society, though I contend that this is not certain. In any event, it is important to call attention both to the unjustified view of so many workers in commerce and the services as unproductive, and to the related view that their class consciousness will remain at a low level. This is all the more important because it is so often women who fall into this category. There may indeed be a male bias underlying the notion that these workers are unlikely to mobilize.

It is of course true that the nature of some women's work in the tertiary sector makes it difficult for them to identify with working-class interests. This is especially notable for the majority of Latin American women workers who acquire jobs as domestic servants. The isolation they experience in middle-class homes and their close association with their employers make a strong identification with workers' issues unlikely. Schmink (1977: 175), however, in her research on women workers in Venezuela, finds this characteristic of domestic servants to be shared by women in the tertiary sector generally. She explains the lack of class consciousness among women in commerce and manufacturing in terms of their indirect relation to the production process, as self-employed and family workers. Moreover, she calls the idea that the services are undergoing proletarianization "illusory" and concludes that women in these occupations are not likely to mobilize.

I agree with the thrust of Schmink's argument, that under the terms of dependent capitalist development, women's incorporation into the labor force will not take the same form as that of men in their societies, nor will it parallel that of women in the advanced capitalist countries. However, in the discussion of Huaraz market women that follows, I depart from the view offered by Schmink, and shared by others, based on my observations and assessment of these women's relation to the production process and their political consciousness.

Market Women in Huaraz

The military coup that brought General Juan Velasco Alvarado to power in Peru in 1968 was met with early optimism as the expropriation of foreign interests and a program of agrarian reform were quickly introduced. Beginning in the 1970s, the military's concern to secure an adequate and cheap food supply for urban Peru made this a key element in domestic policy. In 1970 an agency, the Empresa Pública de Servicios Agropecuarios, was created to control the marketing of basic foodstuffs, and in 1972 the production and marketing of all agricultural products came under state control. By the end of 1974, the Ministry of Food was established to regulate price structures on a regional basis, doing away with marketers' control of basic food prices.[6]

The year 1975, however, marked a downturn in Peru's economy and the transition to power of the more conservative General Francisco Morales Bermúdez, who was willing to take increasingly harsh measures to manage the crisis. With the encouragement of international lending agencies, his government's policy was to reduce public spending, devalue the Peruvian sol, and hold down workers' wages while raising the official prices of primary food items. The result was growing impoverishment for Peru's working class and even greater difficulty for the country's unemployed and marginally employed, who make up the majority of the labor force. The 1980 civilian election, which brought back the president unseated in 1968, Fernando Belaúnde Terry, has meant little relief for this majority of the population. On the contrary, under the terms of the economic policy unveiled in January 1981 and in subsequent economic "packages," the price increases and other measures have been devastating. Sweeping inflation and the lifting of price controls from all but a few staple items have hurt consumers and marketers alike.[7]

I carried out field research in 1977, which was declared the "Year of Austerity" in Peru, through a combination of participant observation and open-ended interviewing in and around the city of Huaraz. I spent considerable time in one of the four markets in the city, Mercado Central, to acquire an in-depth understanding of the nature of market work. I also undertook many informal interviews in the other three Huaraz markets, especially in the sprawling open-air marketplace known as La Parada. In later phases of the fieldwork, I designed a questionnaire for market women and their husbands and made a census of shops along three city blocks.[8] In addition to interviews with some three hundred marketers, I included conversations with market officials, consumers, and producers in my field data. In the summer of 1982, I returned to Huaraz for a restudy, following up on the situation of market women—many of whom I reinterviewed—five years later.

Huaraz is a city of about forty-five thousand Quechua-Spanish-speaking people, and the capital of Peru's Ancash department. It serves as the commercial and administrative center for the Andean valley known as the Callejón de Huaylas. In 1977, the city attracted close to twelve hundred sellers to its markets on the busiest days of the week, and by 1982 this number increased to nearly sixteen hundred sellers. Of these marketers, close to 80 percent are women, and they include rural producer-sellers who come periodically to the city, as well as a much larger number of full-time marketers who live in Huaraz and purchase all or most of their stock from wholesalers. Women, in contrast to men, are highly concentrated in the sale of vegetables, fruits, and prepared foods, which together constitute the bulk of goods sold in the market. Both women and men sell staple foods like rice, pasta, flour, sugar, and salt, as well as meat, fish, live animals, clothing, and household items such as pots and other kitchen utensils, although men generally do so on a larger scale. When men engage in marketing, they often draw on resources generated by other forms of employment, and they may have the greater mobility necessary to travel directly to production sites to buy their goods. Consequently, men often sell larger quantities of goods at lower prices than women, and they are far more likely than women to sell manufactured goods from the coast.

That women make up the large majority of marketers is related to the greater access men have to other forms of casual labor in Huaraz, as petty manufacturers, construction workers, or agricultural day laborers. Moreover, small-scale commerce is seen as befitting women, whose participation in marketing in Peru has a history dating back at least to the time of Spanish conquest. Marketing has the advantage of being one economic activity beyond the household that women can organize around other responsibilities, and that allows them to take along their children. On the other hand, today marketing ranks, along with domestic service, among the lowest-status and most marginalized of occupations for women in Peru. Not surprisingly, given Peru's underdeveloped economy, these are the areas where most women find employment.[9]

Given the scope of this essay, many relevant aspects of the lives and work of Huaraz market women cannot be taken up.[10] Instead I focus directly on three problem areas as they relate to the case of Huaraz: the relation of Huaraz market women to the capitalist economy—that is, their class position; the productive and reproductive nature of their work; and their political consciousness.

Although a small number of sellers in Huaraz come on a periodic basis from the rural sector and are identified as belonging to the socioeconomic category of campesinos, or Quechua-speaking country people, the majority of sellers are urban bilinguals, or mestizos (though many have their origins in the countryside).[11] Mestizos are often described as the Andean middle class, but this undifferentiated usage obscures the marked inequalities among urban residents, who in Huaraz range from the administrative elite down to the impoverished population found in marginal employment such as petty commerce. In order to evaluate more precisely the place of market women in the economy, it is necessary to consider their relationship to the production process as a whole, along the lines mentioned earlier.

The analysis of petty commodity production and commerce discussed earlier usefully illuminates the case of petty marketers in Huaraz. If we agree that there is no necessary analytical separation between manufacturing and commerce, and that the work of marketers is an extension of the productive work that (often) begins in other hands, then the analysis appears suitable here. This conceptual approach has the advantage of allowing us to discern the productive aspect of transporting goods, bulking and bulk-breaking, preparing goods for sale, and, finally selling them. My research in Huaraz revealed that preparing goods for sale may be the most time-consuming part of a marketer's work—ranging from cleaning vegetables for sale on a daily basis to preparing smoked meats or fermented drinks over a matter of weeks. When we place the work of marketers within the framework of the total production process, the valuable content of this work becomes clear.

During the 1970s, however, market women in Huaraz had little control over the prices of the basic foodstuffs they sold, since these were determined by the Ministry of Food in Lima, and the still low earnings they received barely allowed them to reproduce their present conditions. The worsening economic situation in Peru during the past few years has constrained the growth of most small marketers, and I observed during my revisit in 1982 that many are becoming even more deeply entrenched in poverty. It is not because they lack industriousness, but rather because of the external conditions surrounding their work that women in petty commerce in Huaraz act primarily as household provisioners and not as petty entrepreneurs.[12]

Indeed, most small retailers in Huaraz operate without capital. This is possible because wholesalers are willing to extend goods to retailers on credit, coming around to collect debts after the goods are sold. This is essential to women in petty commerce since few have any significant resources to begin selling, and the earnings they acquire are usually insufficient to meet household needs (without the additional income of other family members), much less to reinvest in business.

This feature of marketing in Huaraz calls into question how well the petty commodity form describes the situation in this city, however. Basic to this analysis is the notion of the independence of producer-sellers—that is, of their self-employment. Huaraz marketers display many features of self-employment: for example they have control over when they begin selling and when they take leave of the marketplace, the days and hours they work, what products they sell, and so on. Furthermore, most marketers consider themselves self-employed and value the advantages this offers. However, those petty retailers who told me on occasion that they work only to support the wholesalers may have a point. Since most market women lack capital, they are completely dependent on the wholesalers who offer them goods on credit. In a sense, these retailers may be regarded as commission-sellers, since once their goods are sold they turn over to the wholesalers the earnings on the goods minus the margin they retain as a "commission." (Of course, they are generally held responsible for paying the wholesaler whether they sell all the goods or not.)

Just as in Lima, as described by Scott (1979), in Huaraz too there are differences in the degree of autonomy of workers over their labor process. In addition to the widespread dependence of retailers on wholesalers through the credit institution, there are other forms of dependency operating. A small but not insignificant number of people, for example, work as assistants to other marketers, either on a regular basis or occasionally on a piecework basis. Examples include full-time employees in small restaurant stalls, women who are periodically hired when needed to peel vegetables for those who sell them, campesinas who sew skirts as outworkers for seamstresses who provide the materials, and clothing sellers who hold contracts with Lima factories and sell on commission.

To the extent that petty commodity production has endured in Huaraz, its persistence may be explained by the contribution it continues to make to capital accumulation at the societal level—keeping down the cost of the reproduction of labor power—and by its reduction of Peru's high level of unemployment. On the other hand, the evidence suggests that the petty commodity form may be undergoing a process of subordination to the wage form in the marketplace. During my revisit in 1982, I discovered a growing number of dependent sellers in the city. Particularly striking was the appearance of so many street vendors selling ice cream, candy, prepared drinks, and the like from pushcarts owned by their absent employers. More research, however, will be necessary to document such a transition from relatively autonomous marketing to more dependent forms of commerce.

I have already pointed to what I view as the productive component in market women's work in Huaraz. Here I emphasize that although the work role of the Huaraz marketers is in some ways ambiguous, they may be called productive in the strict sense of contributing to the accumulation of capital. If we regard marketers as operating in the petty commodity mode of production, they are productive insofar as they add value to the goods they market through their own labor. Detailed description of the daily activities of marketers who transport goods and process them for sale can testify to this. If, on the other hand, we deem it appropriate to view some marketers as disguised wage laborers, they may again be understood as productive workers since their labor in the preparation and sale of goods to consumers allows the wholesalers (who in this view engage retailers as workers through the extension of credit) to operate on a larger scale and to see a faster, greater return on their capital. In this latter case, the focus shifts to the social relations of production, identifying the particular way in which surplus value created by retailers is appropriated by wholesalers.

While I emphasize the productive quality of the work of women in petty commerce, it should be noted that their productivity is low when compared to workers in the "modern" sector, and I do not mean to suggest that the present situation is a satisfactory arrangement for the exchange of goods and services. My comments must be understood to describe the situation under the terms of dependent capitalism in Peru, where 99 percent of retail activity is in the hands of small sellers (Esculies Larrabure et al. 1977: 181).[13]

A few words concerning the content of Huaraz market women's work and its resemblance to housework are in order. The content of market work shares much in common with housework, yet in many respects market work requires different skills and involves women in a fundamentally different relationship to the economy. The majority of marketers contribute their labor to the products they sell and thereby save consumers the time they would spend in carrying out these tasks at home: foods are prepared or processed, clothing is sewn, and so on. Nevertheless, many skills necessary to sellers are not learned in the home and are not extensions of housework. Buying and selling must be learned from other marketers or from experience in the marketplace, as must transporting, bulking, bulk-breaking, and other types of market work.

A number of women expressed to me the difficulty they had in beginning to market. Furthermore, focusing on the resemblance of market work to domestic work diverts attention from the fact that housework and marketing are situated at different places in the capitalist social formation, and this has implications for women's views of themselves as workers and their opportunities for political mobilization. Huaraz market women themselves do not speak of marketing as an extension of their role in the home; rather, they describe it in quite a different way, as a separate job that is essential for the earnings it provides. It is important to recognize that, like housework, petty commerce has a reproductive function in maintaining family and society. Nevertheless, it is also critical to examine the distinctly productive features of women's work in the tertiary sector.

This brings us to the question of whether the conditions of work in petty commerce are likely to encourage the development of political consciousness. As noted, it is not well understood what conditions promote or limit the development of class consciousness. Still, insofar as workers' relation to the production process is taken to be a critical factor, I argue that the situation of Huaraz market women differs from the situation of Venezuelan women in the tertiary sector as described by Schmink (1977). Recall that Schmink found that these women are not in direct relationship to the production process and, consequently, have a low political potential. I have suggested that, in Huaraz, marketers are in direct relationship with the production process. They do create economic surplus, and it is transferred through unfavorable terms of trade in the marketplace (where price controls or other economic constraints act to the disadvantage of small marketers) and through exploitative relations with large wholesalers. At the societal level, surplus is transferred from the impoverished sector, in which marketers work, to the urban industrial sector (where both capitalists and workers benefit), because the government's tight regulation of marketing extends only to agricultural products and not to manufactured goods.

Moreover, the working conditions experienced by marketers are very different from those characteristic of domestic servants and other service workers whose jobs isolate them from other workers. Instead of identifying with those whom they help maintain, as isolated workers may, Huaraz market women identify with other marketers. They are in constant interaction with other sellers in the market, and they have ample opportunity to discuss common problems and grievances. Unlike some women in the service occupations who do not easily recognize their exploitation—or who, if they do are reluctant to oppose it because of the immediacy of the human needs they serve—the Huaraz marketers understand their exploitation as stemming from dominant-class interests, and many appear willing to use their collective force to challenge intolerable working conditions. This may be explained by the social character of their work. One woman recalled a time a few years earlier when marketers launched a protest over rising market fees and a higher cost of living, saying, "All rose up together because we were united. And we won."[14]

In the marketplace, women are in fact frequently vocal in expressing their strong dissatisfaction with the conditions of their lives and work. Their wide-ranging criticism is directed at the practices of a few unscrupulous wholesalers, as well as at the increasingly repressive measures of local officials who are attempting to raise the fees marketers pay as a means to augment city revenues, and even at measures of policy makers at the national level. Some marketers, uneducated though they might be, traced their problems to the international debt and its consequences. While marketers occasionally revealed a sense of hopelessness or resignation, I found them to be rarely, if ever, complacent. Instead, I discovered among market women a militant refusal to quietly endure their worsening economic situation. A seventy-five-year-old woman long active in the major market union asked, "How can we provide for ourselves when we don't sell enough to live?" But she told me: "Women must be strong," and she declared herself ready to fight against the conditions that confront poor marketers.

Although only a minority of sellers participate actively in the market unions in Huaraz—many haven't the time—women make up the grassroots of these organizations.[15] Attendance at union meetings grew during the period of my fieldwork in 1977, when the mayor's office proposed a substantial increase in daily and annual market fees. It was the most impoverished of women marketers who pressured the conciliatory male leadership to resist these increases, shouting, "We won't sell! A strike then!" and who won the sympathy of marketers not at the meetings. Their threat of a strike made clear their consciousness of themselves as productive workers whose collective action could be a source of power. In this case, talk of a strike, along with a petition of protest taken to the mayor, resulted in a compromise that was viewed as a partial victory.

In less dramatic fashion, the solidarity and resistance of market women can be seen on a daily basis. Street sellers who help each other evade fee collectors, vendors who assist one another in preparing goods for sale and who alert their neighbors to changing policies, all demonstrate a cooperative base of support among these women workers. "We are *compañeras* [close friends]," they say.

Despite the complexity and ambiguity of the present condition of women in petty commerce in the city of Huaraz, a close examination of the situation of marketers there provides some insights into the way that their workforce participation articulates with the wider political economy. Their social class position, perhaps undergoing a period of change, may be viewed as that of marginalized workers in petty production and commerce, or in some cases of disguised wage laborers. Analyzing market women within the production process as a whole reveals the productive aspect of their work. In social terms, this work is reproductive, for it sustains society over the short and the long term. Finally, the example of marketers in Huaraz shows that being marginalized in the society and the economy has not prevented these women in the impoverished tertiary sector of Peru from developing a consciousness of their situation.

Any conceptualizations of Third World women in commerce and the services must come to terms with the problems of assessing how their social-class position and sexual status are interlinked within dependent capitalist economies. Here I have pointed to some of these problems and outlined my present views, but far more must be understood about women's place in the tertiary sector generally, and about the specific condition of women workers in such areas as petty commerce, before this conceptualization may be refined.

3 Producers and Reproducers

ANDEAN MARKET WOMEN IN THE ECONOMY

This book chapter appeared in the 1986 anthology *Women and Change in Latin America*, coedited by pioneering Latin Americanist feminist anthropologists June Nash and Helen Safa.

· · · · ·

For the last decade, since the florescence of research on women in society, the sexual division of labor has been viewed as a key to understanding women's socioeconomic position. By the mid-1970s, the view held sway that women's cross-cultural subordination could be explained by their universal or near-universal attachment to the domestic sphere of activity, while men enjoyed the higher prestige of the public sphere. A flurry of studies appeared, documenting the unequal and undervalued role of women in the family and household. By calling attention to the previously "invisible" activities carried out daily by women, analysts undertook to transform the androcentric social sciences (see, for example, contributions to Rosaldo and Lamphere 1974; Reiter 1975; Rohrlich-Leavitt 1975).

But just when the domestic/public framework was gaining support by many researchers, it was called into question by others. Evidence was brought forth from fieldwork in a variety of settings that showed women move in a far broader sphere than the term *domestic* suggests. Reports of women's participation in agriculture, marketing, and the wage labor force surfaced, and we began to hear more accounts of women's *dual* work roles, their roles within *and* outside the home (e.g., Sudarkasa 1973; Chiñas 1973). By the late 1970s, the domestic/public framework was regarded by many as inadequate to account for women's socioeconomic position (Young et al. 1981). There were simply too many cases of societies where women had active roles both inside and outside the home.

Even so, it was agreed that significant cross-cultural patterns exist in the work performed by women, and researchers dissatisfied with the available theoretical frameworks undertook to formulate a new one. In the last few years, the production/reproduction conceptual framework has emerged as the most powerful analytical tool that we have to account for women's socioeconomic condition. The identification of production and reproduction as focuses of analysis may be traced to earlier writers, notably Engels ([1884] 1972), but in contrast to scholarly interest in (male) production, serious attention has only recently been directed to the reproductive activities carried out by women (Benería 1979; Safa and Leacock 1981).

The widespread acceptance of this framework seems due in large part to the power of the expanded concept of reproduction. In this context, *reproduction* refers to several levels of women's participation in society: as biological reproducers of children, as social reproducers of labor power on a daily and generational basis, and most broadly as reproducers of society itself (Edholm et al. 1977). There is, then, a recognition of certain cross-cultural patterns in the sexual division of labor; for reasons generally regarded as socially determined, women perform more of the maintenance work in society, freeing men to engage in other, productive, activity.

Beyond this, however, there is less clarity in the distinction between reproductive and productive work. For some (e.g., Deere 1982), the difference lies in whether the work creates use values or exchange values. Women's involvement in subsistence production for family consumption is regarded as reproductive, while men's exchange-value production for the market is more strictly productive. Others (e.g., Schmink 1977; Vasques de Miranda 1977), however, expand the definition of reproductive work to encompass women's income-generating activities, both in and out of the home. It is argued that women's work as domestic servants, laundresses, seamstresses, or sellers of food represents an extension of work carried out in the home and fulfills the same fundamental needs on the societal level. This is contrasted to men's leading roles in such areas as commercial agriculture, manufacturing, and trades such as carpentry and masonry.

While the production/reproduction framework has moved us forward to important new lines of inquiry, taking these conceptual categories as unproblematic may result in some confusion. Let us consider the case of market women in Andean Peru, who illustrate what I view as the strengths of the concepts discussed here, as well as some shortcomings.

THE CASE OF ANDEAN MARKET WOMEN

In many ways, Andean market women appear to be a classic example of women whose reproductive domestic work roles have extended to the public sector. Their involvement in the procurement, preparation, and distribution of basic needs such as food, clothing, and other household items may be viewed as commercialized housework (Jelin 1980; Arizpe 1977). What is more, the marketers often have infants and young children in tow, creating an even stronger impression that these are homemakers who have simply moved their activities to the marketplace. On the other hand, the efforts of market women to provide their families with income brings them into a relationship with society and economy very different from that of unpaid workers in the home. It is this contradictory role of market women that I explore here.

The research that forms the basis for my observations was carried out in the Andean city of Huaraz, about two hundred miles north of Lima. For half a year in 1977 and two months in 1982, I lived with a marketer and her family in Huaraz and, through a combination of participant observation and open-ended interviewing in the city's markets, learned about the work and social lives of market women. My primary interest was in market sellers and street vendors, but interviews with shopkeepers, producers, consumers, and market officials were included as well.

Huaraz is a city of some forty-five thousand Quechua-Spanish-speaking people and the capital of Peru's Ancash department. It serves as the commercial and administrative center for the Andean valley known as the Callejón de Huaylas. The kinds of economic activity generally available to the working class and poor majority in Huaraz include subsistence agriculture, wage labor, and petty commodity production, commerce, and services. Domestic work should be included as well and analyzed, with subsistence agriculture, as unpaid household labor for direct consumption. Consequently, most market women and their families that I came to know in Huaraz depend on several different sources of livelihood. Before I examine marketing more closely, I will consider familial strategies for economic diversification.

Landholdings surrounding Huaraz are generally very small, rarely as large as one hectare. The *chacras* (fields) are important sources of foodstuffs for many families, but far from sufficient to meet household needs. Though men are identified as most actively involved in agricultural work, women perform many tasks on the land and tend household animals.[1]

Housework, of course, must be performed in every household. Unlike middle-class Peruvians who employ domestic help, the poor of Huaraz supply their own household labor, and this falls chiefly to women. In addition to childcare and meal preparation, other time-consuming activities include fetching wood and water (many lack the urban conveniences), washing clothes, knitting, and sewing.

Unskilled and skilled wage work around Huaraz includes agricultural day labor, work in construction, small-scale manufacture of such goods as chairs and adobe bricks, and employment in a soda-bottling plant and a fishery. These jobs are primarily available to men, who may earn about one US dollar daily as laborers. Occasionally, women are hired to work as seamstresses in household manufacturing, and some young women work as domestic servants, earning only marginal incomes.

With unmet family needs and few alternatives for earning an income, many women in Huaraz turn to petty commerce. On the busiest days of the week, the city attracted upward of twelve hundred sellers to its markets and streets in 1977, and almost sixteen hundred by 1982. Close to 80 percent of sellers are women, and they include rural producer-sellers who come periodically to the city, as well as a much larger number of full-time marketers, who live in Huaraz and purchase all or most of their stock from wholesalers. Women, in contrast to men, are highly concentrated in the retail sale of vegetables, fruits, and prepared foods, which together constitute the bulk of goods sold in the market. Both women and men sell staple foods like rice, pasta, flour, sugar, and salt, as well as meat, fish, live animals, clothing, and household items such as pots and other kitchen utensils, although men generally do so on a larger scale. When men engage in marketing, they may often draw on resources generated from other forms of employment, and they may have greater mobility to travel directly to production sites to buy their goads. Consequently, men often sell larger quantities of goods at lower prices than women, and they are far more likely than women to sell manufactured goods from the coast.

Women's earnings in the marketplace are quite low, often around half the earnings of a male day laborer. Still, the need to diversify means that it is common to find families that engage in all three forms of production mentioned here, subsistence farming and household labor, petty production and commerce, and capitalist wage labor.[2]

Many times the skills that a woman takes to the market are ones she acquired at home. She may in fact offer on the market the same product that she prepares at home for family use. Such diverse items as knitted baby caps, shirts, processed grains, cornstarch pudding, tamales, and prepared drinks are found in the markets. It is not uncommon for a marketer to take some food prepared in her household to the market while she leaves the remainder for her family. In the marketplace itself, a seller's work resembles housework. For example, the sellers of fruits and vegetables, who predominate in the markets, generally spend time cleaning and arranging their goods; and some go a step further, chopping portions of vegetables, which they sell in small quantities for use in soups. Other women cook simple dishes over kerosene stoves in their market stalls, offering on-the-spot meals to the public.

The content of marketing work and its serving character have much in common with domestic work. It is not surprising that marketing work is frequently described as a "natural" extension of women's work at home. Moreover, there are other features of marketing that lend themselves to comparison with housework. Market women usually have some flexibility in determining when and where they work and what products they offer.

They can organize marketing activities around other responsibilities, most importantly childcare. Indeed, for many women the principal advantage of marketing is the possibility of taking children along with them. Just as they manage to watch their children while they work at home, women manage to look after their children in the marketplace. Infants may be breastfed, toddlers can play with other young children, and older children can be given breakfast and sent off to school.

In the most obvious sense, then, we see that marketing may be regarded as a reproductive activity similar to domestic work. Besides being similar in content, both kinds of work function to reproduce the labor force and, more broadly, society. Housework provides essential, yet unpaid, services, and marketing brings needed goods and services to consumers at relatively low prices. Together, these activities keep down the cost of reproducing the labor force in Peru and in this way contribute to the accumulation of capital at the societal level.

Nevertheless, I think there may be problems when the limits of the concept of reproduction go unexamined or when reproductive work is taken to be coterminous with women's work. When all of women's work beyond the home is viewed as defined by and reflective of the work women do in the household, we fail to see that many skills necessary to sellers are not learned at home and are not extensions of housework. Locating goods to purchase from wholesalers when retailers are crowding the markets, and successfully attracting regular customers, must be learned from other marketers or from experience in the marketplace, as must transporting, bulking, pricing, and other types of market work. Securing earnings adequate to pay the multitude of daily and annual fees necessary to stay in business, and, sometimes, evading the officials who seem so eager to increase city revenues by fining sellers for minor infractions, also require special skills. Finally, these sellers participating in organized activity in the market unions require experience and knowledge obtained on the job through the work of marketing.

Using the concept of reproduction, we run the risk of failing to differentiate subsistence activities, or the production of use values, from the production of exchange values. It is important to remember, of course, that these are not always clear-cut categories of analysis. While the household may be the center of production for use, we have already seen that marketers often produce or prepare goods at home for market exchange. Similarly, the marketplace is the center for exchange par excellence, but we may discover subsistence activities in that sphere as well. During their hours of work in the markets, women find time to do the family shopping, care for their children, and spin or knit for their families as well as for sale. Furthermore, it is common practice for food sellers to take some food home to their families, especially when it is about to spoil or is not selling well, turning one of the risks of selling perishable goods into an advantage. One woman, who operates a small restaurant in the marketplace, told me that she chose that particular area of commerce because it meant that her husband and young daughter could come and have a good meal at her stand. In this way production for market exchange generates use values as well.[3]

The point I emphasize here is that calling women's work at home and in the market "reproductive" in an undifferentiated way obscures the degree to which women participate in production for exchange. Where women are principally engaged in income-generating activity, as in marketing, the label *reproductive* may divert attention away from the significant role of market women in the national economy.[4] Huaraz market women themselves do not speak of marketing as an extension of their role in the home but, rather, describe it in quite a different way, as a separate job that is essential for the earnings it provides. This has implications for women's views of themselves as workers and for researchers' understanding of women's work in society.

Furthermore, with so broad a concept of reproduction—one which encompasses work that reproduces labor force and society—it is difficult to see where to draw the line. Almost all productive work, it would seem, could be subsumed under reproductive work. Certainly, it would be hard to claim a significant analytical difference between the work of female and male marketers, even if the latter sell larger quantities, travel greater distances, and deal in different products.[5] Like women, men who sell provide essential services and help maintain society. Men and women in other lines of work, in the trades, as agriculturalists, and as wageworkers, may also be regarded, in the fullest sense, as reproductive.

It may be most useful to consider the reproductive *and* productive aspects of both women's and men's work, in as well as outside the home.[6]

In the discussion that follows, I suggest that we view production and reproduction in dynamic relationship, as integrated social processes.

PRODUCTION AND REPRODUCTION AS SOCIAL PROCESSES

Just as the controversy over the relation of domestic work to the production process—or the "housework debate"—was laid to rest, the concept of reproduction came to the fore, challenging us to see how far we could progress in theorizing about women's work. Unlike the debate over whether women's unpaid work was productive, which revolved around Marxist categories that could be supported, refuted, or revised, the current discussion over women's reproductive work calls for clarification of a concept that only recently came into use.

The power of the concept of reproduction lies in the way it explains the sexual division of labor as the cultural elaboration of women's role in biological reproduction; women's diverse economic activities are seen as extending from and linked to their role in bearing and nursing children. Whether the cross-cultural tendency for women to engage in reproductive work is adequate to explain their subordination is another question, and it may be only in class-based societies that such activities are devalued (Leacock 1978). Some writers have suggested that women's subordination may be explained by their reproductive roles (e.g., Benería 1979: 222), though they note the weak separation of productive and reproductive roles in noncapitalist societies (Benería and Sen 1981: 292; Deere and León de Leal 1981: 360). Leaving aside the problem of the universal applicability of this framework, let us consider how it may be most useful in examining dependent capitalist societies, where most market women are found.

As mentioned before, it appears more fruitful to view productive and reproductive activities as integrated in society than as sharply divided along sex lines. Like other forms of dualist thinking,[7] the production/reproduction dichotomy may veil the interconnectedness of these social processes. On the other hand, understood dialectically, these categories of analysis permit us to examine the way that the division of labor in society and household allocation of labor are fundamentally linked. For example, several writers (e.g., Deere 1982) have noted that if women more often than men carry out subsistence activities, this may be explained by more than cultural tradition or male dominance; often familial strategies for economic diversification are based on rational assessments of the greater income-generating power of men in capitalist society. Even so, when women are drawn into the labor force, their workload may double as they continue to meet major responsibilities in the home. Consequently, it is essential that our analysis encompass the total context within which women and men work and make work-related decisions in society.

Bujra (1982: 20) has called for attention to "interlocking productive and reproductive processes." Arguing against the descriptive, and polar, categories of domestic and public, she presents a case for analysis of the articulation of domestic work with different modes of production. Bujra's emphasis on the need to investigate the *relationship* of these spheres of social action pertains closely to the issues raised in this chapter.

The task ahead, it seems to me, is first to clarify our use of the terms *production* and *reproduction* and then to accept the likelihood that social activity cannot be neatly divided into these two distinct spheres. Mackintosh (1981: 10) makes this point, noting that the concepts in question are not of the same order, with reproduction subsuming many productive activities. From this point, as Mackintosh shows, we may turn to the issue that most concerns us: the concentration of women in so many of the undervalued activities in dependent capitalist societies—in the household and in the labor force.

As the suppliers of society's basic needs, Andean market women—often pictured with babies carried on their backs—appear to present a classic case of women's reproductive role extended to the wider socioeconomic sector. It is certainly true that a distinct advantage of marketing is that it may be organized around domestic responsibilities, notably childcare. Looked at another way, however, market women present a clear example of the way that reproductive and productive work roles may be integrated when women enter the workforce. In this chapter I have suggested that a recognition of the reproductive aspect of women's work in petty commerce should not force us to compartmentalize work in society in such a fashion that women's share in production for exchange is rendered "invisible."

The theoretical progress signaled by the reproduction/production model should not be diminished. As used by feminists, and often Marxists, it has added to our understanding of the sexual division of labor, familial economic strategies, and the subordination of women. Like the domestic/ public spheres model before it, the reproduction/production model makes sense of much cross-cultural material that previously seemed confusing. The earlier model was found limiting, however, in its ahistorical form and inadequate for analysis of such categories as market women, which seem to defy classification. For the conceptualization of women and work throughout societies, the "new" model offers the advantage of describing the character of women's work rather than narrowly delimiting the place where it occurs, and its analysts have generally considered the historical context of reproduction and production in society. However, there may be a tendency once again to rigidify our concepts in a way that obscures our view of the interrelatedness of social processes.

All of this concerns most closely how we view women as workers in society. In Huaraz, market women themselves reveal an identification as workers, important to both family and the national economy. When they told me, "Without marketers, Huaraz couldn't survive," they were expressing themselves, perhaps, as sustainers or social reproducers, but they were also recognizing their productive contribution to the economy and society.

4 Market/Places as Gendered Spaces

MARKET/WOMEN'S STUDIES OVER TWO DECADES

The following appeared as a chapter in the 2001 anthology *Women Traders in Cross-cultural Perspective: Mediating Identities, Marketing Wares*, edited by Linda J. Seligmann.

·   ·   ·   ·   ·

My research among Peruvian market women began some twenty years ago, and so it may appear to be a certain conceit to frame this chapter around the last two decades of scholarly work on women marketers. I was hardly the first to research and write on the subject. But when I carried out my doctoral fieldwork in 1977, there were just a few pioneering studies to guide me (Babb 1981). Ester Boserup's well-known *Woman's Role in Economic Development* had noted that "in no other field do ideas about the proper role of women contrast more vividly than in the case of market trade" (1970: 87). More attention to market women was offered in Judith-Maria Buechler's (1972) dissertation on peasant marketing in Bolivia, Beverly Chiñas's (1973, 1975) books on Mexican women traders, and Niara Sudarkasa's (1973) monograph on Nigerian women marketers. A relatively small number of articles had appeared, including Sidney Mintz's (1971) classic essay on Caribbean women and trade.

The approaches of the 1970s ranged from functionalist to structuralist, but in general they were critical of the historical impact of Western development on women's marketing. Studies of market women in the 1980s and 1990s have built upon the early works, but they have also benefited from the growth of feminist analysis and reflect changing currents in anthropology and related fields. For purposes of discussion, I consider the emphasis on history and political economy through the eighties and the turn toward cultural analysis in the nineties. I do not wish to suggest any rigid scheme, but rather to trace several currents in recent research. I conclude by offering some remarks concerning my own changing perspective over twenty years spent conducting research among market women in the Peruvian Andes.

HISTORY AND POLITICAL ECONOMY

Emerging from earlier critiques of development, a significant body of research has examined market women as economically important yet socially marginalized participants in Third World economies. Some studies have been distinctly historical in orientation, arguing that capitalist development may account for women's involvement, but also their exploitation, in marketing work. A few authors have emphasized the opportunities afforded women entrepreneurs (Milgram, this volume[1]), but more have identified the inadequate livelihoods and the struggles of market women (Bunster and Chaney 1985; Robertson 1984) and their confrontations with the state (Clark 1988). Several have considered the growth of the urban informal sector and women's trade within it (Hansen 1980a; Babb 1985a, [1989] 1998).

A number of us were drawn to examine women in marketplaces because they were located strategically at the intersection of household work and the wider economy. As feminist analysts of the 1970s and 1980s sought to document the value of housework and the formerly unassessed informal sector, a few of us debated the utility of the Marxist-feminist analysis of production and reproduction to see what it might offer to studies of market women (Babb 1986). Despite the limitations, it enabled us to take into account the full sweep of women's work in and out of the home and to theorize the contribution of women to the national economies of which they formed a part (Babb 1987b).

Claire Robertson's (1984) *Sharing the Same Bowl,* a socioeconomic history of women marketers in Ghana, challenged some prevailing models of analysis, including modernization theory, "Marxist ethnocentrism," and the dualistic usage of formal/informal sectors. Like a number of researchers of the time, Robertson looked to class analysis within a historical framework to account for the changing fortunes of women traders. She united individual life histories, with attention to both the local (marriage and family relations) and the national (state-level political economy).

One may see a continuing interest in historical approaches to market women's lives, often with a greater attention to cultural identity, in some recent work. In the anthology *Ethnicity, Markets, and Migration in the Andes,* edited by Brooke Larson and Olivia Harris (1995), historians and anthropologists examine changing relations of Andean peoples to economic exchange from precolonial to twentieth-century times. Critical to their analysis is a challenge to persistent notions of peasant conservatism in the face of growing market exchange, as well as attention to the historical construction of ethnic identities that were often central to the economic and political struggles being waged. In one essay, Marisol de la Cadena (1995) looks at the recent implications of economic "development" for gender and ethnic identities in one Peruvian community. She argues that women are increasingly perceived, and perceive themselves to be, "more Indian" than men, since men have greater access to economic opportunities in the wider mestizo society. She acknowledges that women have access to urban culture when they work as marketers or domestic servants, but she judges these to be areas in which women's work is undervalued and, hence, in which women's indigenous identity goes unchallenged. This view may underestimate women's agency and their success in negotiating identities in both urban and rural marketplaces, although in other respects de la Cadena's analysis has deep resonance for rural Andean women.

In the present volume, Judith Marti draws on historical material from nineteenth-century Mexico as she examines conflicting images and identities of marketers and street vendors. Her work demonstrates that struggles over cultural meanings, social identities, and political spaces for women's marketing are nothing new. Images of market women in newspapers and other popular accounts, as well as the legal petitions of vendors themselves, suggest contradictory views of marketers: as respectable businesswomen and as marginal, vulnerable members of society. Marti's reading of the petitions suggests that these women were sometimes clever strategists in their appeals for mercy in avoiding debt payments and other legal problems. She makes rich use of the textual evidence and gives us a look at past negotiations over meanings and identities among market vendors.

CULTURAL IDENTITIES AND CULTURAL POLITICS

Having established the importance of women's market trade and informal commerce in rural and urban areas around the globe, scholars are now turning their attention to some other key questions. No doubt influenced by broader currents in anthropological thought, they devote more of their attention to less strictly economic, and more specifically cultural and political, concerns. Just as a growing number of anthropologists are turning from studies of "economic development" to studies of social movements and cultural politics as potential sites of struggle and change, so too this is emerging among scholars examining market women.

Questions of gender and ethnic identity are central in much of the current research on market women, and the contributors to this volume have been influential in that development. Linda Seligmann's article "To Be In Between: The Cholas as Market Women," appeared in 1989 in the journal *Comparative Studies in Society and History*. My own book on Peruvian market women, *Between Field and Cooking Pot* (Babb [1989] 1998) was first published the same year, and I recall that when I read Seligmann's article I knew she was raising some important questions that I had barely addressed. In that article, she looks at the way highland Peruvian marketplaces have been sites of negotiations over Andean and national identity, and the fact that chola market women—in transition from Indian or campesino status to mestizo status—claim political power as brokers in the process. A later article (Seligmann 1993) further examines how economic transactions and linguistic exchanges in Peruvian marketplaces bring differences over national identity to the fore.

Ruth Behar's writings based on the life history of a Mexican market woman, Esperanza, have made a valuable contribution to our understanding of the subtle and complex ways in which gender and ethnic identities are framed by one's location in economic and cultural contexts and how these identities and contexts are constantly shifting. Beginning with Behar's 1990 article "Rage and Redemption" in *Feminist Studies,* and further developed in her book *Translated Woman* (1993), Esperanza's story is shown to have different meanings when told in Mexico and when read in the United States. In the end, it is less important that the mestiza at the center of this book has traded to gain a living and more important that her life has been made up of a series of experiences, many of them extremely painful, that will be understood in distinct ways on opposite sides of the border.

Another recent work, Deborah Kapchan's (1996) *Gender on the Market,* takes market women as a point of departure for an analysis that is less concerned with economic exchange than with linguistic and cultural exchange. This book offers an ethnographic description of the site of the Moroccan marketplace, principally as a location where women have gained entry in recent years, crossing the divide between private and public spheres. Through oratory performances, these women traders have occupied a physical and discursive domain formerly controlled by men. Kapchan presents a rich analysis of the hybrid expressive forms that women bring to the market as they appeal to the public to buy from them. In the present volume, Kapchan's essay reveals that women's verbal artistry in the marketplace has given them increased power, but this may be undermined by urbanization in the modernizing nation. Even so, they have staked out a new social space for women and thereby redefined what is deemed culturally appropriate.

Gracia Clark's book *Onions Are My Husband* (1994), based on a number of years of research in Ghana, devotes attention mainly to economic aspects of women's marketing, but with an appreciation of cultural questions as well. While it supplies a detailed account of the economics and politics of women's marketing in Ghana, Clark's book also considers the self-perceptions and multiple identities expressed by women and the way these have been used historically and currently in claims for political space. In Clark's essay in this volume, she shows how traders deploy one of their identities—devoted mothers—to legitimize themselves beyond the market and to protect themselves against the national government, which would hold them responsible for rising inflation.

Notably, in the work discussed in this section, a reflexive turn is enriching the scholarship. Just as researchers are becoming more conscious of the mediating of identities found among market women in the places studied, they are also beginning to recognize and discuss publicly the way their own insertion in different cultures follows from shifting identities and intellectual preoccupations. This is especially apparent in the writings of Behar and Clark.

Lynn Sikkink's essay in this volume on women vendors of traditional medicines in Bolivia shows that gender and ethnic identity construction is contingent upon a number of factors. She argues that the particular economic practices of vending influence the way sellers present themselves, whether they emphasize their rural connection to traditional medicine or their urban know-how, and that these self-presentations are played against consumers' expectations. Vendors mediate cultural differences over time, offering their rural ethnic identity for public consumption, to command better sales. This conscious construction of cultural identity to further economic ends has parallels in other areas: for example, among handicraft sellers in the Philippines (Milgram, this volume) and among rural Ecuadorian women in the tourist trade (Crain 1996).

Mary Weismantel (1995) takes up the shifting and rather ambiguous identities of market women in Ecuador. In that context, cholas present a cultural mix, or bricolage, of elements—rural and urban, Indian and mestizo, female and male—which, as she says, disrupts regional expectations and nationalist dreams. As other authors have noted, cholas are both raced and gendered, but Weismantel calls attention to the ways that both feminine and masculine elements are often simultaneously present in the cholas' dress and practices. Indeed, she likens them to cross-dressers in other cultural contexts, who may pass for something they are not. As she suggests, there may be some problems in making this comparison, but there is value in drawing gender and sexuality into our analyses of market women.

Perhaps it was the earlier fascination, particularly among some male writers, with the perceived sexuality of West African market traders, or the image of matriarchal Zapotec traders, that made some turn away from examining sexuality in the marketplaces. But at this point, researchers know more about the force of sexuality in history, culture, and politics. Some contributors to this volume, including Gracia Clark and Johanna Lessinger, have looked at the way sexuality figures in the work and lives of market women in Africa and South Asia. The sexuality, or perceived sexuality, of Andean market women was described much earlier in the writings of novelist and ethnologist José María Arguedas, author of *Deep Rivers* (1978); it is time for us to bring a feminist perspective to this question.

This discussion of the changing approaches to studies of women marketers suggests how wide-ranging the questions are that circulate around market women. This is a point made by Seligmann in her introduction to this volume, and by others (Babb [1989] 1998: 43; Kapchan 1996: 17). While the pendulum has recently swung in the direction of cultural analysis, there has been somewhat less attention to the work relations and economic practices of market women, so one hears less regarding social and economic differentiation among traders. While researchers provide a more complex reading of the ambiguous position of cholas, for example, they may also have an underlying notion that all sellers' identities in a particular marketplace are similarly contingent. However, studies have revealed the heterogeneity of sellers, not only in terms of rural and urban background and ethnic identity, but also in terms of their relative independence or dependence on other economic interests, their participation as wholesalers or retailers, and their domestic responsibilities.

Market women remain one of the major occupational groups in many societies, and their place within wider economies will clearly influence the way they participate in political struggles and social change. In this volume, Lessinger writes of the impact of global restructuring on market women in India, and Clark considers the effect of structural adjustment on market women in Ghana. Éva Huseby-Darvas addresses the economic importance of marketing for middle-aged village women in late socialist Hungary, and concludes by noting that the new market economy following the collapse of socialism has meant the loss of this employment. That scholars are now taking seriously some neglected cultural aspects of marketers is heartening. That they are drawing together perspectives that are at once culturally, politically, and economically informed as they continue to discuss market women is also encouraging.

ANDEAN MARKET WOMEN TWENTY YEARS LATER

My primary field research on Peruvian market women took place in the Andean city of Huaraz in 1977 and was followed by revisits in 1982, 1984, and 1987, a decade that framed my book, which was published two years later. With the prospect of a forthcoming revised edition of my book, I returned to the site of my fieldwork in summer 1997 in order to observe some of the changes of the previous decade and to renew relationships begun twenty years before. The trip also gave me the opportunity to return to Peru with a different outlook and to raise questions I had not thought of addressing during earlier visits. The world had changed over this period of time and so had Peru; my own interest had shifted from a narrower focus on gender and political economy to include cultural questions as well.

My earlier work had emphasized the work of women as marketers in the production process, arguing that these women contributed to the value of the goods they sold and played a key role in the context of the underdeveloped Peruvian economy. I suggested that the national campaign to scapegoat small-scale marketers for the country's economic problems was unjustified given the hidden work these women performed and their self-employment, which relieved the state of the need to provide for them. I was also interested in the link between women's household work and their marketing, theorizing that both were critical to the society. I remain satisfied by and large with my earlier analysis, but I believe there are a number of areas that I may have overlooked.

While I was concerned during earlier visits to examine the Huaraz marketers' strategies for claiming space in the streets and marketplaces, I returned to Peru with a greater interest in struggles over urban space. Just after my trip to Peru in 1987, the major city market was torn down and a large number of marketers were sent to sell in the streets, with the vague assurance of a new model market to be constructed. It was not until 1994, however, that the new market opened, and in 1997 I found that only the most economically privileged sellers were able to sell there. Unlike in the former market, where stalls were rented, the new market stalls had to be purchased, which few people could afford to do. At the same time, city officials were cracking down on street sellers, making the situation most difficult for many marketers. Zones designated for selling were often marginal to the downtown area, and many complained that sales were lower than ever.

A growing number of children, as well as women, had entered marginal areas to sell, some of them wandering the streets to avoid city officials. Interviews revealed how impoverished their conditions were and how they strategized to survive under adverse circumstances. Because the Andean city where I worked was a tourist center, some had fashioned themselves and their trade to appeal to travelers' interests. From innumerable shoeshine boys who capitalized on the dusty shoes of visitors to the area, to small children begging to have their photo taken alongside a baby alpaca for a "tip," to fruit drink vendors with signs proclaiming the value of "vitamin C," many had adapted to a changing cultural climate. My attention was thus drawn to the ways that sellers sought to make themselves more marketable when the economy itself appeared intransigent. As elsewhere in Latin America, Peru in the 1990s was experiencing the harsh effects of neoliberalism, with its structural adjustment measures, privatization, and reduction of social services.

Most marketers feel fairly powerless to improve their own and their families' situations when economic and political conditions conspire against them. When marketplaces, like other institutions, are undergoing privatization, only a minority will benefit from the management's effort to build "community" among them. And when a member of the city council advises that the townspeople suffer from low self-esteem and need to work on "self-identity," many find their situation worsening daily, with little to feel good about. Yet there are still ways that marketers forge cultural identities rooted in traditions resistant to the onslaught of neoliberalism. Not wholly dependent on economic success in the manner of late-twentieth-century capitalism, Andean market women continue to find ways of enduring and of imagining another future.

My interest in Peruvian women marketers continues to gravitate to the conditions of economic hardship they are experiencing and how they manage to get along under current circumstances. But more than before, I turn my attention to the ways that market women and others come to terms with persistent poverty in the face of an apparently modernizing urban space. Newly paved roads, impressive plazas, and thriving tourism all contribute to the appearance of a town making progress. But how do low-income marketers assess the abundance of high-priced restaurants lining city streets? How do shoeshine boys compare their experiences of low-paid work with the evident leisure time of middle-class schoolchildren who share the same space with them in the video arcades? How do street vendors and marketers interpret the efforts of city officials to "clean up" the streets and restrict their activity to fairs? What new cultural identities will emerge in these neoliberal times? Will some market women who are carving out a space in the free market economy move beyond individual success and press for systemic change? These are questions that I now ask.

When I showed copies of my book to marketers and their families in Huaraz, I discovered how painfully close they were still to the events of a decade ago. My *comadre* and her daughter, my goddaughter, remembered the tearing down of the old central market as though it were yesterday. When I read aloud from the preface the words of my goddaughter, who had written the details of that time in a letter to me, their eyes welled up with tears. "The market was demolished, as though there had been another earthquake," I read, translating back into Spanish for them. Now, in the revised edition, I provide further details about the new privatized market and how urban commercial space is more tightly controlled in the interest of the local middle class and the tourist industry. I also give more attention to the various discourses of development that are invoked to make authoritative claims at the local and national levels. Finally, informed by current studies of market women, I consider the ways that Andean sellers are negotiating far more than their economic survival in the marketplace: they are negotiating the terms of their very lives and cultural identities.

The current scholarship on market women, including that of authors in this volume, has taken research and writing in directions I would not have imagined when I began my work in Peru two decades ago. When I returned to my field site recently, I had the advantage of a far broader perspective informed by these authors and others, enabling me to reconsider market women in the context of cultural politics and globalization at century's end. I look forward to seeing what promising new approaches to studies of market women will be taken in the years ahead, building upon and perhaps challenging the impressive scholarship to date.

PART III Gendered Politics of Work, Tourism, and Cultural Identity

Commentary

The two journal articles that appear in part 3 of this book were written at vastly different times in my career and in the history of feminist and anthropological thought. The first was published in the journal *Urban Anthropology* in 1990 but originated in a conference paper presented in 1984,[1] while the second came out in *Latin American Perspectives* in 2012, along with other works first presented at a conference in 2008, and was based on research conducted for my book *The Tourism Encounter* (Babb 2011). In the period between these publications, Peru was experiencing a protracted time of fear and violence, and I turned my attention to research in Nicaragua on the gendered impacts of postrevolutionary neoliberalism (Babb 2001a). Nevertheless, I made several visits to Peru in the 1980s, during the years of conflict, and I returned a decade later, in 1997, resuming much more frequent travel to Peru by 2006.

I bring the two articles together here because they raise related questions concerning how we can assess the nature of women's participation in economies and societies when so much depends on the suppleness of our interpretations. The first piece was written at a time when feminists still needed to make a case for the inclusion of women and gender in social analysis, while the second, written a couple of decades later, could take the legitimacy of gender analysis for granted and argue some of the finer points regarding ways in which indigenous women in areas of Peru and Mexico are inserting themselves in the work of tourism development.

Both pieces had somewhat mixed responses as a result of the rather novel positions I took, and so I begin this commentary by looking back to discover where the heat was in those debates. I go on to discuss the "impossibility of women" as taken up by contemporary feminists who wish to dismantle fixed notions of gender. From there, I raise related questions concerning cultural representation and identity among Andean women. I conclude this commentary with some observations about the politics of the transnational Latin American women's movement in the current context.

In 1984, anthropologist Rhoda Halperin invited me to take part in a panel at the annual meeting of the American Anthropological Association, "Units of Analysis in Economic Anthropology," asking me to address gender as a unit of analysis. I happily agreed to do so, as I considered myself both a feminist anthropologist and an economic anthropologist, and bringing the two together was a key concern of mine. I set to work in my paper to establish that feminists had put gender on the map as a key vector of social analysis, and then I showed its efficacy by directing attention to various modes of production in Peru. After our presentations, and during comments from the audience, I realized that some had found my paper polemical in asserting that economic anthropologists needed to take gender seriously as one unit of analysis among others that differentiate social and economic experience. I remember feeling set back on my heels as a recently minted PhD in my early thirties when I was suddenly made to feel, by an established male scholar nearing sixty, that despite the invitation to address gender, my subject was unwelcome. It didn't help that earlier in the year at the annual meeting of the Society for Economic Anthropology, two Andeanist male colleagues had chatted audibly during my talk on Peruvian market women in the economy; and one of them later let me know how little he thought of "ladies, uh . . . specialists" doing research on gender and economic development and placed an unwanted hand on my knee.

Just as my work in the mid-1970s on the Cornell-Peru Project vexed some participants in that project (discussed in my commentary in part 1), so too did I experience pushback a decade later from economic anthro-

Cooperative members of the Club de Mujeres Yurac Yacu (Yurac Yacu Women's Club) knitting items for sale near Huaraz, 2015. Photo by author.

pologists who did not appreciate a young female scholar's suggestion that their subfield had been slow to recognize the value of gender analysis. To cite one prominent example of thought of that time, anthropologist Anthony Leeds, in a special issue of *Anthropological Quarterly*, "Women and Migration," was given the final word in a piece that seemed to undermine the project of all the other contributors as he took an orthodox Marxian class analysis and pronounced gender analysis to be a "reductionist outlook" that considers only the individual and cannot account for structural relations in society.

As I argue in the next chapter, gender is as "structural" as class, race, and other social vectors, even though Leeds was unable to see it that way. Interestingly, he wrote of the other contributors: "All were compelled to see the complementarity of male/female roles" (Leeds 1976: 70). His view should not be confused with the feminist notion of gender complementarity or with the decolonial feminist rejection of gender as a constructed and colonialist category of analysis; instead, he reflected an old-school notion of the universality of gender roles and the gender division of labor in society. All this is simply to establish that it was not so very long ago that the foundational concept of gender, and even the desirability of giving specific attention to women in society, was challenged by heavyweights in the field.

In the years between my conference presentation and publication of the article that follows here, I strengthened my argument and changed my title from the cautious "The Analysis of Gender in Economic Anthropology" (Babb 1984a) to the rather playful, yet serious, "Women's Work: Engendering Economic Anthropology" (Babb 1990). As I read the work today, I remain committed to deepening gender (and intersectional) analysis, but I am more critical of the implicit evolutionary outlook embedded in my examination of changing modes of production in society. My perspective at that time was shaped by Marxist feminism, and while I offered a historical materialist analysis, I now recognize the Western bias of hinting at any sort of "natural" progression in modes and relations of production (from foraging to horticultural work, from peasant to wage laborer, and so on). Nonetheless, I believe that I organized the piece in a way that usefully highlighted the contributions of those scholars, including myself, who were beginning to engage in fine-grained gender analysis in a number of Peruvian settings, with the objective of calling on economic anthropology to bring gender into the discussion.

In contrast to these earlier experiences of sexism and dismissive attitudes in the discipline, my later article included in this section met a friendlier and more constructive critique, as well as a measure of praise. That work, drawing on my recent research on tourism in postconflict and postrevolutionary Latin America, assessed how regions that had gone through periods of dramatic change were using tourism to rebuild economies and refashion nations. While my book project was not focused squarely on gender and indigenous identity, these were among several key elements I considered to have been frequently integral to the process of commodifying culture and marketing tourism. In the article included here, gender and race were at center stage as I considered research findings from Andean Peru and Chiapas, Mexico.

Vicosinos in the tourism project dressed in traditional finery for a
pachamanca (Andean feast), 2011. Photo by author.

What some regarded as controversial was my suggestion that in spite of
enduring legacies of colonialism and sexism, rural and indigenous women
were in some cases making good as they traded on their gender and cultural identity in the tourism market. In making that case, I knew I might
run the risk of provoking criticism for not keeping my focus on exploitation brought on by tourism development, but I considered it important to
show the ingenuity of historically dispossessed people working the system
to their own advantage. In both the conference session on tourism where
I first presented this work (Babb 2008b) and in the published version

presented here (Babb 2012), I heard from those who worried that my interpretation of the situation might not be critical enough of the fraught balance of power that is characteristic of Latin America. I shared this concern yet remained committed to showing both exploitative relations and mobilization from below, even when that mobilization might veer toward capitalist commodification of female indigenous bodies and cultures.

In their introduction to the *Latin American Perspectives* special issue "Tourism, Gender, and Ethnicity," Tamar Diana Wilson and Annelou Ypeij (2012: 11) noted, "Babb stresses the importance of both using and creating an indigenous identity for tourist consumption as a form of empowerment." And in his commentary following the eight articles in the journal issue, my colleague Andrew Canessa, with whom I have collaborated and whose work includes decolonial feminist approaches to indigeneity in the Andes, offered the following: "Florence Babb's contribution is a fascinating discussion of two contrasting examples of tourism in which local people try to meet outsiders' demands for the 'authentic' as this is diversely interpreted. Tourism, she points out, may throw into relief the intersections between identity and gender as tourists seek out the authentically indigenous. Thus it has the potential to invert the negative status associated with being indigenous and female" (Canessa 2012a: 111).

Yet Canessa goes on to express some puzzlement over why, given that "some women will parlay their embodied Indianness into cultural and economic capital," they have not already had more success in doing this; he concludes that my work "clearly points to the need for further research on women's continued marginalization even when conditions appear to be propitious" (Canessa 2012a: 112). Notwithstanding this flicker of doubt, he concludes with the following regarding the journal contributions:

> The common element of these examples across Latin America, I would argue, is that they all participate in a (neo)colonial economy of desire and consumption in which the Western sovereign individual can seek to satisfy his or her desire for the exotic, the "Other," and the premodern on a very uneven playing field. And yet, despite these hierarchies and inequalities, many of these contributions demonstrate that there is a capacity to subvert the gendered colonial model and carve out new spaces in which the contributions of women are publicly valued and can be translated into real and not simply symbolic gains. (Canessa 2012a: 114)

I agree with this assessment, as it grapples with the dilemma of making sense of and interpreting what are often ambivalent sources of evidence—and as it recognizes the potential for women to make good on opportunities that present themselves, even if compromises must be made.

WOMEN AND GENDER AS CATEGORIES OF ANALYSIS

I began this commentary by noting the resistance among some economic anthropologists to viewing women and gender as valid units of analysis. My examples from the 1970s and 1980s suggest that this stemmed from deep-seated notions of sex difference as natural, immutable, and not particularly worthy of study. During that period when feminist scholarship was emerging, some researchers were unaware, or unconvinced, of the transformational potential of bringing attention to women, and then gender, though by the later 1980s it was becoming harder not to notice the sea change occurring across the disciplines and in the new field of women's studies. Historian Joan Scott (1986) famously wrote a masterful essay on gender as a category of analysis—showing how our historical understanding is fundamentally changed when women and gender relations are made visible—and the work continues to be cited as a milestone. The journal *Feminist Studies* for many years informed prospective contributors that work submitted should recognize gender as a category of analysis, and I blithely wrote in an endnote to the next chapter (first published in 1990), that "it seems unnecessary to quarrel over terminology [of gender]."

This remark appears terribly naive today, as it became clear that not only would critics of women's and gender studies challenge the foundational premises of the field but so would some feminists. Just two decades after the formation of the field of scholarship and the florescence of academic programs around the United States and well beyond, a debate arose over whether the interdisciplinary field had a viable subject of study. Political theorist Wendy Brown (2008: 21) argued that women's studies "may be politically and theoretically incoherent, as well as tacitly conservative—incoherent because by definition it circumscribes uncircumscribable 'women' as an object of study." Here she referred to the growing awareness, following the 1980s interventions largely by women of color, that women do not comprise a singular category, that gender is instead crosscut by race, class, sexuality, and nation. Intersectionality and "multiple subjectivities" better described the experiences of women who were positioned across the social spectrum and often were divided, even if they shared a gender identity.

In response to Brown, who claimed that identity is not sufficient to define a field, feminist theorist Robyn Wiegman (2008: 39) summed up the 1990s discussions of women's studies that "settled most contentiously in debates about the category of *women* and its saliency as a guarantee for knowledge and political movement." She describes the fracturing this produced among US feminist scholars but, ultimately, suggests that far from rendering women's and gender studies impossible, understanding the field's historical development and the *contingency* of its identity categories keeps the field relevant and gives it an edge. Wiegman (2012: 54–69) has furthermore called into question the way that the move from discussion of "women" to "gender" has served as a progress narrative, with an implicit tale of redemption embedded in it. After *gender,* she suggests, *intersectionality* may substitute as the preferred terminology, offering still greater satisfaction to those who embrace it. She interrupts the narrative to draw attention to the possibility that instead of abandoning the concept of women, this foundational concept might have been remade to be capacious enough to truly include all women regardless of their race, sexuality, and national identity.

More feminists agreed with Wiegman than with Brown, which is borne out by the continued presence, and often the growth, of women's, gender, and sexuality studies in US universities. If this debate regarding feminist terms of analysis and related conceptions of gender difference and inequality took place largely on US soil, however, how is it relevant to the lives of women elsewhere, particularly in the global South? Postcolonial scholar and anthropologist Saba Mahmood (2008) entered the conversation by addressing the way that Muslim women's perceived inequality has been mobilized in the global North, not only by political interests seeking to intervene militarily, but also by feminists who are certain that these women are failing to recognize their own oppression. Recalling Gayatri Spivak's earlier critique of colonialist white men seeking to save brown women from brown men, Mahmood shows that even well-intentioned northern feminists are guilty of framing veiled women's lives as circum-scribed and the women as in need of rescue. In the name of freedom and women's rights, liberal feminists join the chorus of those holding culture and religion accountable for these women's perceived difference.

Mahmood agrees that there are gender inequalities in the Muslim world, but she insists that the question is: By whom and for what purposes is there an outcry for women's freedom? She poses the challenging question that decolonial feminists in general might productively engage regarding the "arrogant certitude" of some strands of feminism in their "world-making projects": "Does the confidence of our political vision as feminists ever run up against the responsibility that we incur for the destruction of life forms so that 'unenlightened' women may be taught to live more freely?" (Mahmood 2008: 108).

Turning more specifically to Latin American feminisms and decolonial perspectives on Andean women, we can comment further on the relevance of northern feminists' debates over the terms of scholarly analysis and their political implications. First, it is important to say that theory from the North does, of course, circulate to the South and has an impact on thought and activism there as it is selectively appropriated or repurposed. At the same time, independent developments in the South have given rise to lines of political development among feminists that are both similar to and different from those in the North, a point made frequently by south-ern feminists who reject the criticism by the Latin American Left that they have been overinfluenced by bourgeois northern feminism. Thus even if the consternation over the discovery that women do not constitute a homogeneous category was largely a (white) American problem, the turn toward intersectional analysis has had strong Latin American reso-nances—recall Marfil Francke's early recognition of "braided" forms of gender and racial dominance in Peru.

It is worth noting that *Feminist Studies* (2016) has an updated state-ment on the journal's subject matter, that it "views the intersection of gen-der with racial identity, sexual orientation, economic means, geographical location, and physical ability as the touchstone for its intellectual analysis. Whether drawn from the complex past or the shifting present, the work that appears in *Feminist Studies* addresses social and political issues that intimately and significantly affect women and men in the United States and around the world." Indeed, there has been growing cross-fertilization of ideas moving from both North and South, with more international contributions to US journals, and more US feminists challenging their own geopolitical blind spots by engaging theory and research from the South.[2]

There is still another parallel here: the critique by women of color and poststructuralists (and those who are both) of the notion of *women* as a unified category and the critique of decolonial feminisms' challenging the concept of *gender* as a colonial construction. While the former emanates mainly from the North, the latter is both inspired by and generated, in large part, in the South. The critique by US women of color, who showed that by and large the category of "women" in the United States has referred to white, middle-class, heterosexual women, led to a call for scholarly attention to intersecting forms of difference and inequality.

In a related way, decolonial feminists, including María Lugones, have argued that gender, like race, is a constructed category introduced with colonialism and Eurocentrism. Much of this work is philosophical or historical in focus, however, and what has remained unclear in the critique is how we should understand and assess gender and race today. I have found it useful in my ethnographic analysis to bring together both the insights of decolonial feminisms, which provide historical perspective on how gender and racial inequalities emerged (or deepened over time), and intersectionality, which I have referred to as braided inequalities, as we know it in recent decades. Just as I have found these approaches to be generative in rethinking the work I discussed in parts 1 and 2, so they are generative in thinking about the two articles appearing in part 3.

I have traced the case I made for considering gender a foundational unit of analysis in economic anthropology and in scholarship more generally, though today I would draw on decolonial feminisms and emphasize that gender is always contingent and must be understood in its historical context; moreover, I would draw on intersectional feminisms, and go beyond my earlier focus on gender, class, and cultural difference, to address racial and sexual difference in a more profound way. In the second and more recent of the two pieces that follow, "Theorizing Gender, Race, and Cultural Tourism in Latin America," I anticipated and incorporated the preoccupations of intersectional and decolonial feminisms. In that later work, I considered the involvement of rural, indigenous women of the Andes and of southern Mexico in cultural tourism practices. Moving beyond the question of these women's insertion in local economies and societies, I examined how, in each case, women were at times able to capitalize on opportunities and trade on their gender, racial, and cultural identities in order to benefit themselves and their families. The new social purchase in iconic indigenous women and the products they sell has accounted for a good deal of touristic interest in these regions, and for the women themselves there have been some advantages worth noting.

My ethnographic research in Peru and Mexico suggested certain differences between women's participation in the two regions. Andean women, viewed by tourists as emblematic of the "exotic" Peruvian nation, could quietly provide services to tourists or more actively sell them the "Andean experience" by posing for photographs or selling artisan crafts deemed to be "authentic." In contrast, some women in the Chiapas region of Mexico, particularly those who had been active in the Zapatista rebellion, were still more proactive in relation to tourism, revealing the self-assertion they had acquired through social mobilization and, at times, catering to a market of tourists who wished to discover indigenous activists and consume a part of their experience. These women might host solidarity tourists in their communities or sell Zapatista dolls and related paraphernalia, for example. Despite whatever differences I could perceive in the two regions, I found that these indigenous women were embracing their gender and cultural identities, instrumentalizing them in order to make gains in the tourism market. This is not to say that they were overcoming the legacies of colonialism in Peru and Mexico, but that they were cleverly turning the tables on some assumptions regarding "subordinated" indigenous women and trading on their newfound cultural capital.

CULTURAL REPRESENTATION AND IDENTITY AMONG ANDEAN WOMEN

In my recent work on tourism in Latin America, I was particularly interested in the encounters between tourists and toured, and how different parties to tourism encounters parlayed their interests into desired outcomes. While tourists often hoped to acquire intimate knowledge of

Casa de los Abuelos (Grandparents' House), a small museum in Vicos, 2015. Photo by author.

cultural difference through tourism experiences, local women and men in economies dependent on tourism were often willing to provide the simulacra of such experiences—offering their own time as guides, artisans, and performers, or the products that seem to embody such experiences. Thus a tourist in Peru might be intrigued by "Inca shamans" around the iconic site of Machu Picchu, or by the often-reproduced paintings and weavings of *chismosas*, representations of Andean women wearing hats, long braids, and full skirts seated together with their backs to the viewer, signifying women gossiping or sharing secret knowledge.

By the time I conducted comparative research on tourism in Peru, Nicaragua, Mexico, and Cuba, I was giving far more attention than I had earlier in my career to cultural questions, which I often framed as cultural politics.³ Some of the ways that gender and race have figured in my discussion of cultural and political currents were shaped by world developments, as well as by intellectual currents in anthropology, feminist studies, and tourism studies. The framing of my interest in tourism as a subject of study was inspired by the way tourism functions both as an economic development strategy and as a mechanism for the cultural and political refashioning of regions and nations. I was struck by how frequently tourism was enlisted during transitional periods in postconflict and postrevolutionary societies, and how this was experienced at the local level by those who might (or might not) stand to benefit from the growing attention to their cultural difference. Peru was an unusual case, as it had undergone a long period of conflict and violence that was seen as anathema to tourism development. With the passage of time, however, tourists started coming back, and eventually some sought out more intimate experiences by getting to know Andean people in their own settings.

Significantly, cultural anthropology had gone through a period of soul-searching from the later 1980s, the "postmodern turn" marked by publication of the edited volume *Writing Culture* (Clifford and Marcus 1986). This anthology signaled (and helped produce) the crisis in representation—blowing the lid on what remained of an authoritative voice in ethnographic practice and writing. It also, and famously, slighted women's writings as exemplars in the field. Feminist anthropologists responded with their own landmark anthology, *Women Writing Culture* (Behar and Gordon 1995), which addressed women like Zora Neale Hurston and many others, often overlooked in the discipline, who presaged the postmodern turn and innovative writing that came into vogue by the 1990s. Their work assessing the current state of the field, like that of their male colleagues, expressed a recognition of contingency and ambivalence in conventional categories of analysis, but they went beyond that to critique the relations of power behind gender, race, and sexual differences found in research and writing. Relatedly, the new wave of tourism studies likewise directed critical attention to cultural representation, to the "tourist gaze," and to the ways that power figures in the tourism encounter. While much of the recent scholarship on tourism points to cultural commodification under conditions of neoliberal globalization, other studies, including my own, observe instances of local hosts working to redefine the terms of the tourism encounter. Where race and gender are so often concerned in these exchanges, as my article in part 3 reveals, we find local indigenous women struggling against a host of assumptions regarding their "inferior" or "backward" ways, even as they are celebrated as their nation's emblematic symbols of cultural heritage.

Engaged postcolonial scholars like Saba Mahmood, mentioned earlier, have shown that liberal feminists are not exempt from colonialist thinking, and so they may unwittingly make assumptions about the ability of rural, often-uneducated women to represent their own interests. Whether they are northern or southern scholar-activists, feminists may underestimate these women as knowledge producers and social protagonists in their own right. In Peru, during the 1990s under Alberto Fujimori's presidency, many thousands of rural women were subjected to forced sterilization, and urban feminists appeared to disregard the practice and its deep injustices (Ewig 2010). If forced sterilization was Fujimori's draconian strategy for reducing poverty, why were feminists not decrying the policy as an assault on indigenous women's bodies? Did they view rural women as in need of "progress" in the form of reproductive control? It seems hard to avoid concluding that urban coastal feminists had accepted the modernist narrative that controlling these women's fertility was a route to development.

A decade later, and after the 2003 release of the report of the Truth and Reconciliation Commission, President Alan García had to be convinced to take proper action to address the decades of violence perpetrated by Sendero Luminoso and the Peruvian military. Only now does a national museum, Lugar de la Memoria, commemorate the lives lost, the sexual violence directed against women in particular, and the devastating impact on families and communities. In recent years, Lima's feminists have honored the memory of María Elena Moyano, the Afro-Peruvian activist who was martyred because she dared to defy Sendero and organize for better conditions in Lima's shantytowns. However, the differences between coastal cosmopolitanism on the one hand, and urban and rural poverty on the other, remain immense, representing incommensurable epistemic communities. Urban middle-class Peruvians, including many feminists, have only gradually recognized the profound injustices and the gendered consequences of the time of violence.[4]

In her work in rural Ecuador on indigenous women and development initiatives, Sarah Radcliffe (2015) sets out a far-reaching framework for examining postcolonial development, an approach she terms "postcolonial intersectionality." Bringing together postcolonial theory and intersectional analysis, she hopes to overcome the limitations of the latter, which may still rely on identity categories that have more resonance in the global North. I find Radcliffe's approach and insights to be congenial with those I advance in this book based on feminist decolonial thought and intersectionality, although she might judge my work on tourism to be overoptimistic in its assessment of prospects for entrepreneurial indigenous women. Rather like Canessa in his response to my work, in which he questions why rural women catering to tourism have not done better for themselves up to now, Radcliffe (2015: 11) calls attention to the "ambivalent and contested effects" of neoliberal representations (in tourism and beyond) of indigenous women as bearers of "folkloric culture and arcane environmental knowledge." I believe that she and I agree that this representation of rural indigenous women is colonialist and most often serves the interests of more powerful social groups; where we may disagree is in how to assess women's agency in maneuvering within these constraints. I find staging this current conversation to be productive and illuminating— even if I do ask myself whether I have been wrongheaded, whether I have pushed my point too far or overlooked countervailing evidence. I find much to admire in Radcliffe's deep ethnographic inquiry into these critical questions, and I am inspired by her recent work, along with that of Bueno-Hansen (2015), Canessa (2012b), Rivera Cusicanqui (2012), and others who have labored to decolonize Andeanist scholarship on race and gender through participatory methodologies and research collaborations.

FEMINIST QUESTIONS AS FRAMED BY THE CONTEMPORARY WOMEN'S MOVEMENT IN LATIN AMERICA

While I have organized this book around key debates in the scholarship on Andean women from the 1970s to the present, my thinking has been deeply influenced by closely related feminist activism over these decades.

In the final section of this commentary, I discuss some recent developments in Latin American and transnational feminisms in order to clarify
what is at stake in the scholarly debates. As one strand of activism, some
Latin American feminists have been participating in the World March of
Women, held in various corners of the globe since 2000. These World
Marches appear to be reworking several of the central concepts that
emerged in feminist analysis in the 1970s and 1980s (e.g., production and
reproduction) just as they embrace newer currents in feminist political
thought (e.g., care work, the body, and territory).

For example, one platform statement declares, "We are working to
build a feminist, solidarity-based economy, one that alters patterns of production and reproduction, distribution and consumption, in addition to
recognizing and appreciating domestic and care work, as something that
is crucial to the sustainability of human life."[5] Several of the core principles outlined as organizing platforms on various websites draw attention
to the body; women's work, including care for families and communities;
and forms of violence and exploitation under conditions of patriarchy and
global capitalism. In the preparations for the most recent World March of
Women, in 2015, we saw a concern to identify gendered legacies of colonialism and struggles over territory, sovereignty rights, and responses from
the global South in confronting empire in the face of increasing precarity.
Thus we discover that feminists active in the World March have sought to
bring gender and power to the table in discussions about social justice and
globalization.

Cajamarca, Peru, was the site of the fourth regional gathering of the
World March of Women of the Americas, as about a hundred women from
North, Central, and South America came together in October 2015.[6] In
addition to addressing the region's broad agenda, the group marched in
solidarity with the women in Cajamarca who struggled in response to mining development and the implications for land use, water, and environment.
One local woman who has attained international recognition for her heroic
efforts to defend her family's land against the incursion of the Yanacocha
mine, Máxima Acuña, participated in and was honored at the gathering.
The World March and transnational feminism in this instance seem to have
lent crucial support to local initiatives. Much of the discussion around the
recent Andean concept of *buen vivir* (living well) has shed light on the onto-

logical turn toward cosmopolitics and the rights of nature, bodies, and territories that are very much at stake in the Peruvian struggles.

While we can see in the World March of Women traces of earlier strands of feminist thought, I suggest that the fingerprints of a more current decolonial feminism also appear on these new agendas. Thus we see greater awareness of indigenous women's knowledge, of new epistemic communities in which "tradition" is no longer viewed simply as a drag on "progress" but is instead regarded as cultural heritage that may be enlisted to help craft the sort of alternative societies or "worlds" that decolonial theorists have been talking about. Feminist voices from the South now include those of indigenous-identified feminists such as Silvia Rivera Cusicanqui and Julieta Paredes from Bolivia, and Tarcila Rivera from Peru, whose diverse politics coincide in calling for territorial rights, the rights of nature, and the right to maintain collective cultural practices.

In Peru, rural and indigenous women like Máxima Acuña have been among those most critical of the impact of mining and other extractive industries, and of the contamination of water and other resources vital to Andean communities. Some have used cultural identity practices to their own advantage; these practices provide indigenous women with new social capital in such contexts as the promotion of biodiversity and tourism development. This is not to ignore the fact that these women have also experienced the durable inequalities that have long accompanied being female, indigenous, and rural or urban poor—which is the dilemma of being both culturally emblematic and socially marginalized in Peru.

One other signal event for Latin American feminism that I attended, the thirteenth Latin American and Caribbean Feminist Encuentro, was held in Lima in November 2014, thirty-one years after the city had played host to the second continental gathering in 1983. This time, the number had risen to some fifteen hundred in attendance. At the opening plenary, prominent feminist activist-scholar Virginia Vargas set forth key questions to be addressed in the days ahead: (1) interculturality and intersectionality, (2) sustainability and environment, and (3) body and territory. While some exclusionary practices at the encuentro were identified (men and trans women were not admitted, and Afro-descendant women felt they were marginalized in the program), indigenous women, including Bolivian Aymara communitarian lesbian feminist Julieta Paredes,

The Latin American and Caribbean Feminist Encuentro in Lima (the T-shirts declare women's rights to their own bodies), 2014. Photo by author.

played a notable part, calling for a recuperation of feminism and for a "revolution of our peoples."

From the start, the encuentro addressed sensitive and significant issues that have yet to be resolved in Latin American feminism—or in feminism more broadly. Cultural diversity and the politics of location were taken up in nuanced ways as the gathering addressed issues facing rural and urban indigenous women. Contingents of household workers, sex workers, and individuals identified as lesbian, gay, bisexual, transgender, and queer (LGBTQ) were highly visible. Theoretically sophisticated questions, including, "What is the feminist subject?" and "Is gender a colonial category that must be decolonized?" were paired with feminist activism that ultimately took to Lima's streets in a show of strength at the end of the encuentro.

Some of the most memorable discussions revolved around what it will take to have a truly intercultural feminism that recognizes how body and territory are implicated in specific settings in Latin America and the Caribbean. The Afro-descendant women were riveting as they marched onstage during a plenary to present a declaration, chanting, "Negra sí, negra soy," and transgender and sex-worker participants were passionate in voicing their rights. Some rural indigenous women, identifiable by their traditional dress and use of language, were outspoken on panels and in private conversation. One woman told me that as several of them sold arti-san goods at the event, other conference participants asked to pose for pic-tures with them (recalling the tourist desire to document their experience with "native culture"), and that she had informed them: "No—I'm here for the conference!" Andean women had a presence at the encuentro and on the plenaries, and they expressed their commitment to activism as women, if not necessarily as feminists—suggesting ongoing differences between popular women's organizations and feminist movement organizations.

A strong advocate of indigenous women of the Amazon and the Andes was Tarcila Rivera, the Peruvian founder of the NGO Chirapaq, who headed up sessions where she called for the inclusion of these women in any broad-based feminist initiative. But surely the most vocal champions of indigenous women in the region were Julieta Paredes and her Bolivian colleague Adriana Guzmán, who held workshops to promote communi-tarian feminist thinking and activism. These sessions attracted both rural-identified women and some urban supporters, including a few interested participants like me from the global North. The two advocated adopting the Andean cosmovision, decolonizing feminism, and freeing society of patriarchal relations. Julieta and Adriana dramatically intervened at the closing session, proposing that the next Feminist Encuentro, in 2017, be held in Bolivia, where the focus would be on indigenous feminism. While this drew some animated responses from the large gathering, the better organized Uruguayan feminists carried the vote for the next venue— prompting Julieta to provocatively declare that the first *indigenous* femi-nist encuentro would then be held a year before the meeting in Uruguay.

Notwithstanding fierce debates and moments of tension over social inclusion and the decision-making process, the thirteenth Feminist Encuentro was a rich and productive meeting of women from many parts of Latin America and the Caribbean. In the Declaración Final at the closing event, a number of accomplishments and emergent questions were identified as the organizers called for further discussion of capitalism, heteropatriarchy, and colonialism, which continue to constrain lives, bodies, and environments. They also called for ongoing discussion of the ways in which some women experience greater challenges than others; of race, sexuality, reproductive rights, disability rights, and political rights; of *feminicidio* and other forms of violence; of extractive industries and their gendered impacts; of armed conflict; and of migrant experience. Edmé Domínguez, in writing of the encuentro, quoted another participant as saying, "We want a world in which all feminists fit (*todos cabemos*), where individual and collective rights are inseparable."[7] For me, too, this captured the spirit of the encuentro and provides a suitable closing for this commentary, suggesting both positive directions and hard work still ahead. These feminists will be building on political frameworks emergent in the 1970s and 1980s, repurposed and rendered more inclusive with recent insights from popular, transnational, and decolonial feminisms. Scholars might wish to do likewise.

5 Women's Work

ENGENDERING ECONOMIC ANTHROPOLOGY

This work was first published in 1990 in the journal *Urban Anthropology*.

.   .   .   .   .

Over the last fifteen years, a number of anthropologists have called for greater attention to gender relations and, especially, to women's position in society (e.g., Rosaldo and Lamphere 1974; Reiter 1975; Young et al. 1981; Caplan and Bujra 1982; Shapiro 1983). The recognition of distortion in theories and research that take the male as the universal measure and, as a consequence, underestimate the social, economic, and political participation of women has led to some serious rethinking in the discipline. Nevertheless, the subfield of economic anthropology has been surprisingly slow to take advantage of the new scholarship on gender. Although this new work has often focused on precisely those matters of concern to economic anthropologists—the division of labor, social relations of production and distribution, economic development—gender has rarely been appreciated as a primary category of analysis in the mainstream of economic anthropology.[1]

Attention to gender and specifically to women's experience implies more than a simple addition of new material to old research designs. Once gender is understood as a socially conditioned way that relationships are organized between women and men across societies past and present, far more is required in order to produce gender-informed analyses. Once "men" and "women" are themselves revealed as social constructs whose attributes vary greatly cross-culturally, all social analysis takes on a new dimension. Lest we underestimate the complexity of gender as a fundamental element in social organization, we may recall the words of Rosaldo (1980: 401), who stated that "gender is not a unitary fact determined everywhere by the same sorts of concerns but, instead, the complex product of a variety of social forces." In this essay, I explore how a self-conscious approach to gender in economic anthropology can change the way we apprehend social and economic phenomena.

Economic anthropologists typically select units of analysis that are sociological (e.g., individual, household, social class, economic sector) or geographical (e.g., community, region, nation, or even world system). When I suggest that gender should be viewed as fundamental to analysis in economic anthropology, I do not question the importance of examining other units of analysis.[2] But I argue that whether we examine households, social classes, occupational sectors, or modes of production, our analysis will be incomplete if we disregard gender. By now, gender should have attained the sort of analytical standing held by class and ethnicity, though it is rarely recognized as critical to an investigation of economic phenomena.

In the first part of this essay, I assess the status of gender analysis within theory and research in economic anthropology. Some will disagree with my classification of works in the mainstream versus those in the margins of economic anthropology and may, therefore, question my conclusions. Admittedly, the distinction between center and periphery in economic anthropology must remain a rather subjective one. However, I have relied on several key series and texts in the subdiscipline as an indication of the degree to which gender analysis, and specifically attention to women, is being incorporated in economic anthropology.[3] While my treatment of the subject is by no means exhaustive, I hope to lay the groundwork for further discussion.

Although I am critical of the degree of attention that gender has received in economic anthropology, in the second part of this essay I point to a number of encouraging developments in research. I suggest that several new directions taken by researchers may prefigure a more gender-conscious approach. Following this discussion, I turn in the third part of this essay to consider the significance of gender in Peru's informal economic sector as an illustration of the problem before us. Rather than providing an extended case study, I draw selectively on several studies conducted in the Andean region to demonstrate the difference that gender analysis can make. I argue that attention to gender relations in our research designs is essential to the advancement of theory and research in economic anthropology, and that it will substantially enhance our understanding of the societies we study.

GENDER ANALYSIS IN ECONOMIC ANTHROPOLOGY

Gender has been recognized as a critical organizing principle and element of social differentiation by a number of sociocultural anthropologists. As noted by Fernandez-Kelly (1983: 16), there is abundant historical and empirical evidence of "the significance of gender as a category which has powerful analytical and explanatory value in the study of social, political and economic processes." She and others provide further evidence through their own research that "generalizations about classes, groups or nations remain partial unless qualifications by gender are effected." Even so, this fundamental understanding is slow to gain hold in the academic mainstream. Harris and Young (1981: 117–18) attribute this to theorists' persistent use of the concept of the individual agent who, "although supposedly neutral, is in point of fact almost always conceived as male." Another reason why gender analysis may be slow to work its way into the mainstream of social analysis is that incorporating gender "does not simply add another dimension to sociological, anthropological, or economic studies, but forces us to reformulate the points of departure of a socio-scientific tradition that is often biased" (Fernandez-Kelly 1981: 415).[4]

Up to now, this question has been discussed by those concerned with the anthropology of women, or with the political economy of women's work, but only peripherally in economic anthropology. In part, this may be due to influence from the field of economics—called by two economists "the oldest, the most established, the most quantitative of the social sciences—and the most dominated by men" (Ferber and Teiman 1981). Perhaps as a result, much of women's activity has been regarded as "noneconomic" and has gone unexamined (Benería 1981), while men's activity has taken center stage as the presumed universal measure. Unpaid domestic work and child-rearing, and underpaid work in the wage labor force and the informal sector, are frequently left out of the picture.

Neither the forefathers of economic anthropology (e.g., Herskovits 1940; Firth 1967), nor those who later came to be associated with the formalist-substantivist debate (e.g., contributors to LeClair and Schneider 1968; Dalton 1967; Schneider 1974) appreciated the importance of gender in their writings. The early writers began to apply neoclassical economic theory to the diverse societies they studied, while later participants in the debate that evolved in the 1960s argued over the suitability of such universal concepts as maximization, rationality, and indeed, "economy" itself to anthropological research in nonmarket societies. However, while they disagreed among themselves about the concept of an "economic man," they retained a socioeconomic man whose activities appeared far more important than those of any woman in the societies they studied.[5]

This is not to say that women are totally absent in these earlier writings, for they are not. In the ethnographic contributions of the first economic anthropologists, descriptions of the sexual division of labor and women's activities appear often enough; but rarely do gender relations of power and production figure as fundamental to social and economic life, and rarely is gender taken as a problematic category of analysis. As a result, gender has not been brought into the theoretical discussions. In this respect, the formalists and substantivists differ very little.

While it is true that these forerunners wrote at a time when gender issues had hardly been explored in the social sciences, at least one anthropologist acquainted with the pioneering cross-cultural research on women forcefully opposed it. Leeds (1976: 69) challenged the "spurious reification of 'women' as a unit for analysis." Calling the category of women "personalistic," he went on to decry "the reductionist and individualistic outlook" of gender analysis. He argued that such analysis is advanced "at the expense of the structural, the organized, the collective, the socio-culturally determined." Theory and research have made it abundantly clear, however, that "women" as a category *is* structural, organized, collective, and

sssocioculturally determined. And it is precisely the reductionism of analyses that take the male as universal that gender analysis seeks to counter.[6]

Followers in the 1970s and 1980s have not fared much better in drawing women into the analysis. Though they have distanced themselves from
the old debates in economic anthropology and offered alternative
approaches, such authors as Sahlins (1972) and Gudeman (1986) have
generally presented women only in relation to men, whom they identify as
the central actors in the economy. Influenced by structuralism, their culturalist perspectives allow for some treatment of women's position, but on
the whole women's place goes unquestioned in the "domestic mode of production"; metaphorically, they are cattle in men's exchange.

Other writers in recent years have pursued various tendencies in economic anthropology, but few have considered the gender question. In the
first five volumes of *Research in Economic Anthropology* (Dalton 1978, 1979,
1980, 1981, 1983) and the first volume of conference proceedings of the
Society for Economic Anthropology (Ortiz 1983), none of the contributors
focus particular attention on gender differences or on the special roles filled
by women. However, in several recent volumes of these two major series in
economic anthropology (Isaac 1984, 1985; Plattner 1985; Greenfield and
Strickon 1986), each contains one article concerned with the economic participation of women (Weinpahl 1984; Barlow 1985; Babb 1985b; Schildkrout
1986—this last focuses more on children than on women).[7]

Moreover, as the current editor of *Research in Economic Anthropology*,
Isaac (1984: 3) has stated that "the overwhelming emphasis in economic
anthropology upon exchange-distribution, which is often carried out in the
'public' realm dominated by men, at the expense of production-consump-
tion, in which women's activities are typically vitally important[,] ... has
given our economic models a decidedly androcentric bias. I submit that the
simultaneity of anthropology's discovery of production and women—in
this last regard, the transformation of Homo economicus into Hetero economicus—was not at all fortuitous." A recent volume in the *Research in
Economic Anthropology* series (Isaac 1987) devotes the first of five parts
(articles by Kurz and Peletz) to "women's roles in the economy." And the
recent published proceedings of the Society for Economic Anthropology
(Maclachlan 1987) includes an article on the sexual division of labor
in agriculture (Burton and White). This acknowledgement, in the

mainstream of economic anthropology, of the importance of gender analysis to research is encouraging, though it is still just a beginning.

Marxist writers emerging on the scene in economic anthropology since the 1970s have breathed some new life into the subdiscipline, but they have contributed fairly little to our understanding of gender. This is somewhat surprising, given the intensity of the recent Marxist debate over domestic labor and women's contribution to the creation of surplus value in capitalist society (Fee 1976). A special issue of the British Marxist *Critique of Anthropology* (1977) takes up such important questions as the origins of women's oppression (Reiter 1977), the significance of Engels's work for the construction of a gender-conscious anthropology (Aaby 1977), and the conceptualization of women's work as "reproductive" (Edholm, Harris, and Young 1977). Called the "Women's Issue," this small volume unfortunately stands alone in recent Marxist anthropology.

European scholars such as Terray (1972), Bloch (1975), Godelier (1977), and Seddon (1978) bring the concepts of class and mode of production to the fore but offer few insights on the question of gender. Meillassoux (1972, 1975) has been rightly hailed for recognizing the importance of relations of reproduction in lineage societies; however, he is criticized by feminist anthropologists for borrowing from Levi-Strauss the notion that women function as the mere pawns of men who appropriate women's reproductive powers and for underestimating women's importance as agricultural producers whose influence may extend to other domains of social life. Clammer's *New Economic Anthropology* (1978), despite its fresh perspective on underdevelopment and articulating modes of production, presents nothing new where gender is concerned. Recently, Clammer (1985: 82) has noted the centrality of "the issue of women" and states, "Certainly within Marxist anthropology this question [of women] cannot be avoided much longer if credibility is to be fully achieved." Yet Clammer himself mentions women only in the context of reassessing Engels's work and in reference to the concept of reproduction.

North American Marxists have not, in the main, attempted to set new agendas in economic anthropology. Perhaps sensibly, they have tended to stand aside from the controversies that consume the energy of so many others and, instead, address broad problems of political economy. However, Diamond's (1979) collection (which includes international contributors) notes the work of feminist Marxists and in one article calls for bringing both women and changing family forms to the center of Marxist analysis (Leacock 1979). Another collection by US Marxist anthropologists (Hakken and Lessinger 1987) also draws on insights of feminism for developing theory and politics, and includes work on gender relations (articles by Babb and Keren).

Generally speaking, it is necessary to go outside the mainstream of economic anthropology to discover any examination of gender differentiation. Kahn and Llobera (1981) include a feminist critique of the analysis of reproduction (Harris and Young 1981) in their collection of articles on precapitalist societies. And Leons and Rothstein (1979) include several articles attentive to gender questions—one (Rothstein) focusing specifically on the topic—in precapitalist and capitalist societies. But these works do not claim to set forth a program for economic anthropology, and they may be identified with the reemergence of political economy rather than with any subdisciplinary activity. Similarly, Berreman's (1981) collection on social inequality and Wallman's (1979) anthology on the anthropology of work consider the special features of women's and children's work, but these have apparently failed to make their mark in economic anthropology.

More studies that take up gender issues may be located as we depart from economic anthropology (e.g., Cohen et al. 1979; Zimbalist 1979; Nash and Fernandez-Kelly 1983), but such divergent tendencies are rarely found in the work of those authors who claim to be defining and delimiting the subfield. Moreover, when researchers do turn their attention to gender questions, their work is more often identified with the anthropology of sex roles or women's studies.

Economic anthropology would benefit from more analyses that do not presuppose the centrality of men in all areas of economic and social life; that ask what activities women engage in and how these contribute to the maintenance of family and society; that question how decision making and control of resources are allocated by sex as well as by class, ethnic affiliation, and so on; that examine cases of women's marginalization (e.g., exclusion from certain areas of work, relegation to the least remunerative positions, etc.) to see what material conditions and ideological supports allow for the perpetuation of inequality; that do not turn findings from present-day societies into cultural universals but investigate historical antecedents and cross-societal variability; and, finally, that consider women as active agents in social and economic change.

POSITIVE DEVELOPMENTS IN RESEARCH

While past and present formulations of the subject matter and theory of economic anthropology have by and large ignored the issue of gender, some areas of research suggest more positive developments. This is nowhere more apparent than in the study of hunter-gatherer, or foraging, societies. Since the time of the well-known "Man the Hunter" conference in 1966 (Lee and DeVore 1968), much has changed in the thinking about foraging societies. At that time, research was beginning to show the considerable economic contribution of women among hunter-gatherers. Even with this knowledge, it took some time before anthropologists were willing to let go of man-the-hunter as the moving force in human history from the time of the early hominids through contemporary society. Indeed, that same year, Service (1966: 10) justified titling his book *The Hunters*— though he acknowledged the importance of women's work—by asserting that "neither men nor women . . . in any society, find their interest much aroused by a description of domestic tasks."

However, a powerful critique of androcentric thinking in anthropology (e.g., Slocum 1975; Rohrlich-Leavitt et al. 1975), as well as the expanding base of empirical research, has been effective in challenging earlier assumptions about foragers. Now it is not surprising to find books appearing with such titles as *Woman the Gatherer* (Dahlberg 1983). Lee's work on the !Kung shows the strong influence of the new scholarship on women as active members of society. Of course, Lee's own findings since the 1960s on the importance of gathered food helped inform this scholarship, but by the late 1970s his perspective was enlarged as he wrote *The !Kung San: Men, Women and Work in a Foraging Society* (Lee 1979). There, Lee undertook to examine women's work not only in gathering, or productive activity, but also in childrearing and what he termed "housework," or reproductive activity. The result is an enriched understanding of !Kung economy and society.

Others have contributed in significant ways to the discussion of the sexual division of labor and gender relations in hunter-gatherer societies

(Draper 1975; Leacock 1978; Halperin 1980; Sacks 1982). Unfortunately, such a thoroughgoing reanalysis has not occurred in the research on other social forms. It is nonetheless possible to point to new anthropological approaches to horticultural, peasant, and industrial societies.

Rohrlich-Leavitt (1975) and Friedl (1975) have each taken a broad view of gender roles in foraging and horticultural societies, albeit from different perspectives. The former sees horticultural societies as containing many of the same egalitarian elements as hunter-gatherer societies; the latter takes women's subordination as a universal and sees its slow disappearance as a correlate of social evolution in the direction of industrial capitalist society. Other authors have discovered important economic roles among women in specific horticultural societies, to complement— and sometimes revise—what is known of men's economic roles in those societies (e.g., Weiner 1976; Strathern 1982).

Although many studies of peasant societies are still written as though women do not exist, or as though they exist only as wives of "peasants," some research is beginning to reconceptualize women's involvement in agricultural production. Notable within this current is the new recognition of women's work not only in the fields but also in the provision of meals to workers on the land, the processing and marketing of agricultural goods, and so on—all as part of the agricultural process (Deere and León de Leal 1981). Such a broad definition of agricultural work, along with a recognition of domestic, or reproductive, work, is utilized in several studies of women in peasant societies (e.g., Bourque and Warren 1981b; Bossen 1984), but the impact of this far-reaching new scholarship is barely felt in most studies of rural societies.

Finally, we may turn briefly to rural proletarian and urban industrializing societies, traditionally outside the purview of most economic anthropologists. When these changing societies are investigated, it is most often to examine male experiences. However, some studies are showing that notions of males as breadwinners and females as homemakers are not adequate to account for the large-scale impact of multinationals on women in the global food, textile, and electronics industries (Arizpe and Aranda 1981; Fernandez-Kelly 1983). Nor can they account for the growing presence of women in domestic service and such informal-sector activities as petty manufacturing and trading in Third World cities, where men hold the modern industrial-sector jobs (Trager 1976–77; Nelson 1979; Hansen 1980b; Bunster and Chaney 1985). The uneven effects of capitalist penetration, as well as the uncertain advantages of the socialist alternative (Wolf 1985), are beginning to receive more attention from anthropologists concerned with the dynamics of gender relations.

Notwithstanding these developments, however, few economic anthropologists have yet brought their thinking in line with the recent empirical findings or brought gender relations critically to bear in their analyses. This is so whether they investigate strategies for labor allocation at the household level or patterns of labor force recruitment at the societal level; rural peasant or urban proletarian participation in the economy; or production, distribution, or exchange in society. Without such an analysis of gender relations, we continue to underestimate women's central involvement in the economy and to put forward incomplete and inaccurate interpretations of the societies we study.

A gender-conscious economic anthropology might be expected to inspire research in some important new directions. We might go beyond a critical recognition of women's gathering activities in foraging societies to a view of "domestic" tasks and childcare as equally significant work. We might reexamine gender relations in horticultural societies to see what historical and economic conditions can account for often-reported sexual antagonism. An expanded economic anthropology could contribute to the ongoing interdisciplinary research on rural women and development, adding the expertise of those trained in cross-cultural fieldwork methods. A focus on gender will be essential as we examine changing modes of production in society, since changes in the sexual division of labor almost invariably accompany such economic transitions. In the rapidly urbanizing context of Third World cities in which a number of anthropologists are now investigating small-scale production and commerce, it will certainly be necessary to ascertain why so many women are entering the informal sector.

A gender-conscious approach in economic anthropology might dispel or redefine some of the most contentious problems in the subfield. Does the long-disputed formalist notion of maximization have meaning in the neglected context of household production or domestic work? Can we formulate a unified economic theory that is both gender sensitive and cross-culturally applicable, or must we agree with the substantivists that such a project is misguided? Do the Marxist categories of productive and non-productive labor (or the revised feminist categories of production and reproduction) shed light on the sexual division of labor, or must we construct analyses that go beyond dualist thinking? These are only a few of the issues that might be raised within the framework of an economic anthropology that critically analyzes gender in theory and research.

PERU'S INFORMAL ECONOMIC SECTOR AND THE ANALYSIS OF GENDER

Whether we examine lowland horticulturalists, highland peasants, or the urban working class on the coast, gender differentiation is evident in Peru. For the purposes of this brief discussion, I focus on the significance of gender as a category of analysis in the informal sector of the Peruvian Andes. By *the informal sector*,[8] I mean those economic activities (numerous in many Third World cities and towns) characteristic of small-scale manufacturing, commercial, and service enterprises in which individuals with low levels of skill and capital are typically self-employed.[9]

Before turning to my own research on women in petty commerce in the north-central Andes of Peru, I consider several important studies carried out in the central Andean region of the country. The first study, a major project on informal enterprise and development, illustrates some limitations of anthropological research that does not examine gender. I show that other studies in the region have advanced in the direction of gender-conscious scholarship.

Research on small-scale enterprises in the Mantaro Valley, centered on the principal city of Huancayo, was carried out under the direction of Norman Long and Bryan R. Roberts.[10] They and their collaborators report findings in two edited collections (Long and Roberts 1978, 1984), as well as in a number of journal articles.[11] Their work stands as one of the few efforts to investigate the relation of a regional economy to the dominant capitalist economy in Peru. The research is especially notable for its recognition that local-level entrepreneurs may actually sustain growth and influence the national-level economy, rather than fall victim to it.

However, despite their sensitivity to economic differentiation in the Mantaro Valley generally, Long and Roberts are remarkably inattentive to gender differences—indeed, they sometimes seem unaware of women's presence in the region. Their analysis begins with households as primary units, then follows the activities of (male) "heads of households." This has the unfortunate consequence of leaving unexamined the widespread activity of market women in and around Huancayo, a city famous for its huge marketplace, as well as other work performed by women. In recent writings, Long and Roberts indicate that their data come from sample surveys directed only to men (e.g., to "economically active males," the "male population," etc.), yet no explanation is offered for this restricted approach.

Women, in the rare instances when Long and Roberts mention them, are generally the sisters and wives—the helpmeets—of men who claim the center of attention. In an article by Long (1979), the author considers the successful economic career of one male entrepreneur who has managed to combine diverse subsistence activities with income-generating work in the capitalist sector. In the process of describing this career, Long notes the significant collaboration of female kin. However, in emphasizing the individual, Long appears to underestimate the level of family involvement and the degree of male dependence on female support. Furthermore, had he investigated women's career patterns, he might have qualified his optimistic conclusions regarding entrepreneurship and upward mobility.

Long and Roberts (1984: 3) could have benefited from following, to its logical end, their own advice "to 'disaggregate' the analysis of development by taking into account the more immediate life circumstances of the populations of underdeveloped countries." They refer here to regional differences, however, and never disaggregate the family or household by sex. The sexual division of labor is mentioned only briefly (pp. 132–33) as another dimension of differentiation. Women, once again, appear in relationship to men in household enterprises (e.g., pp. 157–59), or in special cases, such as in an account of a village from which men have emigrated (pp. 133–34), or in a story of one woman's abject poverty (pp. 172–74). Where men are surveyed and enumerated, women are treated anecdotally.[12]

We may compare the analysis of the researchers described above to that of Florencia E. Mallon (1983, 1987), whose historical research in the same area of central Peru included ethnographic fieldwork and interviewing of peasants, miners, and entrepreneurs. While Mallon's (1983) earlier research did not focus on women, it is informed by an analysis of gender relations so that gender is "problematic." Men are most evident in the historical record, yet Mallon makes it clear that this region is populated by women as well as men. It is notable that in Mallon's (1983: 24) first case study, she presents the example of a peasant woman whose success as a farmer and petty merchant made her self-sufficient.

Recently, Mallon (1987) has united her strong class analysis with an equally powerful analysis of gender. She examines the interlinkage of gender relations with precapitalist and capitalist relations in the transition from the nineteenth to the mid-twentieth century. She looks at internal change in the household, where the domestic economy is organized primarily by gender as a basis for controlling and allocating labor power. In contrast to the impression given in the foregoing scholars' work, Mallon demonstrates that, since the colonial period, women of the region "were a strong presence at all levels of economic activity" (1987: 382). She cites evidence that through recent times women have been important actors in independent and family enterprises. While elite women have often managed commercial properties, women of the popular classes have also been highly visible in commercial relations, often as merchants.

These precursors to today's petty producers and traders did not, however, enjoy equality in gender relations. Mallon (1987: 384–86) argues that despite women's prominent roles in the local-level central Peruvian economy, men alone had access to commercial networks in the broader economy and to legal and political institutions. Moreover, women experienced patriarchal control at the level of the household, where men had control over women's sexuality through marital arrangements and through an ideology of "proper" behavior for women; this sometimes translated into a strategy for accumulation as men gained control of property brought into marriage by their wives. In such a way, men were guaranteed control over the product of women's labor, economic decision-making in the family, and the accumulation of wealth.

One wonders how many male entrepreneurs studied by researchers in the central Andes depended for their success on female family members. Mallon cites interviews with a number of men and women who indicate that the contributions of property and labor made by women were decisive to any success their families had. Mallon (1987: 397) concludes that the transition to capitalism in central Peru provided new "openings" for women, yet as men were increasingly drawn into commodity production, women's substantial economic activities were marginalized.[13]

In my own research in Peru, I have attempted to apply the new thinking about gender relations to my study of women in the informal sector.[14] During four periods between 1977 and 1987, I conducted field research in the provincial city of Huaraz, located some two hundred miles north of Lima. The city's predominantly mestizo population of Quechua-Spanish-speaking people numbered about forty-five thousand a decade ago, but is now estimated to be twice that. Huaraz serves as an administrative and commercial center, and it is also the point of entry for the growing number of tourists in the Andean valley known as the Callejón de Huaylas, drawing to the city many who are looking for employment opportunities. While the urban middle-class elite finds employment in a variety of government posts, in the schools, in the hospital, or in business, the working class and poor majority generally work in subsistence agriculture, wage labor, petty commodity production, small-scale commerce, and the service industries.

To explore further the economic opportunities and social constraints experienced by this majority in Huaraz, it is necessary to disaggregate the population by sex. Then it becomes apparent that women's economic participation, while extensive, is substantially restricted. Though men, particularly in recent years, experience hardship, they frequently combine agricultural work on small plots of family land with occasional wage labor on others' fields or in construction; with small-scale manufacture of such goods as adobe bricks, chairs, and clothing; and with employment in a soda-bottling plant and a fishery. There is little industry in Huaraz, but the unskilled and skilled wage work that exists in the city goes chiefly to men. Women, who usually have important responsibilities at home—including work in the family fields, housework, and childcare—have fewer opportunities for paid employment. Those women who seek employment generally find it in one of two areas: small-scale marketing or domestic service. The inequality apparent in the gender division of labor in the Huaraz workforce becomes clear when we consider that women often earn only half the income of male day laborers—who themselves earn as little as one US dollar daily.

My research has examined marketers and street vendors in Huaraz, a group whose number expanded from around twelve hundred in 1977 to two thousand in 1987, and particularly the women who make up 80 percent of sellers in the city. Like others who have carried out research on women, I have found it essential to examine women's lives and work in relation to the lives and work of men in order to provide a fuller picture of socioeconomic activity in the region. As a result, my approach does not bring with it the implicit bias of studies focusing only on men. I emphasize, however, that while women should be viewed in relation to men and the wider society, they ought not be seen as the adjuncts of men. Furthermore, in my view, it is sometimes most appropriate to place women at the center of study so long as mainstream research fails to offer equal treatment of male and female experiences.

In Huaraz, women predominate in the city's three covered markets and in the sprawling open-air marketplace. Yet when we consider the gender division of labor in the markets, we see that women do not have the advantage. Women tend to be concentrated in the retail sale of vegetables, fruits, and prepared foods, which together constitute the bulk of goods sold, but which generally result in meager incomes. Both women and men sell staple foods like rice, pasta, flour, sugar, and salt, as well as meat, fish, live animals, clothing, and household items such as pots and other kitchen utensils, although men usually do so on a larger scale. When men engage in marketing, they often draw on resources generated from other forms of employment. and they may have greater mobility to travel directly to production sites to buy their goods. Consequently, men often sell larger quantities of foods at lower prices than women, and they are far more likely than women to sell manufactured goods from the coast. While women work occasionally as wholesalers, men are the major wholesalers in the region. Although there are significant areas of overlap in the nature and scale of women's and men's commercial activity, the division of labor by sex in the Huaraz markets is quite pronounced.

Gender differences are not the only basis for structural inequality in marketing, however. Market women themselves are a heterogeneous group, and internal differentiation is apparent among them. After my more recent visits to Huaraz, this socioeconomic differentiation became one of my principal concerns. I considered, for example, the relations of independent market women and the less fortunate women they sometimes employ. These included the owner of a small restaurant stall and the impoverished woman she hires for little more than a hot meal; the seller of crushed garlic who pays an elderly woman by the piece to peel her garlic; and the absent marketer who hires another woman to attend her stand.

Deeper inequalities are evident where differentiation has accelerated in Huaraz marketing. During the last few years I have observed an increasing number of market women whose autonomy has been undercut by larger commercial interests. For example, four young women "independently" selling hot drinks on a street corner receive their wages from the same individual, a man who rarely makes an appearance; marketers who sell ice cream from barrows pick up their merchandise daily from stores that hire them on commission; and vendors of such diverse items as candy, clothing, and kitchen goods are supplied by coastal manufacturers who keep the sellers dependent on the extension of credit. Taken together, such cases as these suggest that a gradual process of subordination to the wage form may be occurring among marketers in Huaraz. Emerging class differences within marketing in the informal sector and growing links between the informal and formal sectors need to be examined further.

Nevertheless, the gender question arises once again as we discover that the larger the commercial interests that erode the autonomy of petty marketers, the more likely men control them. Thus, even as we consider the general pattern of socioeconomic differentiation, we must ask a series of gender-related questions: Why are women concentrated among the most impoverished of sellers in trades generating the lowest incomes? Why are men more often able to expand their enterprises and occasionally to employ others? How are structural conditions rooted in gender and class (and perhaps ethnic) inequalities responsible for the differential experiences of women and men in petty commerce?

To answer these questions, it is essential to consider the broader context within which women and men engage in commerce. Gender differences within the family and household are critical to this analysis. While men find the support in families that permits them to devote themselves to work outside the home, women must generally provide that support. In Huaraz—and cross-culturally—women have primary responsibility for the care of home and family. Food preparation and childcare are often the most time-consuming duties, but the tasks are far more numerous. Both men and women in Huaraz comment that while men usually have one job, women have many jobs. We must disaggregate the household to view the structural inequality present within it.

For women who seek paid work outside the home, the extra burden they shoulder is obvious. In addition to the sheer physical difficulty of maintaining the household and working outside it, they must manage to integrate these very different responsibilities in their daily lives. Often, women select marketing as one of the few areas of employment in which children may be taken along and which may be combined with other domestic tasks. While this may offer an advantage to individual women, the extra effort required to meet household needs places women as a group at a structural disadvantage relative to men in commerce.

Of course, Huaraz women's unequal experience in marketing can be connected ultimately to the wider Peruvian society that benefits from the second-class status of women in the home and in the workforce—that is, society benefits when the costs of social reproduction are kept down. Here I have emphasized the importance of investigating gender differences in one area of Peru's informal economic sector, but it is clear that we must consider the differential position of women and men at every level, from household to national society, if we are to understand the many forces that come to bear on any one economic sector.

Gender is critical to our analysis in economic anthropology, whatever our "unit" of study may be. Our unit or units of analysis vary from the single mode of production to articulating modes of production (Foster-Carter 1978), and from the local or even societal level to "world system" analysis (Wallerstein 1974), depending on the problem we investigate. Many of the questions we desire to examine require that we consider broader, and interlinking, units of analysis. But what remains consistent is the differential experience of men and women at every level of analysis.

In general, the field of anthropology has seen increasing attention to gender issues during the last two decades.[15] The subdiscipline of economic anthropology has also seen a steady, though slower, growth in research and theory that is more gender-conscious. To date, however, this has taken the form of isolated articles on women or gender appearing in volumes that otherwise do not often reflect the far-reaching and transformative implications of this new scholarship. Furthermore, the scattered references to women found in the mainstream literature do not generally reveal an understanding of gender as a relationship, shaped by historical and social processes, comparable to class or ethnicity. If gender is to be recognized as a primary category of analysis, then an awareness of gender differentiation must inform the work of all economic anthropologists, whether our central research focus concerns men or women.

I have discussed several approaches to examining men's and women's participation in Peru's informal sector in order to argue that economic anthropologists need to take seriously the issue of gender. I have maintained that analyses are incomplete and often distorted when they disregard gender, and they are enriched to the extent that they acknowledge the differential experiences of women and men in society. Yet there is another reason to recognize gender as a fundamental category of analysis: as anthropologists, we have a responsibility not only to produce useful research but also to identify, discuss, and sometimes confront those issues that affect most directly the lives of the people we study. Gender, as the basis for one of the most persistent forms of inequality cross-culturally, deserves our serious attention.

6 Theorizing Gender, Race, and Cultural Tourism in Latin America

A VIEW FROM PERU AND MEXICO

First appearing in 2012 in the journal *Latin American Perspectives*, in the special issue "Gender, Ethnicity, and Sexuality in Latin American Tourism," this work is based on a chapter of my 2011 book *The Tourism Encounter: Fashioning Latin American Nations and Histories.*

.   .   .   .   .

Cultural tourism—tourism that favors intercultural encounters and promises an inside experience of cultural difference (Baud and Ypeij 2009: 4)—in Andean Peru and Chiapas, Mexico, has drawn travelers seeking locally "authentic" experiences with indigenous women and men. In Peru, tourists often desire to experience "traditional" and "remote" indigenous communities, while in Mexico that desire may be coupled with a yearning for "real" revolutionary culture in the Chiapas region. In both cases, romantic or exoticized images may be used—by the state or by indigenous people themselves—to entice travelers, who expect to find cultural difference on prominent display. Drawing on ethnographic research in the two areas since 2005 and focusing on initiatives in cultural tourism, I consider whether, in spite of the durability of gender and racial inequalities, there is nonetheless greater purchase in being female and indigenous; this may be as a result of cultural tourism, education, and opportunities brought about through urbanization and indigenous social movements that are pressing for greater inclusion and cultural rights. I suggest that, while unequal social relations are still at play, being indigenous and female in these regions may provide, to a greater or lesser extent, new cultural capital, understood as qualities of the individual (for example, appearance, dress, language, artistic ability, and everyday practices) that may be converted into economic advantage (Bourdieu 1984).

Scholarly attention first turned to gender and ethnicity in the Americas in the 1970s, in part as a result of the first UN Conference on Women, held in Mexico City in 1975. At that time, the lines were often sharply drawn between those who viewed indigenous Latin America as an age-old cultural hinterland in which gender inequality was firmly entrenched and those who maintained that gender complementarity was disrupted when European interventions introduced new inequalities from urban centers (Bourque and Warren 1981b; Harris 1981; Isbell [1978] 1985; Silverblatt 1987). Globalization has brought further disruptions and both new challenges and new opportunities for indigenous communities. John and Jean Comaroff (2009) have usefully identified a widespread phenomenon of our day as "Ethnicity, Inc.," in which "authentic" cultural identities are commodified and marginalized peoples may find contradictory openings for entrepreneurial success.

While we might take a cynical view of these developments, this is also a time of emergent indigenous social movements, both in the Andean region and in southern Mexico, and the valorization of cultural identity that accompanies such movements is not so much about commodification as about social struggle. Indeed, when in 2009 the Peruvian city of Puno played host to over six thousand delegates from twenty-two nations at the Fourth Continental Summit of Indigenous Peoples, the conference was preceded by a two-day women's summit in which more than two thousand indigenous women made it clear that their voices would be heard. In the cases I present here we will see that, while rural Peruvian women remain largely behind the scenes with regard to local tourism initiatives, women in Chiapas are in some cases playing a more significant part in tourism that may reflect their activism in the region.

Nearly two decades ago, after the earlier debates on Latin American gender and ethnic relations had sedimented into differences over complementarity versus inequality, Marisol de la Cadena (1995: 343) offered an assessment of Andean women that appeared to support the latter view: "It is in the intimacy of everyday relations in the street, marketplace, and village that implicit decisions and identities are made about who is, and who is not, Indian. . . . Modernization has reinforced the Indianization of women, while opening the option of cultural mestizaje to most men." Increasingly, she said, it was "common knowledge" that Andean women were considered more "Indian" than their male counterparts, and that as a result they suffered from deeper social inequalities. More recently, however, de la Cadena, writing with Orin Starn (2007), suggested a nuanced understanding of indigenous lives and activism on a global scale that may modify her earlier view. Moreover, she and others, collaborating in a discussion of the current cultural politics of indigeneity in Peru, concluded that indigeneity is part of a process of identity formation in articulation with class, gender, sexuality, and place that is historically produced (García 2008). Only one contributor, however, offered a close examination of the sometimes contentious relationship between gender and indigenous politics in Peru (Oliart 2008).

We need to reexamine gender and indigenous identities in new ways, taking gender as seriously as ethnicity, to see what meanings may inhere in these ever-shifting identities. A number of scholars have examined the politics of race in colonial and postcolonial times in Peru and in Mexico (Mallon 1995; Orlove 1993; Poole 1994) and, more widely, in the Andes and Mesoamerica (Gotkowitz 2011). Several have embraced an approach to identity formation in the region that offers a more subtle reading of cultural meanings and practices involving differences of gender, race, and power (Canessa 2005; Femenías 2005; Seligmann 2004; Weismantel 2001). Yet few have reconsidered the relationship between gender and indigeneity in light of the changing cultural and political landscape in recent years. The intersection of gender, race, and nation is a familiar framework for feminists working around the globe, and it has found considerable acceptance among social analysts and cultural theorists more broadly, but it has not often been historicized so as to reveal the uneven way in which change occurs. Under the new terms of engagement emerging in Andean Peru and Chiapas, I suggest, first, that tourism has become a particularly robust site for reexamining gender and indigeneity, and second, that what has been a social liability, being female and indigenous, can serve in some cases as a form of cultural capital.

In his collection on gender, indigeneity, and the state in the Andes, Andrew Canessa (2005: 4) notes that "'the Indian' has become an international commodity, and Indians are widely recognized around the globe for their 'traditional' lifestyles and as guardians of the natural environment." An essentialized notion of indigenous people may be a form of Orientalism (Said [1978] 2003) or imperialist nostalgia (Rosaldo 1989: 69–74) imposed from outside. However, under the terms of international tourism indigenous women and men themselves deploy notions of "traditional" or "authentic" cultural difference as a strategy to attract more tourists. In some cases they may defy conventional expectations and display more rebellious identities, which may also draw a tourism niche market. Thus it is critical to consider the active ways in which indigenous people on the margins become stakeholders in their own identity construction. Women, notably through their use of dress and language, once again are shown to be the principal signifiers of traditional culture, the indigenous, and the "Other."

Following periods of political upheaval in Andean Peru and Chiapas, there has been a tourism revival in these regions. Well-established tourism industries were halted for a decade by very different political movements in these areas—in Peru during the 1980s and into the 1990s by the ruthless forces of Sendero Luminoso (Shining Path) and the military, and in southern Mexico by the antiglobalization Zapatista uprising that surfaced in 1994. Now tourism is increasing once again, as conflict has subsided and the two nations have sought to promote economic development and refashion regional and national identities. Together, these regions present some marked historical similarities, but the different characters of their recent conflicts present rather different prospects for indigenous women and men involved in tourism.

In what follows, I consider how recent developments relating to culture, political economy, and tourism in postconflict Andean Peru and Chiapas are inflected by race and gender. I discuss ways in which local cultures and tourism industries in these regions market indigenous identity and gender difference, sometimes building on historical practices or ideologies and sometimes making unabashed use of stereotypes of the "Other." I offer examples of these practices in the community of Vicos, Peru, and in Zapatista and Lacandón communities in Chiapas. This is not to say that more balanced and open exchanges between local populations and tourists are unknown but rather to suggest that tourism encounters in these regions as elsewhere are heavily freighted with difference and power.

GENDER, RACE, AND TOURISM IN THE PERUVIAN ANDES

Since the period of violence and conflict when Shining Path militants faced off with the military, tourism has returned to Peru. Specifically, cultural tourism has reemerged, attracting visitors with the promise of exposure not only to spectacular settings and archaeological wonders but also to intimate encounters with rural and indigenous Andeans. While scholars have usefully considered travelers' romanticization of rural Andeans and their spiritual connection to the natural and supernatural world (Hill 2008; van den Berghe and Flores Ochoa 2000), gender differentiation in the tourism encounter is less often examined (Meisch 2002; Zorn 2004).

Compared with the situation in other areas where I have carried out research on tourism (Cuba and Nicaragua), sex and romance tourism is not as prevalent or as widely known, although in recent years Peruvians have expressed concern about the presence of sex tourism in the Amazon area, especially around Iquitos. Moreover, in areas of heavy tourism, especially Cuzco, young men seeking out female tourists for intimate friendships and romance, known as *bricheros,* have become commonplace. As in some parts of the Caribbean, these "Andean lovers" perfect the art of seduction of gringas, often by exaggerating qualities of indigenous difference, wearing their hair long, playing traditional flutes, and adopting a dress style evocative of "Inca" culture. Tourists are said to desire their imagined Andean knowledge and experience. In some cases, women attracted to the "authenticity" of bricheros (who actually work hard to speak European languages and adopt a manner that is pleasing to tourists) may invite the men to leave the country with them. The Peruvian scholar Víctor Vich (2006: 191–94) points to the gendered and racialized dimension of these intimate encounters and argues that the brichero stands in for the nation in the contemporary neoliberal world, in which the nation is up for sale. The tourist's desire is for this figure, at once folkloric and romantic, who appears locked in time, even in the modern city of Cuzco.

"Gringotecas," clubs where locals meet foreign women and men, provide opportunities for sexual encounters and material advantage in the form of entrée into more venues, as well as meals, gifts, and travel. Andean women, less often than men, can also benefit from relationships with tourists, generally not in an explicit form of sex work but in the form of dating or romance tourism. The attraction of Peruvians to international travelers and of tourists to Andean difference is sufficiently well known to be the subject of discussion on various websites, including one for expatriates and travelers to Peru (www.expatperu.com).

Gender differences appear in the performance and delivery of more traditional tourism services in Andean Peru. Jane Henrici (2002) examined how tourism development, cultural heritage, and local economy affect women, particularly when the marketing of traditional arts and practices is viewed as a key to "modernization." Elayne Zorn's (2004) work on Taquile Island in Peru offered a rare example of community-based tourism that met with some early success. Interestingly, while men were centrally involved in transporting tourists to the island, women had an equally important role as the main producers of the celebrated textiles on sale to visitors. Women were prominent in social and economic exchanges with tourists, even when this contributed to tensions that emerged between Taquile men and women over access to tourism's benefits. In the end, however, it was competition from mestizo transporters that led to local men's displacement from the business of tourism, eroding this communitarian project. Just as Walter Little (2004) discovered in Guatemala, cultural tourism here built on notions of indigenous and female difference, and women more often than men presented themselves as *indígenas*. Local identity, marked by dress, language, and demeanor and strongly inflected by gender, has been a critical factor in Peru's tourism development.

The close connection of gender and race or ethnicity in the Andes is clear in de la Cadena's (1995: 329) work in a community near Cuzco, where she reported the perception that "women are more Indian." She found that "gender intersects with status to structure and legitimate eth-

nic inequality within the community and even within households." She
concluded that while both men and women might acquire "modern" skills
and be perceived as less Indian and more mestizo, for women the advantage to be gained from this was more modest. The question animating my
work is whether this is true today, or whether in some instances indigenous women have an advantage in relation to their male counterparts.

My research on Peruvian tourism has focused on cultural and experiential tourism (known locally as *turismo vivencial*) in the Callejón de
Huaylas in north-central Peru, an area best known for adventure travel
and mountaineering. Responses to my interviews in the area indicated
that a majority of travelers come to the region for cultural tourism and
ecotourism. As a Spanish teacher from the United States wrote, she was
most surprised "that it is relatively authentic—though I've only been in the
north so far. The campesinos aren't what I expected—posing in their
quaint dress for a sol. Instead they seem to patiently deal with our tourist
presence spying on their customs—which are not staged." An Israeli man
who came to Peru following his military service captured the elements
that drew him to the country: "Beautiful scenery, amazing people, and as
a backpacker, it's rather cheap." Many are struck by what a French woman
described as "the kindness of people and how helpful they are. The way
they're living with the strict minimum and seem to be happier than people
like us, who have everything so easily." Similarly, a man from the
Netherlands appreciated "the endless solidarity and *cariño* [affection] of
the poor people."

While I have been based over the years in the city of Huaraz, capital of
the department of Ancash, I have observed travel throughout the Callejón
region. In particular, I focus on Vicos, an Andean community that is well
known in the history of applied anthropology, since Cornell University
assisted the Vicosinos a half century ago to become the owners of their
former-hacienda land (Dobyns, Doughty, and Lasswell 1971; Stein 2003).
Recently, Vicos has launched a small tourism project with the assistance
of nearby nongovernmental organizations. I have made short visits to
Vicos over three decades and stayed there for several days in 2006 and
again in 2010 as a guest in order to learn more about how a handful of
families with support to build guest lodges has fared in launching this
project. Those acquainted with the Cornell-Peru Project of the 1950s and

1960s may recognize this enterprise as a logical extension of development initiatives of the past. By now, however, Vicosinos themselves are seeking to manage the business of drawing travelers, largely from the United States and the Netherlands, for stays of a few days or more during which they participate in the everyday activities of the rural, agricultural community. A selling point for potential visitors is the opportunity to get to know about the lives and culture of a traditional, indigenous Quechua-speaking people. To that end, the community has shifted from agricultural modernization to modernization based on cultural difference.

Having conducted archival research on gender relations in Vicos during the time of the Cornell-Peru Project (Babb 1985b), I was eager to see how Vicos community members were approaching tourism as a new means for economic development. In Huaraz, an NGO supporting Vicos's tourism project, the Mountain Institute, had produced an attractive brochure that orients prospective and current visitors to "a direct experience with families that live in the Andean mountains." Images and text offer a brief history of Vicos from the time when it was "a typical Andean hacienda" (1611–1952) to the time of the Cornell-Peru Project. The present is described by reference to the continuing biodiversity and traditional culture in the region. What rivets one's attention are the photos and descriptions of the eight hosts of tourist homestays and other residents of Vicos. All of the hosts and other local specialists are men, and the descriptions emphasize what tourists will experience by staying with or meeting a craftsman, a beekeeper, a musician, a weaver, or a toolmaker—all men. Women are strikingly absent from this portrayal of everyday life in Vicos.

My visits to Vicos brought to light the gendered and racialized nature of the experience, suggesting that these social vectors continue to be salient, as they are elsewhere, and that tourism development efforts have differential consequences for women and men in the community. In part, this may result from the greater difficulty women have in speaking Spanish, given past practices of sending sons to school or the military while daughters remained at home. It may also stem from the perception identified by de la Cadena (1995) that rural women are "more Indian" and less modern, less able to fulfill key responsibilities in tourism development, though, as I have shown, elsewhere in the Callejón de Huaylas women play active roles in the local economy (Babb [1989] 1998).

Only Vicosino men attend the tourism workshops, or *talleres*, in Huaraz. There they are given advice on how to receive guests and interact with them, including the suggestion that family members should eat together and offer commentaries on how things were done in the past and how traditions are continuing in the present. One of my hosts, whom I call "Tomás," explained that relating to tourists was new to them, and that for his wife, "Dora," it produced considerable anxiety, since her Spanish was limited and she was not sure how she would manage. While it might be said that women are the principal conservators of culture and tradition in Vicos, men are the ones who are expected to pass this knowledge on to their guests. Tomás spoke frequently and reverentially of the time of their grandparents, and even as the radio or TV played loudly he emphasized that things were much the same now as in the past. As the male head of household, he played host while Dora provided the critical and labor-intensive services of preparing the guest quarters and meals.

During this visit, Dora remained largely behind the scenes while Tomás interacted with me directly. He called me to meals that she had prepared, except in the case of the *pachamanca*, the traditional Andean feast on my last day, which was prepared by Vicosino men and then served by the women. He escorted me to a local wedding, and Dora joined us only after carrying out work at home. While he delivered a speech at the time of my departure, she was shy and scarce. Both were kind and hospitable, but Tomás performed the role of gracious host and family spokesperson. Women in Vicos may be simply too busy with household responsibilities to play a more active part in the tourism project, but the androcentrism of the tourism project may well be repeating the practices of past interventions in Vicos that singled out men for economic development projects (Babb 1985b; Greaves, Bolton, and Zapata 2011).

On another visit I interviewed women at the long-standing visitor attraction operated by the Vicos community, the thermal baths and hotel at Chancos. Vicosinas are much more in evidence in the Chancos enterprise, playing a significant part in the operation of the baths, rustic hotel, small restaurants, and market stalls that are concentrated along the quiet road that leads into Vicos. The women vendors and restaurant workers I spoke to were more comfortable in Spanish than many other Vicosinas; those I spoke to told me that they were not familiar with the tourism project, though they were interested in hearing about it. They were regarded as cholas, women bearing characteristics of both campesinas and mestizas who had adapted to the world of urban commerce and interacted with a wider social network.

Tourists come to Vicos to see Indians leading "traditional" lives, not savvy women bargaining with buyers in the market. It is to larger towns and cities like Huaraz that tourists go to visit busy markets and haggle over prices. In such towns there is more diversity, and social differences stand out in sharp relief. These differences between rural communities and more urban settings are captured in regional popular culture. A fascinating touristic display of the contrasting provincial Andean and elite cultures in Peru is found in the sales of knockoff Barbies in handmade outfits identified as "chola" (urbanized Indian) and "de Lima" (from the capital city). In Vicos, however, cultural commodification is better concealed than revealed, and there is little need for cash during a tourist's stay unless it is to give a host a small amount to purchase coca leaves for an Andean ritual—until the end of the visit, when there is a quick accounting of the payment due. Tourists are spared learning of families' urgent need for cash for children's school supplies, household items, or transportation to nearby towns and of women's central role in managing household budgets.

It remains to be seen how tourism will fare in Vicos and how men and women will collaborate in this initiative. Although I have noted that men are the designated hosts and play the leading public role in experiential tourism in the community, women are critically important to its success. The complementarity of gender roles in Vicos is arguably as apparent today as it was thirty years ago. Just as the significant part played by women in the community eluded the applied anthropologists some decades back, the supporters of the tourism initiative may also be overlooking the key role played by women. When Tomás told me of his wife's nervousness about his becoming a member of the project, I believe he was also signaling his own anxiety that without her full support he could not make a go of it. A wider recognition of the significance of women in the project and more generally in Vicos might have positive effects going beyond the tourism project.

RACE, GENDER, AND TOURISM IN CHIAPAS

Since the Zapatista rebellion nearly two decades ago, there has been renewed international attention to Chiapas—although anthropologists like June Nash and those in the Harvard Chiapas Project focused close attention on its cultural history beginning a half century ago (Nash 2001; Vogt 1994). Journalists and activists were the first to arrive on the scene in 1994, but mainstream tourism returned later in the decade, and today there is a busy tourism season and visitors come throughout the year.

As in the case of Andean Peru, Chiapas is well known for its rural and indigenous population. Cultural, or "ethnic," tourism (van den Berghe 1994) is a response to the broad appeal of traditional Maya people and culture, and many travelers make the circuit (Ruta Maya) that includes the Yucatan, Oaxaca, Chiapas, and, across the border, Guatemala. The fact that rebels in Chiapas made headlines when the North American Free Trade Agreement went into effect on January 1, 1994, adds to the allure for some who wish to see the place where indigenous people rose up in opposition to free-trade measures that they claimed would further marginalize them in Mexican society. A visit there offers quaint colonial towns, traditional communities, archaeological and jungle tours, and a politicized climate in which market vendors offer the ubiquitous Zapatista merchandise. What tourists do not often recognize is the diversity of the region's indigenous peoples (Eber and Kovic 2003; Gil Tébar 1999; Rovira 1997; Stephen 2002), viewing them instead as essentialized Indians. This is seen in the desire of solidarity tourists to have intimate encounters with idealized indigenous Zapatistas and of other tourists to purchase textiles made by authentic Indians whose specific cultural identities remain unknown to them.

Researchers and some tourists have, however, discovered the gender differences that exist in Chiapas, and some have noted indigenous women's voice. Many women have been empowered through organizing artisan cooperatives in which they control production and marketing. Mayan women who have become involved in Zapatista activism have spoken up about the extra burdens they shoulder at home and in society, with heavy family responsibilities and often unequal access to education and other resources. They have addressed domestic abuse, reproductive rights, and the social discrimination they face as both women and indigenous people—asserting their individual and collective rights (Speed, Hernández Castillo, and Stephen 2006). Their organizing as women and as Zapatistas is now widely recognized, and several *comandantas* have become celebrated figures in the social movement. The Zapatistas' call for indigenous rights includes particular attention to women's rights, and the "Women's Revolutionary Law" is one of the cornerstones of their political platform.

Hernández Castillo (2005) has discussed the strategic essentialism of Mayan women activists who are embracing the ideal of gender complementarity even while acknowledging current gender inequalities. A cultural politics of celebrating gender difference along with Mayan spirituality and worldview not only enables them to hold their male counterparts to a higher standard but also positions them to be cultural standard-bearers. Women participating in the tourism economy have the further advantage of being deemed by outsiders to be traditional and authentic Mayas, embodying cultural heritage and ancestral knowledge and resistance to the homogenizing forces of globalization.

In the course of my research in the region, I joined several groups of solidarity tourists in the cultural center Oventic in Zapatista territory. We met with members of the Zapatistas' good-government council, and each time there was at least one woman present among the indigenous leadership, even if she was a quieter member of the group (having less fluency in Spanish). In this way, women were visible to tourists and broke with traditional gender divisions in Chiapas. The conferences I attended along with numerous international activists also made gender issues central features on their agendas. In workshops and panels, indigenous women and their supporters discussed matters relating to women and health, education, and livelihood.

The iconic Zapatista women in braids and bandannas adorn the most popular items sold to both solidarity and mainstream tourists, including T-shirts, posters, and even ashtrays. Also in abundant supply are male and female dolls wearing wool tunics and masks symbolizing their resistance; both genders have androgynous forms and carry rifles. Female Zapatistas are represented as different from males by the addition of long braids tied with colorful yarn and, in some cases, by small wrapped bundles attached to their backs, often with masked infants peeking out. A newer invention is the "nursing" dolls created by Zapatista women of the regional Women for Dignity collective; these artisans use Mayan textiles designed in their communities to dress larger plush figures featuring snaps on hands that link together, and snaps on each breast to join nursing babies to the dolls. Along with the dolls' braids and masks, this clever innovation draws considerable interest from tourists intrigued by women's place in Zapatista political culture.

Having described the relatively prominent role of women in Chiapas's political culture, I should also note that in places like San Cristóbal de las Casas, where there is a heavy concentration of tourism, indigenous women may be rendered nearly invisible—considered folkloric but bothersome—as they move through the city selling craft items to make a living. As Little (2004) showed for Antigua, Guatemala, women in their indigenous dress in Chiapas are viewed as the repositories of cultural tradition and may be the preferred vendors of items that tourists desire, but tourists often pass them by and pay higher prices in city shops, where they judge the quality of the weavings and traditional articles of clothing to be higher.

During my visit, I observed an example of gender and indigenous difference on display, but nearly invisible, in plain sight in one of the shops ringing the café and cultural center TierrAdentro. In a space with a small quantity of traditional textiles for sale, two women in traditional dress were sitting on the floor talking quietly while one wove on a backstrap loom. There was little movement through this area, where the women worked as part of the Women for Dignity artisan group; they were stationed there as a sort of "living history" cultural performance for the rare tourist who wandered into the shop from the cybercafé. For me, this recalled the way that women and children pose on the roadside for tourists on Andean Peruvian circuits and baby alpacas are brought to high-end boutiques in Lima to boost sales of clothing.

Little has been written about women and gender in the Lacandón jungle area, an important site of early civilization and the cradle of Zapatista political organizing. Travelers go there principally to visit archaeological sites and the jungle, where local men are generally the ones who transport and guide visitors, while women are busy behind the scenes preparing lodging and meals. My stay in a local community catering to tourism in the jungle revealed significant similarities to the gender division of labor in community-based tourism in Vicos. The jungle tour I took, led by a young man as guide, was the most sustained period for more intimate acquaintance with a member of the Lacandón community; women, I was told, rarely served as guides. I needed to seek out a few women to talk to, something that would be difficult for travelers who do not speak Spanish.

During my stay at the camp at Lacanjá, I spoke with a small group of women who were relaxing with their children in hammocks outside their home. All were members of the same large family, which had several camps where it hosted visitors. The women told me that tourism had helped them by enabling them to sell crafts in the camps' shops. However, an older woman among them lamented that younger women were no longer wearing traditional dress, suggesting that this was due to the influence of outsiders and their cultural practices. Nearby, the local Internet place was operated by a Lacandón man and his wife, who was from Oaxaca and nonindigenous. She experienced difficulty as one of only a few non-Lacandón women in the community, because people there generally spoke the Mayan language and not Spanish. She was nonetheless part of the socially diverse fabric of the community, which increasingly was marked by differences of age, language use, gender, and economic opportunity.

Of sex and romance tourism, there is little at present in Chiapas. The prostitution that exists is directed mainly to local men or to soldiers (Kelly 2008), who during the region's recent militarization have been known to draw local women into commercialized sex. Previously unknown in many indigenous communities, prostitution may be related to family violence and abuse of alcohol (Eber and Kovic 2003: 12). Relationships sometimes form between travelers and local men and women, and I heard one account from a European woman who came for a few days and met a man whom she married; she has lived in San Cristóbal for some years now, working along with her husband as a tour guide for a leading tourism office. However, as a travel destination Chiapas does not attract the sort of sex or romance tourism found in Mexico's resort locations.

As in Andean Peru, the intertwining of gender and race in the lives of indigenous women in Chiapas is complex and contradictory. Generations of subordination to those of higher socioeconomic class and racial status and, often, to men of their own communities have put these women at a disadvantage with regard to education, employment, and social position. Mestizos in both regions continue to look down on campesinos and indigenous people and on the in-between category of "modernizing" Indians; women among these groups may be the object of particular scorn. Tourism may reproduce discriminatory practices, even when, in some cases, the figure of the indigenous woman is rebranded as desirable in marketing traditional societies in transition. The iconic woman spinning yarn in the Andes or weaving on a backstrap loom in Chiapas can be a selling point and a particularly reassuring image of cultural continuity in places recently marked by conflict. These women are aware of the power of representation in tourism and may seek to get ahead by enhancing their image as authentic indigenous women, in some cases using websites and other marketing devices to encourage tourism or the direct sale of craft items. In contrast to a short time ago, when it was safer to conceal one's indigenous identity, it is now a point of pride for some, at least in the realm of tourism. In the case of Chiapas, the indigenous struggle for human rights is characterized by women playing a significant role in activism to counter local-level, as well as national-level, injustices (Speed 2008), and this appears to carry over to their participation in tourism.

INDIGENOUS WOMEN AND TOURISM

How does tourism, and particularly cultural tourism, affect the balance of gender relations among indigenous peoples in Andean Peru and Chiapas? When de la Cadena described Andean women as "more Indian," she parted ways with analysts who emphasized harmony and complementarity among Andean women and men. She acknowledged that women who gained experience as marketers were already acquiring the modern urban skills that might enable them to appear less Indian and more mestizo, but she claimed that local men and women devalued such activity as "not really work" (1995: 330). Whether or not Andeans uniformly hold that view, we might ask whether they view work in tourism as meaningful and worthy. We have seen that indigenous women are often viewed as the most culturally authentic members of their communities and, as such, may have an economic advantage in tourism when they produce items and sell them to the public or interact in other ways with tourists. Does this result in higher status for them in local communities? Does marketing their identity as traditional or indigenous benefit them in other ways?

Recent research in the Cuzco area supports the view that women are finding new ways to market their identities as well as their products in the tourism economy. For example, women and children who pose for photos, using folkloric dress and sometimes iconic alpacas to cater to tourist preferences, have become commonplace enough that individuals serving as models are referred to as *sácamefotos* (take-my-pictures). However, as do the bricheros who seek women's affection in the tourism market, these women gain new sources of income without necessarily gaining respect in family and community; the work is not regarded as worthy in the way that the work of artisans is (Simon 2009). In such cases, gender and racial identity are put to work in ways that result in deeply ambivalent outcomes at the local level.

Long-term research at an eco-lodge in the southeastern Amazon area shows that competition for tourism revenues has resulted in local concern to manifest indigenous identity and culture. In this area, characterized by mixed "native communities," gender appears to be less significant than ethnic identity. It remains to be seen to what degree tourism is a benefit, offering new economic resources and validation for indigenous identity, and to what degree it may promote new inequalities as both potential income and ethnic identity become contested sites. In an ironic twist that recalls the tourism project in Vicos, as the Amazonian community seeks "modern" progress it is "considering the possibility that a return to the past [reclaiming traditions, retention of language and dress] may be the best path to a prosperous future" (Stronza 2008: 251).

Research on indigenous women in Latin America suggests that women's position may undergo the greatest change in areas where they participate in local women's movements or in indigenous movements that offer substantial attention to gender injustice and seek to overcome it (Speed, Hernández Castillo, and Stephen 2006). This could account for the greater visibility of women in Zapatista communities than in other areas of Chiapas or in Andean Peru. It may also help explain their active part in organizing artisan cooperatives that direct their sales to the tourist market (Ortiz 2001). In times and places where women recognize the need to assert their rights, they clearly tend to have a more prominent role both in political mobilization and in tourism development. Tourists themselves often seek opportunities to interact with indigenous women, and this may draw women into more active engagement with tourism. To be sure, as women participate more in tourism they may lose some of the apparent authenticity that attracts tourists in the first place. My work presented here supports the view that it is critical to sort through the ways in which identities are shifting in response to both new challenges and new opportunities for those who have been marginalized historically. For indigenous women whose full citizenship rights have been denied in the past, even short-term gains may be used strategically to advance their individual and collective interests.

Peoples and nations that increasingly look to tourism for economic and political stabilization frequently refashion their cultural identities and histories to draw travelers. The emergence of indigenous social movements in southern Mexico and in countries like Ecuador and Bolivia and, to a lesser degree, Peru has the double advantage of asserting rights at the national level and capturing the interest of international travelers and supporters. Chiapas and the Andean region thus have a higher profile for those considering their options for travel destinations. They have the cachet of having recently made international headlines and the security of having emerged from deeper conflict. Women, whether exoticized for their cultural difference or simply admired for their artisan skills and newfound activism, are coming to play a more important part in the tourism encounter in these postconflict and transitional societies. Being "more Indian" can become a source of cultural capital. These women's growing visibility, their social and political participation, and even their marketing of Zapatista dolls and chola Barbies, suggest that in some cases women are making gains under the new terms of engagement with tourism.

Conclusion

TOWARD A DECOLONIAL FEMINIST ANTHROPOLOGY

In the opening pages of *Women's Place in the Andes,* I discuss the Congress on Research on Women in the Andean Region that I attended in Lima in 1982, and the dinner I had thirty years later with several friends who also had been there. Our host that evening, Jeanine Anderson, had written the final report from the congress. When I recently reread her account of how the event was conceived, I was surprised to discover that her remarks resonated with a number of the concerns addressed in this book (Anderson de Velasco 1983: 7–13). The idea for the conference came out of one of the early meetings of the National Women's Studies Association, held in 1979 in Kansas City. Present there were some of the leading feminist scholars working in Peru, including Susan Bourque, Elsa Chaney, Cornelia Butler Flora, Carmen Diana Deere, Blanca Figueroa, Margo Smith, and Marta Tienda. Anderson noted in the report that women's studies was still in its infancy in North America and Europe and was scarcely on the horizon in Latin America at the time. The new knowledge and debates were understood as having been generated from outside the region studied as a result of better resources and opportunities in the North, though that was beginning to change. Thus, the idea of a conference on Andean women held in and drawing scholars from the region, as well as internationally, had powerful appeal.

Blanca Figueroa, based in Peru, would organize the Lima event, while feminists based in the North would secure the needed funding. The objective was to promote Andean women's studies (with heavy emphasis on Peru) and "to repatriate studies of women in Peru to their legitimate owners [*dueñas*]" (Anderson de Velasco 1983: 8, my translation). This desire to reclaim their rightful knowledge, at least symbolically, prefigured the decolonial feminisms that emerged a decade later; indeed, such radical questioning of scholarly imperialism was fairly common among some feminists as early as the 1970s, as I have suggested elsewhere in this volume. Notwithstanding the organizers' embrace of a decolonizing outlook and the presence of a large number of urban Latin American participants, there were few if any rural Andean women at the congress, and Amazonian and Afro-Peruvian women were rarely part of the conversation at that time (Anderson de Velasco 1983: 9). Even so, the final report's recognition of the omission speaks to the era's growing attention to social, racial, and place-based inequalities as these intersected with gender inequality.

The congress achieved a number of important objectives, including the opening of feminist theoretical debates concerning women in the Andean region to a diverse group of interlocutors, the recuperation of research that was made available in Spanish for the first time, and the formulation of priorities for future research. The organizers had put decolonizing theory into practice *avant la lettre*, as each major panel included a Peruvian, a Latin American from outside Peru, and a participant from outside the region. As a northern participant myself, I can add that presenting at the congress, my first time sharing research results with a largely Peruvian audience of scholars and activists, was both humbling and exhilarating. I would be hard-pressed to think of another conference where I have been asked such far-reaching and urgent questions requiring me to make clear why my work matters.

DECOLONIZING SCHOLARSHIP ON ANDEAN WOMEN

As I complete this book, I am marking forty years since my first trip to Peru to carry out doctoral research. When I traveled to Lima for the 2017 Congress of the Latin American Studies Association, I participated in a sponsored session I conceived, "Feminists Rethinking the Andean Region: South-North Dialogues." This was the most recent in a number of conference sessions I have organized on the theme of reframing conceptualizations of gender and race in the Andes, a series that began with "Are Andean Women Still 'Más Indias' [More Indian]? The Re-circulation of Gender and Indigenous Identities" at the 2010 conference of the American Anthropological Association in New Orleans. At that time, we took up de la Cadena's much-cited pronouncement made two decades earlier that Andean women *are* perceived as more "Indian"; the panelists' responses to this declaration ranged widely.[1] Following on the commentary chapters in this book, my own answer to whether Andean women still experience the same forms of intersectional disadvantage as in decades past is both yes and no. Certainly, among rural Andeans in Peru gender and race discrimination, along with socioeconomic discrimination, prevail as colonial legacies couple with urban modernist prejudices. This is experienced in manifold everyday ways by women who are multiply situated, whether as rural community members, workers in local market economies, guardians of "heritage" in tourism settings, or migrants to cities, including the national capital, Lima.

However, to move beyond "additive" notions of intersectionality and come to terms with the historically shifting geopolitics of knowledge production, we must recognize instances where women have made gains over the generations—for example, through education, social mobilization, and opportunities for gaining a livelihood in the cultural heritage industry. These gains are often compromised by durable forms of inequality and social injustice, but they are gains nonetheless. I have argued that a decolonial feminist standpoint enables us to advance toward a more inclusive anthropology of Andean-ness and indigeneity that questions the received wisdom. This includes some feminist views regarding the deficits of Andean womanhood and gender relations—those positing that the abject conditions of rural women have burdened them so heavily that they are diminished as knowledge producers and actors in their own right.[2]

One of the principal challenges of embracing a decolonial perspective is identifying and acknowledging the internal disagreements among feminist analysts of North and South. I refer not only to the more commonly cited North-South differences but also to the differences *among* southern feminists, just as we find among northern feminists. It would be a mistake, something akin to the earlier view that there was a singular "Third World woman," to expect anything less in the South than the complexity and tensions found more broadly among feminist activists and scholars worldwide.[3] As I have redoubled my commitment to placing my past work in conversation with Peruvian analysts, I have contended with incommensurable views expressed in different social and geographic locations in the nation, which made my objective of rethinking my work in dialogue with Peruvian feminists that much more fraught. Would I conclude that some critical responses to my work from urban coastal feminists represented lingering colonial legacies and assumptions held by privileged interlocutors regarding subaltern Andean women, or would that mean letting myself too easily off the hook? For example, could I write off some critiques of my early work on the Vicos Project, and of gender complementarity, as civilizing narratives of urban feminists who could not fathom rural Andean women as knowledge producers whose experience of gender and gender relations might differ radically from their own?

I have found myself caught between seeing (as urban Peruvian feminists often do) the evidence of deep-seated gender inequality in rural Peru and then being struck by the evidence that colonial penetration and contemporary neoliberal capitalism have given rise to emergent inequalities that have not always and everywhere been in place. In general I would agree with the decolonial feminism advanced by Aymara sociologist Silvia Rivera Cusicanqui (2010), who shows persuasively that in the Bolivian case colonialist re-visioning and disparaging of what had been greater equilibrium between Andean men and women began to turn productive and reproductive activities into binary realms of unequal value. Likewise, where rural women's domestic activities in the "private" sphere were earlier in balance with men's "public" activities, this division of labor was, over time, freighted with the unequal gender politics of more cosmopolitan urban society. However, whereas Rivera Cusicanqui concludes that rural indigenous women in Bolivia were left with, at best, symbolic value and little power, I have taken into account the ever-shifting values and meanings attributed to those individuals, including rural indigenous women, who seize opportunities for attaining an education, participating in the heritage industry of tourism, and so on. I do concur that the playing field is uneven, and that women are now struggling against the odds to ameliorate colonialism's legacy and neoliberalism's penchant for reinscribing social inequalities.

It may be instructive to consider a Latin American Studies Association session I organized in 2013 in collaboration with Peruvian sociologist Patricia Ruiz Bravo, titled "Gender, Race, and Ethnicity in the Andes" and featuring panelists from three Andean nations and the United States.[4] Mercedes Prieto questioned how to build a research agenda from the South relating to indigenous women in Latin America. She drew on history and anthropology to examine the emergence of Ecuadorian women as political actors and indigenous intellectuals, addressing relations between indigenous women and the nation-state. She considered women's bodies, health, and human rights—areas of significant tension between urban feminists and indigenous women over such issues as gender complementarity and women's role as guardians of indigenous culture. While many feminists have dismissed such gender practices as essentialist, Prieto pointed to emerging spaces for intercultural dialogue.

Patricia Ruiz Bravo discussed perspectives held by and about indigenous women in the Andean and Amazon regions in Peru. She examined the diverse strands of racialized experience in the country in light of the changing demographics in Peru since 1940, as decades of migration reduced the rural indigenous population and contributed a growing number of urban indigenous-identified Peruvians. Whereas the Andes and the Amazon have generally been considered worlds apart, NGOs and social activists in Peru have begun to address the two together (Afro-Peruvians concentrated on Peru's coast are still less frequently part of the discussion). Drawing on interviews with activists and analysts, Ruiz Bravo discovered what my own research has shown: indigenous women may embrace the premise of gender complementarity without subordination to men.

For her part, Pamela Calla addressed masculinist party politics and gender mainstreaming from below in Bolivia, and Amy Lind considered how the state governs identity in the case of Ecuador by resignifying gender, race, ethnicity, and sexuality in the nation's Citizen Revolution. While Calla brought needed attention to men's relationship to gender politics, Lind's work paid critical attention to sex and sexuality in the Andean region, notably including nonheteronormative sexuality in her discussion of development and citizenship rights. These feminist scholars have proposed lines of scholarly research that I contend build toward a decolonial feminist practice, advancing our understanding of braided inequalities of gender, race, class, and sexuality in the Andes.

Four years later, and as might be expected, the 2017 Latin American Studies Association congress in Lima drew an unprecedented number of participants from Peru. The session I co-organized with Cristina Alcalde, "Feminists Rethinking the Andean Region," engaged productively with the conference theme, "Diálogos de Saberes, Dialogues of Knowledge," in relation to the host nation. In recent years, the association has featured forums challenging the geopolitics of knowledge and proposing serious engagement with ideas generated among indigenous, Afro-descendant, and other marginalized peoples; at the same time, the association has been a venue where feminists have advanced decolonial theory in order to account for ways in which gender, race, and sexuality are constituted in Latin American contexts.[5] With our co-panelists María Elena García and Eshe Lewis and discussant Patricia Ruiz Bravo, we brought these conversations together so that feminist, antiracist, and decolonial theory from the South commingled with theorizing from the North, and called for a more robust means to apprehend contemporary Latin America. Our papers concerned decolonizing views of Andean gender and sexual relations, intimate-partner violence among Afro-descendant couples in Lima, nonhuman and human rights in Peru's gastronomic boom, and lesbian, gay, bisexual, and transgender Peruvian experiences in migration.

We need more opportunities for scholar-activists, including indigenous scholar-activists, to come together and engage with some of the most urgent questions that have often divided us, but which, over time, have created a foundation for collaboration and knowledge exchange.[6] Whether our concern is Andean women or gender, race, and ethnicity more broadly in Latin America, we must reflect more deeply on our research practices and analyses in relation to others' commentary and constructive criticism. The most fruitful ideas may emerge organically in some cases; but given what we have seen historically as the powerful legacy of colonial thought, we should subject our thinking to the collective scrutiny of those who have the most at stake in the marketplace of knowledge. We will not always see "the world" in the same way, but we can agree that a recognition of the workings of Andean *worlds* will be made richer by our open and inclusive dialogues.[7]

To deepen the discussion of these vexing questions, it is worth returning to earlier scholarly efforts to assess the historical evidence of how the Andean and colonial worlds collided in the period through the eighteenth century. Historian Ward Stavig (1995) offered keen insights into the culture clash of indigenous and European normative practices, based on early legal records that he understood to represent the perspectives of Spaniards on gender, heterosexuality, and marriage. His discussion of the criminalization of *naturales* (indigenous persons) for such normative Andean practices as trial marriage and premarital sex (in Quechua, *sirvinacuy*—or in Vicos, *watanaki*), a period when couples establish whether a marriage will be successful, is instructive regarding what has endured in the Peruvian Andes. Stavig (1995: 606–7) sheds light on the colonialist view that trial marriage was not only sinful but also "diabolical," "noxious," and "pernicious," and that gender complementarity in the form of balanced male-female participation in household formation and the division of labor was an aberration. He finds ample evidence that during the colonial era, European intervention and the impact of Christian proselytizing led to a "syncretic intertwining" of cultural practices and beliefs, yet Andeans resisted the challenge to their long-established ways of defining marriage, family, and household relations. There was a notable and selective appropriation of those European ideas that might fit into Andean systems of thought and ways of life. Stavig consulted twentieth-century ethnographers such as Irene Silverblatt, Billie Jean Isbell, Olivia Harris, and Penelope Harvey, discussed earlier in this book, to show that such continuities are found from colonial to contemporary Peru, even in the face of the "civilizing mission" and generational changes in the Andean region.

In a recent feminist analysis of the legal trial and confession of Micaela Bastidas, wife of Tupac Amaru II and his collaborator in the last major indigenous rebellion against Spanish rule in Andean Peru in 1780, anthropologist Ella Schmidt (2016) similarly argues that we must recognize the complex negotiations of the indigenous and colonial worlds of that period. Bastidas, called at her trial "a savage, indigenous woman" (Schmidt 2016: 41), was widely known as a forceful leader in the uprising, and yet she presented herself as a subordinated and innocent wife who remained ignorant of her husband's objectives. If this was her only hope for avoiding the death penalty, she was unsuccessful, as she and many other women involved were subjected to torture and horrible deaths. Schmidt contends that this was a strategic response to norms of that time as indigenous women were hardly credited with independent action and decision-making authority in the colonial era. She shows that Bastidas, who was located between indigenous and mestiza social worlds, was negotiating the terms of Andean gender complementarity, whereby households could be viewed as two-headed, with male-female couples sharing power and responsibility; nonetheless, colonial records labeled such units as male-headed and viewed rebellious women as monstrous. Schmidt's refusal to reduce subaltern lives to one-dimensional representations of accommodation or resistance is an important reminder for those of us undertaking to assess the still-complex and ambiguous present in Andean Peru. Like Stavig, Schmidt underscores the need to decolonize our thinking around gender and race in the Andes, as Euro-American categories of analysis would have little meaning, or very different meanings, in past and present indigenous cultures and societies.

While it may seem as if the analytics of gender complementarity and of reproduction and production in Andean Peru are no longer useful to thinking about the present, I emphasize that some of the most far-reaching discussions among decolonial thinkers currently take up just these analytical questions. Cultural theorist Freya Schiwy (2010: 125), contributing to a leading volume on the "decolonial option," notes that "indigenous movements debate concepts of gender complementarity while, at the same time, using gender complementarity as a template for thinking [about] decolonized relations." Indeed, Peru's indigenous organization Chirapaq, discussed earlier, currently sets forth the following on its webpage on indigenous women and gender equity:

> Our proposal for equitable gender relations is based on the principle of complementarity of indigenous peoples, where despite our differences in sex, age, size, strength, or differences of whatever kind, we are equals in dignity and rights.
>
> Indigenous cosmovision conceive[s] of gender relations as based on duality, complementarity, and equilibrium, and . . . harmony, understanding, and mutual respect. None of [cosmovision's] parts is more important than another, and rather [the parts] need one another . . . to exist.[8]

And, as noted earlier, the World March of Women has recently utilized the production/reproduction framework to identify and build on developments in transnational feminism.

The analytics of gender complementarity and production/reproduction, which frame much of this book, are flawed insofar as they appear to rest on binary and heteronormative assumptions about households and divisions of labor; thus I have argued that it is essential to push beyond what may be colonialist impositions in naturalizing gender and sexual differences as male-female binaries. Bolivians María Galindo and Julieta Paredes (whose work was mentioned earlier) sought to do that with their radical lesbian and indigenous political interventions.[9] For her part, Schiwy has called on decolonial thinkers to treat gender as seriously as race so as not to reinscribe the coloniality of power relations. While many would agree that colonialism "feminized" indigenous men in relation to European men, less attention has focused on the dehumanizing effects on indigenous women, who were even further "subalternized" in the colonial era. Schiwy (2010: 138) makes the crucial argument that while gender complementarity is often an idealized and "contested concept in the politics of decolonization," it nevertheless "becomes one model for thinking [through] an alternative modernity."

In the current context, more writings on gender, race, and power from Andean women themselves in Peru (such as writings found in neighboring Bolivia and Ecuador) would afford a counterpoint to the far more prevalent urban, Lima-centered feminist contributions. We can, however, draw some conclusions from various forms of political practice in the coastal cities and the Andean highlands. As a case in point, recall my commentary in part 2 concerning the responses during the 1990s to President Fujimori's thinly veiled eugenicist policy of imposing sterilization on rural Andean women in the guise of reducing poverty and supporting women's reproductive health. While the indigenous women subjected to the practice struggled with the personal and social consequences of such intervention, the coercive measures were notably overlooked by many urban middle-class feminists in Lima. We may rarely find such harshly consequential examples of epistemic differences among feminist activists and women more generally in Peru (or anywhere), yet they are part and parcel of the widespread, long-standing stereotypes and assumptions regarding rural indigenous women that have shaped the analytics of gender and race in Peru and the Andean region (Ewig 2010; Rousseau 2009; Radcliffe 2015). Decolonial feminisms stand to deepen intersectional analysis and afford more critical perspectives that might overcome the racialized geographies that often divide us, not only along a North-South axis, but also *within* northern and southern regions.

I do not claim that a decolonial perspective can resolve all uncertainty around persistent disagreements such as whether gender complementarity accurately represents an Andean world based on epistemic principles that are at variance with northern feminist thought. However, I contend that this perspective can effectively counter critics' dismissive views of alternative ways of thinking and being in the world. A decolonial skepticism regarding the view that Andean women will not see improvement in their lives short of a wholesale transformation in their gender relations can move us beyond sedimented thinking about women remaining almost inevitably "más indias." Indeed, de la Cadena herself (2008: 345) appears to have moved away from her earlier observations in Andean Peru, commenting that "being mestizo is not as hegemonically empowering as it used to be, being Aymara, or Quechua, or Ashaninka, or Maya does not denote wretched Indianness anymore. This emergent and alternative bio-politics results from political struggles, and its significance is historical. It expresses a decolonizing effort strongly grounded in local formations smaller than the nation yet backed by the growing presence of transnational indigenous movements." She goes on to note that in the present political context of social struggles, indigeneity has become a "new political actor" in Peru that cannot be reduced to ethnicity alone but, rather, exceeds it (de la Cadena 2008: 347).[10]

PUBLIC DISCOURSES AND ACTIVISM SURROUNDING RACE AND GENDER IN PERU

In Lima during my sabbatical, the film *Choleando* (de la Puente 2011), named for the practice of racial one-upmanship in Peru, was getting a lot of media attention as part of a Latin American series showing in venues around the city. Having read about the semidocumentary film, which poses the question "Are we or are we not racist in Peru?," I arrived early for a showing in the MALI (Museo de Arte de Lima) art museum's packed auditorium. The audience was largely young to middle-aged, students and intellectuals, with some degree of racial diversity. Sitting next to me were three women who could have been from the Amazon region. The anticipation was palpable before the feature-length film began. Staged as an exploration of race and racism by two Peruvian students, the film introduces us to Mariananda, who is middle class, white, and convinced that racism is a serious problem in the country, and Julio, who is darker-skinned and self-identifies as a cholo, and believes racism is no longer the problem that it once was in Peru. The two, who notably serve to unsettle binary thinking about white racism and nonwhite perception of racism, set out to take the measure of racism among Peruvians.

Former president Alan García appears early in the film and depicts Andean people chewing coca leaves and wearing ponchos and traditional full skirts (*polleras*) as "sad" (*triste*) in temperament, a stereotype that is widely held on the urban coast. The two young protagonists call on social scientists to clarify the meanings of *race* and *racism*. Nelson Manrique comments on the relationship of race and class, and the process by which money whitens, known as *blanqueando,* in Peru. Psychologist Jorge Bruce (2007), author of *Nos habíamos choleado tanto* (We had put each other down [racially] so much), on the psychology of racism in Peru, refers to postcolonial racializing and the disrespectful use of *cholo,* even if it is sometimes used affectionately among friends. The film uses animation to show a series of individuals, each calling the next one "cholo" but never considering himself a cholo. These views appear to support Mariananda's position.

Although much evidence of racism is presented, Julio finds support for his position that racism is on the decline in Peru when he interviews sociologist Martín Tanaka, who maintains that racism is less prevalent now than before, and that it is less about appearance and origins than in the past. Likewise, a theater professor refers to *diversidad cholo* (cholo diversity) in Peru, which Julio takes to suggest that many in the country are proud to be cholo, and that, indeed, Peru may be called *un país cholo* (a cholo nation). The film devotes only brief attention to Afro-Peruvians, who reveal that they are often asked if they are from another country because they do not "look Peruvian." The relationship between gender and racial differences is given little notice, except in a brief segment that moves from

Lima to Cuzco, where Andean men known as bricheros, motivated by a desire for gifts, visas, and foreign girlfriends, seek out and attract tourist gringas. The film ends with the two young interviewers face to face in downtown Lima. Finally, they agree that Peruvians are still far from treating everyone alike, and they leave the audience with the question "Are we going to change this situation?" The anthropologist-filmmaker, Roberto de la Puente, and the two actors playing the protagonists took the stage after the film showing, participating in a lively conversation with the audience about their pioneering effort to generate wide and public discussion about racism in Peru.

The timing could not have been better, as there were several incidents of racism in Lima around this time. One occurred in December 2011, when a young man, an artisan from Cuzco visiting Lima and dressed in impeccable Andean textiles, was not allowed back into the multiplex cinema in the high-end Larcomar commercial center, where he had been watching a movie with friends, after leaving to use the restroom. He and his friends complained, and this became a cause célèbre leading to protest by Limeños, including some youth who used social networking to gather for a street performance, donning polleras and *chullos* (Andean caps). The movie theater was forced to close for several days, and the incident was widely covered by the media. Thereafter, commercial establishments at Larcomar posted the municipality's nondiscrimination ordinance prominently.

Around the same time, in a less publicized case, three women with children, in Andean dress with polleras and hats, were approached by an official and apparently directed to leave the same commercial center overlooking the seacoast in Lima's fashionable Miraflores district (Gonzalo Portocarrero, personal communication). This case did not attain public visibility, probably owing to the women's more humble demeanor and class status, their gender, and their timidity when confronted by a man in uniform. A third incident occurred in another Lima movie theatre. In that case, when a woman in the audience asked a nearby adolescent to lower his voice during the movie, he responded by calling her by the racialized epithet *serrana*. She in turn reacted by slapping the boy. The boy's parents, well-known musicians and politically progressive, were likely embarrassed by his behavior but charged the woman with abuse, bringing considerable media attention to the matter. The public was divided over where to place

Cuzco weavers demonstrating their work at the Larcomar commercial center in Lima, 2012. Photo by author.

blame, but many defended the woman, saying that the boy's racism (and sense of middle-class entitlement) deserved an emphatic response.

Two years later, I was surprised to learn of still another controversy over racial injustice and exploitation at the Larcomar commercial center. This involved rural indigenous women who were skilled weavers from Cuzco and whose collective had long sent women in pairs to spend a month at a time demonstrating their expert weaving for shoppers in the luxury store Sol Alpaca. I had informally interviewed several of these women in the alpaca clothing store in the past and knew that they were proud to showcase their craft in Lima. However, they were also keenly aware of the double standard of Limeños, who valued the best examples of Andean cultural heritage but would not have expected to see these same weavers in traditional dress in the streets of their city (still less, at Larcomar). The women had explained to me that they accommodated this reality of modern life by wearing more urban attire until they arrived at the store for a public performance of their rural cultural identity. When some well-known journalists became aware of

In place of women weavers from Cuzco, mannequins and photographs are now on display in the Larcomar shop, 2016. Photo by author.

the perceived cultural commodification of these women, who were ostensibly unpaid for their work, they launched a protest and wrote articles and blogs to call attention to the alleged exploitation. Despite the store's assurances that the women's expenses were covered, and that this was a way to promote the women's own artisanry as well as enhance the store's sales, they were forced to end the longtime arrangement and began using mannequins and photographs of Andean weavers in place of the "living history" display. I solicited opinions among a number of Limeños, as well as retail workers in several Sol Alpaca shops in the city, and found a range of views as diverse as the population itself. Some were indignant about what they felt was an unjust burden on these women, and others simply felt the store had given the artisans an opportunity that the women had openly accepted.

What do these public ruminations on race in Peru have to do with gender? So far, in these examples I have given little explicit attention to the way that gender can complicate interpretations of race and racism in Peru, yet gender can be understood as salient in all these narratives. In the film

Choleando, the filmmaker has stated that he deliberately chose to have the "white" interviewer view racism as a serious problem and the "cholo" see it as having less significance today. But what of their gender difference? Was Mariananda's greater sensitivity to race discrimination represented as a consequence of her gender, if not her racial and class, identity? Was Julio's initial denial of a race problem an expression of masculine and working-class toughness, if not his racial position? In the first pair of incidents at Larcomar, was the young man who was prevented from returning to the theater empowered to stand up to authority, whereas the women who left the mall quietly with their children were not, even if in both cases there was unfair treatment based on ethnic identity and self-presentation? Does the example of a woman literally striking back at racism read differently because she was an adult woman who struck a teenage boy? And finally, were the weavers considered by protesters as particularly vulnerable to exploitation as women, and should they instead have been recognized as decision-making agents in their own right, rather than viewed paternalistically as women waiting to be rescued from the ravages of a masculinist market economy? All are complex cases, particularly when we factor in differences in age, language use, and evident wealth or poverty, yet gender appears to play a significant part in all of them.

Peruvian popular culture has both reflected and reinforced the intersecting forms of discrimination by race and gender in Peru. It is not uncommon for indigenous women to be singled out for ridicule, as exemplified by the controversial TV program *La Paisana Jacinta,* which aired intermittently over the past two decades and portrayed its Lima "hillbilly" title character (played by a male actor in braids and chola dress) as ignorant, dirty, and unattractive.[11] And both the media and the public have expressed scorn for the rapid rise of the internationally acclaimed actor Magaly Solier, who hails from Andean Peru. Despite protests pointing to the racism and sexism in such representation and treatment, stereotyped notions are deep-seated and they persist in the wider society.

While examples of gendered and racialized discrimination abound in Peru, public consciousness of the problem has gradually shifted. This change has come about not only because of growing awareness in urban environments but also because, in the last decade or so, indigenous women activists have mobilized in both rural and urban settings. A catalyst for this activism has been those Peruvians who have expressed growing concern for, and protested the devastating consequences of, extensive mining and other extractive industries in the Andean and Amazonian regions. In 2011, the government passed the Law on Prior Consultation, which recognized the right of indigenous communities to participate in discussion of projects that would affect them and their lands; this mobilized communities to assert their indigenous identity. While Presidents Alan García and Ollanta Humala resisted acknowledging Andean communities as indigenous, effectively excluding them from the law's protection, some men and women have laid claim to the identity and demanded their right to sovereignty. A number of women found their voices but discovered that their concerns were often drowned out by their own men, so they began forming independent organizations, including several that drew together indigenous women of both Andean and Amazon regions (Rousseau and Morales Hudon 2017). To do so, they risked being labeled "inauthentic" indigenous women and even "feminists"—a term that only a few openly embrace, even when they find that their communities have fallen far short of the ideal of gender complementarity and have devalued women. Nonetheless, these activists have demonstrated that they remain fiercely dedicated to preserving land rights, food sovereignty, and their ethnic identity.

In a hopeful sign for the future, the first Continental Summit of Indigenous Women was hosted in Puno, Peru, in 2009.[12] The six thousand women who met discussed a far-reaching agenda that called for establishing a clear connection between collective indigenous rights and the human rights of indigenous women; reasserting fundamental principles of gender complementarity and equilibrium, and demanding that their cosmovision not be "folklorized"; demanding the elimination of machismo and racism; bringing women into greater political participation; questioning global development and its effects on women, territory, biodiversity, and food sovereignty; and ending violence against women, in part through intercultural education and communication. There can be no doubt that these women were full-fledged knowledge producers and social protagonists sending a signal to indigenous men, indigenous women yet to be organized, and national governments, expressing their

Installation with Andean references at the Latin American and Caribbean Feminist Encuentro in Lima, 2014. Photo by author.

readiness to play an active part in addressing some of the most urgent issues throughout the continent.

The continued activism of indigenous women and of feminist organizations in response to widespread forms of discrimination and exclusionary practices is sorely needed, yet the two groups have rarely come together to address common interests. Thus it is encouraging to note that the Latin American and Caribbean Feminist Encuentro held in Lima in 2014 raised many of the same concerns addressed at the first Continental Summit of Indigenous Women held in Puno five years earlier. A majority of those at the 2014 event were urban feminists from throughout Latin America and the Caribbean whose agenda included the rights of sex workers, lesbians, and other marginalized women; yet their final proclamation, read by Virginia Vargas, also emphasized such themes as interculturality and sustainability, bodies and territories, and called for diverse feminisms to recognize colonial legacies and pluricultural cosmovision.[13] This convergence of political desires and objectives among indigenous women activists and participants at the Latin American and Caribbean Feminist Encuentro offers the promise of future collaborations—something that visionary feminist scholars will endorse and embrace as well.

REVISITING WOMEN'S PLACE IN THE ANDES

In this volume I have used my past writing on Andean women and gender relations to stage conversations concerning the utility of feminist frameworks from the 1970s to the present as analytics for deepening our critical understanding of intertwined and persistent inequalities of gender, race, sexuality, and nation. I have argued that a decolonial feminist anthropological perspective will enable us to reexamine past research frameworks in a way that brings to light new dimensions of enduring debate and disagreement. Whether such a reconsideration will vindicate long-debated concepts like gender complementarity remains to be seen, but rethinking long-held and often rigid positions will surely yield richer results in the future. Looking anew at the last four decades (now going on half a century) of research on Andean women and gender, including more recent turns toward understanding racial formations, masculinities, and sexualities in the era of postneoliberalism, can reopen discussion of power and social relations in a time of dramatic change. In Peru, that period saw the abolition of the hacienda system and the introduction of agrarian reform on the cusp of the 1970s. This time of transition preceded two decades of national conflict and prolonged violence, which was followed by the turn of the millennium, when the nation stabilized and the economy experienced growth, albeit limited. I have argued that the political economic framing of this history, while critical, should not deter us from examining the social, cultural, and other dynamics of everyday life that have undergone just as significant a change. Where gender, race, and other forms of social difference and inequality are concerned, we need to make sense of the full sweep of historical change and where it may be leading.

When I returned to the Callejón de Huaylas in 2017, the fortieth anniversary of my doctoral work, I relished the opportunity to stay again with

The author with her *comadre* Socorro, her goddaughter Magaly, and Magaly's sister Beatriz in Huaraz, 2016. Photo by Rafael Castro Ramírez.

my compadres in Huaraz and to revisit people and places that have long called me back. For the occasion, I gave a talk hosted by the regional office of the Ministry of Culture, presenting from my current book project and especially from ideas mapped out in the introduction. The challenge was to address an audience that would likely include members of the local elite, as well as personal friends and associates, who would have differing degrees of familiarity with feminism and gender studies; as such, I aimed to use the "F" word sparingly while still calling for a decolonial feminist perspective in order to shed light on race and gender in Andean Peru. Indeed, those who came out that evening ranged from individuals from the ministry, institutes, and local universities (including several anthropologists), to a social movement calling for food sovereignty, to a fledgling group of young feminists I had not heard of before, in addition to my goddaughter and other family members.

Following my talk, the first comment came from a prominent older woman in Huaraz who had long played an active part in women's civic and other organizations and whom I had met years ago. Although she acknowledged differences in the value placed on women and men, she suggested that any need for feminism had passed now that women had attained greater rights; and she added that, in any event, feminists just want to replace machismo with another ideology. I did my best to convey the desire of decolonial feminists to address various forms of difference and inequality while recognizing women as protagonists in their own lives, and I was soon joined by a young Spanish anthropology graduate student I had met the year before, who was still more forceful in arguing that feminism is needed now more than ever. This received enthusiastic applause from the young Huaracina feminists in the auditorium. One more comment came from another acquaintance, a middle-aged male activist identifying as "100 percent Quechua," who seemed to have grasped my point when he asserted that problems of gender violence and inequality, like other inequalities, grew out of the legacy of colonialism and must be countered as such. I navigated the terrain of the passionate discussion that ensued, until a small and friendly group accompanied me to a nearby restaurant. There, we went around the table, and each related what had brought him or her to my talk that evening and to the work each was dedicated to doing. My qualms about the mixed responses to my talk and audience members' ambivalence to feminism and gender analysis were allayed by the animated oratories of the dozen who honored me by coming together that night.

However, I was once again reminded that not all the Peruvians I interact with in my research settings agree with me about the value of using a feminist framework to examine local intersections of gender and race in the Andes. Although I take pains to decolonize my knowledge base and analytical approach, and to convey my commitment to a deep understanding of the history and geography of gender and race inequalities in Andean Peru, there are those who doubt that a transnational feminism can advance either scholarship or activism. Thus it may be worth stating as I conclude this work that I am well aware of the limitations of my intention to be collaborative in relation to both my methodology and the work that emerges from it. At a time when activist, decolonial, and world anthropologies are

The author giving a lecture hosted by the Ministry of Culture, Huaraz, 2017. Photo by Eva Valenzuela.

increasingly under discussion, I have sought to rethink past feminist debates by closely attending to theory from the South and by staging conversations between my own scholarship and that of others, particularly of Peruvian and other Andeanist writers and activists. As I expressed earlier, southern theorists and political activists often disagree among themselves, and it is little wonder if my work does not always resonate with theirs; nonetheless, subjecting my work to their critiques has been most illuminating.

Ideally, I would have found more research collaborators among Andean women themselves, but I have had little expectation that the Andean people I came to know through my studies of marketers, tourism providers, and rural agriculturalists—aside from the occasional research associate from Huaraz or Vicos—would embrace my projects as their own. Nor were many of them activists with whom I might form practical alliances.

I argue that this in no way diminishes the significance of examining the intersecting ways in which they are affected by and confront gender and racial injustices on a daily basis. By establishing meaningful connections with those I have met through my field research, I have aimed to make their concerns and experiences central to my work. Even so, I have rarely presumed to take their time beyond our conversations in households and markets—where our collaboration frequently has focused on mundane things such as peeling potatoes while we shared personal stories and observations about life in the Callejón. I can only hope that in the long term I am doing justice to the complex lives of the many individuals who generously have given me their time during my many visits to Peru. Without a doubt, I still have far to go in decolonizing my research and writing, and this will be a lifelong process.[14]

The day after my talk at the Ministry of Culture, May 13, 2017, was my last in Huaraz that year. The timing provided a kind of poetic closure for me inasmuch as my first day in the city's Mercado Central was exactly forty years earlier, May 13, 1977. As I described in the opening pages of my book *Between Field and Cooking Pot* (Babb [1989] 1998), on that day so long ago I was surprised by a lively procession with musicians and dancers that I encountered in the aisles of market stalls and around the small chapel in the market. I later came to realize that this colorful folkloric display was no everyday occurrence but, rather, the culmination of annual events honoring the Virgen de Fatima, patron saint of Mercado Central. Four decades later, I looked forward to the days of celebration marked by religious masses, processions, music, dance, and feasting. The host, or *mayordoma*, of the series of events in 2017 was an unmarried woman, the owner of a dry goods stall, who told me she had committed to the vast undertaking out of her faith, motivated in part because this was the hundredth anniversary of the Virgin's presence as patron saint of the market. On my departure day before my overnight bus ride to Lima, I paid my respects to the generations of marketers who came along decades after my earliest forays in Huaraz, Vicos, and the Callejón de Huaylas. I was moved once again by the resilience and initiative of these Andean women and men who still contend with so much uncertainty in their lives.

In *Women's Place in the Andes*, more than simply offering a collection of my past essays, I have engaged in a self-critical process of locating my writings in the historical contexts in which they were written and then reexamining them from the present vantage point of emergent decolonial feminisms. Ultimately, my objective has been to work toward a decolonial feminist anthropology of gender, race, and indigeneity that recognizes culturally diverse individuals in all their complexity, as neither saints nor sinners, neither iconic heroes nor pitiable victims. If I inspire others to undertake their own reflections and contribute to what I hope will be a growing and vigorous discussion of gender, race, and other axes of power in Latin America and beyond, I will be more than satisfied.

Notes

INTRODUCTION

1. Among the many sources on the period of political conflict in Peru between 1980 and 2000, a useful place to start would be González 2011.

2. One of the earliest feminist researchers in Peru, Violeta Sara-Lafosse (1983, 1984) wrote several short pieces in the 1970s on Peruvian women and families, though she is best known for her work a decade later on Andean migrant women working as seamstresses and in communal kitchens in Lima.

3. Much writing has grown out of the feminist gatherings during this period, from the small but significant one held in Buenos Aires, Argentina, in 1974 involving pioneering feminist Latin Americanist scholars, to the large-scale UN conferences over two decades that began with Mexico City in 1975. Continent-wide Latin American feminist encuentros began in 1981, meeting every two to three years through the present; see Sternbach et al. (1992) for an appraisal of the early Latin American feminist gatherings.

4. During this early period, there were fewer Peruvian contributors to the debates on gender relations in the Andes. One writer of note was Daisy Irene Núñez del Prado Béjar (1975a, 1975b).

5. Orin Starn (1991) took anthropologists to task for overlooking the stirrings of unrest leading to Sendero Luminoso's emergence in 1980. Although some Andeanists had long documented the dissatisfaction over impoverished lives in

the Andes, by the later 1980s most were more attentive to conditions that favored instability and even war.

6. Notably, Duke University's department of women's studies devoted a year to the theme of "The Future of the Feminist 1970s," with courses, seminars, and post-doctoral fellowships to advance understanding of "how some of the major interventions of the 1970s . . . continue to have an impact on feminist thought, offer important interventions into contemporary questions, or map the futures of feminism" https://today.duke.edu/2012/06/feminism (accessed December 27, 2017).

7. I generally pluralize *decolonial feminisms* because I do not wish to suggest that there is a single unitary decolonial feminism, any more than there is a unitary feminism or a unitary category of women. In some instances, however, I refer to "a decolonial feminism" with the understanding that there are multiple ways that decolonial feminisms have been addressed.

8. I have had generous funding from the University of Iowa, the University of Florida (Vada Allen Yeomans endowment), and the University of North Carolina at Chapel Hill (Anthony Harrington endowment) in support of my research in Peru over the years. Because of family and other commitments, my trips have often ranged from one to five months, and my total time spent in Peru through the present is approximately two years.

9. I do not mean to overemphasize the geographic binary of global North and South, as there is tremendous movement in the world today and many who cross borders. It may be more useful to speak, for example, of the Americas as a broad region with shifting populations. Nevertheless, I occasionally find it helpful to refer to geopolitical differences using these terms.

10. Arguedas's life (1911–69) was celebrated in 2011, the hundred-year anniversary of his birth, with a number of events, including a seminar held at the IEP. That same year, the hundredth anniversary of the scientific discovery of Machu Picchu by Hiram Bingham, the Yale anthropologist, was commemorated. Both are considered emblematic and national treasures of Peru.

11. We can find still earlier contributions to a feminist decolonial anthropology in the work of such leading figures as Zora Neale Hurston and Eleanor Leacock, among others.

12. These are questions that feminist anthropologists have debated over several decades and which I discuss in later chapters. I argue that decolonial feminisms could be deepened by inclusion of some earlier contributions that worked through questions of egalitarianism versus universal oppression in the historical and archaeological records. Etienne and Leacock's (1980) anthology of essays on feminist ethnohistory and ethnography is one that examines the impact of colonization cross-culturally and concludes that greater egalitarianism predated colonialism in many parts of the globe.

13. There are other important contributions relating to notions of gender complementarity. Ivan Illich's (1982) early and provocative intervention argued

that "vernacular gender" relations in preindustrial societies revealed that gender differences could be in harmony and free of sexism. Feminists took issue with him largely based on Western histories of sexual inequality, but it might be worth revisiting his work in light of recent indigenous feminist theorization on the subject. Arturo Escobar (2008: 241), writing about black and indigenous communities in Colombia, notes that they are "characterized by gender relations that are different from those of modern societies, and patriarchy is not seen as operating on the same basis, given the very different configuration of family, territory, and kinship. The most common idiom to explain this difference is that of vernacular gender relations, or gender complementarity of tasks." And Silvia Rivera Cusicanqui (2010: 32) considers "gender" as a construct in Bolivia's history, particularly since the time of colonialism; she discusses the enduring Andean symbolic order based on male/female difference whereby women maintain social-spatial autonomy from men, though this is challenged by modernity.

14. Figures from the World Population Review, "Lima Population," October 20, 2017, http://worldpopulationreview.com/world-cities/lima-population/ and "Peru Population," November 10, 2017, http://worldpopulationreview.com/countries /peru-population/.

15. See Eshe Lewis's (2012) documentary *Negro soy: Voces Negras del Pacífico Peruano* for interviews and narration on the history and current situation of Afro-Peruvians.

16. See Albó (1991) for discussion of this phenomenon.

17. See Tanaka's blog postings, discussing his views on race and racism in Peru and contrasting them with those of Jorge Bruce and others, in *Virtù e Fortuna,* http://martintanaka.blogspot.com/2008/03/blog-post.html.

18. For a recent and productive discussion of these questions in the Bolivian context, see Burman 2011.

19. I once found a small notice about a meeting of homosexuals buried in a local paper in Huaraz, and there was an occasional homophobic reference to a male hairstylist and the like, but these were exceptional in my experience and concerned men more than women. For more on queering development studies, see Lind 2010 and Cornwall, Corrêa, and Jolly 2008.

PART I. GENDER AND RURAL DEVELOPMENT

COMMENTARY

1. See *Chacarera* (1997), based on an interview with Peruvian anthropologist Luis Millones (discussed later in the commentary), who examines how male bias and cultural bias have produced seriously flawed notions about Andean families and gender. He states that these notions, and particularly one expressed by

outside observers in the stereotyped phrase "Más me pegas, más te quiero" (The more you hit me, the more I love you), are twentieth-century ideological constructions of those who do not recognize the active part of Andean women in love and gender relations.

2. Indeed, in a published reference to Aida Milla de Vázquez's involvement at Vicos, Mangin (2011: 35–36), who was serving as Peace Corps director, notes that she "had started wearing Indian clothes and identifying strongly with the Vicosinos, had been antagonistic to the Peace Corps volunteers in Vicos as Yankee imperialists and had clashed with volunteer leader Roberts." He reported that tensions in Vicos had escalated to the point that some Vicosinos shouted, "Kill the gringos," something generally overlooked in the Vicos literature.

3. Ironically enough, it was during a lecture given by Richard Price many years later at the University of Iowa, when he was discussing his rereading of Malinowski's notes on Surinam, that I had the revelation that this was none other than the person whose undergraduate field report (Price 1961) and journal article (Price 1965) I had read decades before. I was struck then as I am now by the scholarly genealogies hidden away in the CPP archives—in this case, an early contribution by the anthropologist who would become without a doubt the most distinguished of any of the US participants, though he is not generally identified with the project.

4. Stein became persona non grata within the CPP circle as a result of his critical engagement with the archives and the material he collected in Vicos. As my mentor in graduate school, he never showed disrespect for the CPP participants, but he departed from the "party line" at a time when few were challenging the received wisdom on the unalloyed benefits of the modernization project.

5. Jason Pribilsky's (n.d.) history of social scientific experimentation and the modernity project in Vicos makes an important contribution to the discussion of the CPP and its legacy. In addition, Rowenn Kalman's (2017) doctoral dissertation at Michigan State University, based on her research on political ecology in Vicos, is a valuable resource.

6. That volume's inclusion of several contributors without experience in Vicos, and the omission of others who had offered earlier critiques of the CPP's success, may suggest the politicized nature of Vicos's past as a testing ground for modernization theory and social scientific experimentation.

7. Among the contributors to the volume, Doughty, Bolton, and Mayer belong in the first group, who defend the CPP against the critics, while Barnett, Ross, and Pribilsky fall in the second group, who offer needed critical assessments of the broader historical context of the Vicos project. In addition, Mangin and Mitchell offer thoughtful reflections on some of the entanglements of this experiment in applied social change. Isbell and Zapata bring the reflection on Vicos up to the present day, something that is critical to the account. For more on contem-

porary Vicos and its engagement with cultural tourism as a development strategy, see Babb 2011.

8. See the website at https://instruct1.cit.cornell.edu/courses/vicosperu/vicos-site/.

9. This is expressed by Bolton (2011: 244) in regard to critics of modernization and applied social change in the Andes and more generally.

10. The three principals I refer to are all deceased, as is my advisor, William W. Stein. While I never met any of the first three, I attempted to write respectfully of their central involvement with the CPP.

11. See Kalman 2017 for a detailed discussion of environment, new technologies, and cosmovision in contemporary Vicos. She compared the favorable views of gender complementarity espoused by the NGO Urpichallay with views held by Vicosinos. While the Vicosinos may practice forms of gender complementarity, they rarely named it as such during the period of her research in the previous five years. Like Kalman, I have found that the NGO has made well-meaning interventions based on mestizos' understanding of Andean reciprocity and complementarity. Their initiatives and training programs remind me of the CPP interventions more than a half century ago, even if the NGO appears to be resisting some of the modernist assumptions of the CPP.

12. For more discussion of feminist debates over collective cultural rights in relation to women's individual rights, see R. Aída Hernández Castillo and Liliana Suárez Navaz ([2008] 2011). Women's rights may also be viewed as collective rights, though they may sometimes be at odds with perceived cultural rights (particularly if male-defined).

13. See de la Cadena 2015 for further discussion of Andean cosmopolitics, the interactions of human and nonhuman actors, and the incommensurability of indigenous and nonindigenous worlds in the southern Peruvian Andes. As an important contribution stemming from the ontological turn in anthropology, this work reveals much of significance to our understanding of Andean notions such as gender complementarity.

14. There may well be other reasons for the silence around my work on gender relations in Vicos. The fact that the published versions began as a master's thesis, and that I was a newcomer to Andean anthropology, no doubt made the work rather easy for some to dismiss. My work also might have had more impact had I pursued publication in a more mainstream journal, but by 1977 I was in Peru for my doctoral research and was simply gratified that the Vicos monograph came out in the years that followed in new versions—if not in prominent venues.

15. This remark was made in Mannarelli's (1992) essay reviewing Silverblatt's (1987) book, which was translated into Spanish. Her essay makes a case similar to Barrig's, discussed in this commentary, expressing concern that the gender complementarity perspective idealizes the past.

CHAPTER 1. WOMEN AND MEN IN VICOS, PERU

I owe special thanks to [the late] William W. Stein, who encouraged me to write the original monograph, and to all those who offered their comments and criticisms at various stages: Elizabeth Kennedy, Margo L. Smith, Elsa M. Chaney, Meredith L. Brown, Andrés Gallardo, Barbara Nowak, Laura Sholman, and the editors of the University of Michigan Occasional Papers in Women's Studies. I am grateful to the Department of Manuscripts and University Archives at Olin Library, Cornell University, for access to the archives of the Peru-Cornell Project during August 1975. This paper could not have been written without the use of field data gathered by the following researchers: Clifford R. Barnett, William C. Blanchard, Teresa Egoavil Escobar, Allan R. Holmberg, Aida Milla de Vázquez, Stephen R. Nelson, Norman Pava, Harold Skalka, and Mario C. Vázquez. It was the cooperation of the people of Vicos, of course, that made the research project possible.

1. Translations of fieldnotes from Spanish to English are my own, and editing has been minor. The names of Vicosinos have been changed to protect their privacy. Dates given for fieldnotes are complete wherever possible; however, in some cases only the month and year, or the year alone, was recorded.

2. For this reason, and for clarity, the ethnographic present is used in this section.

3. "PCP" before fieldworkers' names indicates unpublished field data from the archives of the Peru-Cornell Project.

4. Núñez del Prado Béjar (1975b: 625) notes that in Huaro, Peru, a yoke of oxen will replace a husband, but only another woman will replace a wife.

5. The situation of younger women without husbands is sometimes just as difficult when there are children to raise. One woman with young children was abandoned by her husband, an absentee peon whose land was confiscated, leaving her to cope with the situation (Stein 1975b).

6. Boserup (1970: 56) shows that, in Africa, where in many cases women do most of the farming, Europeans' ignorance of women's role led to the deterioration of their position in production when modern techniques were introduced only to men. She writes, "Such a development has the unavoidable effect of enhancing the prestige of men and lowering the status of women. It is the men who do the modern things."

7. Holmberg (1967: 7) writes that "hacienda overseers and their assistants employed whips on slow or recalcitrant serfs, probably from early colonial times." He (Holmberg 1971: 37) indicates, "Whipping serfs by labor bosses reportedly ended about 1928 when an Indian protest over this practice brought a central government order to end it." Perhaps this refers to the purpose of punishing persons who did not attend prayer services during Lent (Holmberg 1967: 7). At any rate, whippings by the hacienda staff did occur during the early 1950s.

8. In another listing of skills by sex (PCP: Holmberg 10/8/53), the men's list includes thirty-nine skills, the women's list includes eight, and a third list of skills performed by both sexes includes nineteen skills. It is revealing that the men's list contains a good number of skills introduced by the project, while none of the eight skills of women are new ones. Furthermore, the men's list is highly specific, with such skills as "casket carrying" and "scissors using," while the women's list includes only the broad categories of women's work—for example, "spinning" and "cooking." In addition, the majority of skills in the third list are generally performed by women. We must conclude that, not only did the project overlook women when it introduced new skills, but also members were uninterested in, or unaware of, the work women traditionally performed.

9. DeWind (1975) describes how wives of miners in Peru were taught homemaking skills to keep them "happy" (nonmilitant).

10. As a field-worker, Milla de Vázquez (PCP: 9/30/57) was offered a separate room in which to eat apart from her host family. This suggests that eating apart is not strictly a male prerogative but a sign of respect—which most Vicos men do not expect in the home.

11. Enrollment records taken by Vázquez in 1954 show that only 11 women relatives substituted regularly for men among a total of 245 peons (Stein 1975b).

12. It should be remembered that Vicosinos were not completely outside the cash economy before the project, since periodic wage labor goes back to colonial times. For a discussion of wage labor from the sixteenth to the eighteenth century in Peru, see Spalding (1967: 56–58). Vázquez (1971: 82) notes that the wage rate increased from twelve to fifteen soles for men, and from five to eight soles for women, working in surrounding towns during the years of the project.

13. See Sacks (1974) for a reconsideration of Engels's explanation of the decline of women's position when men enter social production.

14. Benston (1971: 282) writes, "In a society in which money determines value, women are a group who work outside the money economy. Their work is not worth money, is therefore valueless, is therefore not even real work. And women themselves, who do this valueless work, can hardly be expected to be worth as much as men, who work for money."

15. See Illich (1973) for a discussion of this situation as it applies to Latin America as a whole.

16. The Vicosinos, however, twice mobilized and obtained changes in the school, in 1961 and 1971 (Stein 1975a: 39).

17. A lack of machismo among peasant men has been noted by Chiñas (1973) and Elmendorf (1972) in Mexican communities.

18. See Arizpe (1975b) for a discussion on this subject.

19. For a consideration of women's position in other parts of rural Peru, see Bourque and Warren (1976, 1981b).

20. I use the concept of underdevelopment as discussed by Frank (1969).

PART II. GENDER AND THE URBAN INFORMAL
ECONOMY

COMMENTARY

1. For years I had a Peruvian poster from that time on my office wall saying, "¡No a los concursos de belleza!" See the film *Miss Universe in Peru* for a critical view of Peru's 1982 indulgence in the global pageant during the period of violence in the country.

2. See anthologies coedited by June Nash and Helen Safa (1976, 1986), which made use of this analytic yet also went beyond it. My own contribution to the latter volume appears as chapter 3 in this book. In it, I challenge the production/reproduction binary in relation to marketers' work. For Marxists and Marxist feminists, *production* generally refers to work that has exchange value in the capitalist economy, while *reproduction* generally refers to unpaid domestic labor that serves to reproduce society (housework, childcare, meal preparation, and so on).

3. See Sternbach et al. 1992 for discussion of the first decade of feminist encuentros in Latin America and the Caribbean.

4. I thank Pascha Bueno-Hansen for directing me to Francke's work.

5. See Babb 2017 for more on gender and racial geography in Andean Peru.

6. A decade later, Peruvian economist Hernando de Soto (1989) published his book *The Other Path*, which issued a neoliberal call for formalizing the informal sector by cutting bureaucratic red tape. The work was translated into a number of languages and had an outsize influence, championing informal-sector entrepreneurs but failing to address the structures of inequality that prevented many from succeeding.

7. It is a mark of my respect that I discuss these authors' work at some length here and in other chapters, even if I come to different conclusions in some cases. Indeed, I organized a conference panel for the 2010 meetings of the American Anthropological Association titled "Are Andean Women Still 'Más Indias'? The Re-circulation of Gender and Indigenous Identities," based on de la Cadena's pivotal work. She herself was unable to attend as discussant, but offered thoughtful remarks.

8. Notwithstanding my critique of the public/private binary, there have been some important feminist interventions recently that take up Latin American women's activism in the public sphere, and which use the concept to stress the ways in which women have gained space in areas conventionally considered masculine arenas. See, for example, Phillips and Cole 2013.

CHAPTER 2. WOMEN IN THE MARKETPLACE

Funding for fieldwork in Peru in 1977 was provided under a grant-in-aid awarded to William W. Stein by the State University of New York Research Foundation.

My return to Peru in 1982 was made possible in part through the generosity of the organization Perú Mujer, which provided travel funds to Lima. I thank Bill Stein, Liz Kennedy, Karen Sacks, and Jane Collier for their comments on earlier versions of the material presented here (Babb 1980b, 1981). The paper has undergone revision, based on my revisit to Peru and the recommendations of reviewers for the *Review of Radical Political Economics*, for which I am most grateful. Most of all, I am indebted to the marketers of Huaraz, Peru, whose friendship and cooperation enabled me to carry out my research. Any shortcomings are my own.

1. Important examples of this research are Katzin's (1959) research on Jamaican "higglers," Chiñas's (1973, 1975, 1976) work on Isthmus Zapotec women who trade, Sudarkasa's (1973) study of Yoruba women's trading and domestic activities, and Jellinek's (1977) account of one Jakarta street seller.

2. For discussion of this imprecision in the terminology and conceptualization of small-scale marketers, see Bromley (1978a, 1978b) and Bromley and Gerry (1979).

3. While these producers direct themselves toward household provisioning or reproduction of subsistence requirements, this is not due to any underlying psychological orientation. I agree with Deere and de Janvry's (1979) criticism of the view that the simple reproduction of petty commodity producers is behaviorally motivated. As they point out, the inability to accumulate must be explained by reference to surplus extraction (e.g., unequal terms of trade, taxation through market fees).

4. See Edholm, Harris, and Young (1977) for clarification of the concept of reproduction as it is used to theorize the situation of women and women's work. In this paper, I refer to the process of social reproduction, particularly as it concerns the regeneration of the labor force.

5. I agree with those critics (e.g., Fee 1976) of the debate over whether women's work, especially housework, is productive or unproductive, who note that the discussion is often beside the point and does not contribute to an understanding of the relationship of women's work to the wider economy. However, insofar as the differentiation of productive and unproductive labor has remained a central question for Marxists (e.g., Meiksins 1981) *and* the issue has divided analysts of petty marketing—as discussed in this paper—I take it up here.

6. Fitzgerald (1976: 50) and Strasma (1976: 310) comment on marketing policy during this period. Stein (1978: 140–150) discusses Peruvian government concern with food prices, before and during Velasco's presidency, in terms of the problem of national underdevelopment. For a discussion of economic policy through the recent period of military rule, see Thorp and Bertram (1978) and Fitzgerald (1979). Grompone (1981) and Osterling (n.d.) review the current situation of Lima's *ambulantes* (street vendors) in terms of uneven development in Peru.

7. For reviews of recent developments in Peru, see Petras and Havens (1979), Bollinger (1980), and articles in the *Latin American Working Group Newsletter* (1980).

8. This questionnaire, administered to twenty-seven individuals, may be found in Babb (1981). Questions that were asked concerned personal background and work history, marketing activities and relations with wholesalers and customers, and views on women's and men's work and recent developments in Peru. The questionnaire was designed to supplement the data collected in my more numerous informal interviews.

9. For recent analyses of Peruvian women's activity in commerce and in other sectors of the subsistence and capitalist economy, see Mercado (1978), Figueroa and Anderson (1981), Bourque and Warren (1981b), and Bunster and Chaney (1985).

10. Elsewhere I have described the situation of Huaraz women in petty commerce within the socioeconomic context of Peruvian underdevelopment (Babb 1979), and the recent government campaign against marketers (Babb 1982).

11. See Stein (1974) for a class analysis of Andean social structure. For an analysis that considers class, ethnicity, and sex in the Andes, see Bourque and Warren (1980).

12. See Schmitz (1982) for a discussion of the structural constraints (e.g., access to resources, relation to large-scale enterprises) that limit the growth of small-scale enterprises.

13. The *control* of retail activity often lies elsewhere, however. See Babb (1982) for a discussion of national and international control of marketing in Peru.

14. This quotation and others in this section are taken from my original fieldnotes, collected in Huaraz in 1977. Translations from the Spanish are my own.

15. I was aware of five market unions in Huaraz in 1977. The two principal unions each had several hundred members. The largest was the Union of Market Workers, founded in 1965 and, by 1977, affiliated with the Confederation of Workers of the Peruvian Revolution, a labor organization sponsored by the Peruvian government as an alternative to party-affiliated labor unions. The second largest was the Union of Retailers and Sellers, in existence for over a decade and affiliated with the General Confederation of Peruvian Workers, the labor union federation connected with the Communist Party in Peru.

CHAPTER 3. PRODUCERS AND REPRODUCERS

Earlier versions of this chapter were presented in Lima in 1982 at the Congress on Research on Women in the Andean Region, organized by Perú Mujer, and in Mexico City in 1983 at the Congress of the Latin American Studies Association. I gratefully acknowledge the useful comments of participants at these conferences. Gabriela Núñez offered constructive criticisms of the present version. Field research in 1977 was supported by a grant-in-aid awarded to William W. Stein by the State University of New York Research Foundation. In 1982, travel funds were provided by Perú Mujer. I am especially indebted to the marketers of

Huaraz, Peru, for without their friendship and cooperation this research would not have been possible.

1. For discussion of male bias in assessing women's work in agriculture in the Andes, see Bourque and Warren (1981a) and Deere and León de Leal (1981).

2. Household diversification may be viewed at the family level as a strategy for coping with poverty and for spreading the risk of failure in any one endeavor, but it should be viewed at the broader level as a response to economic underdevelopment in Peru (Babb 1981).

3. This occurs in a way parallel to that described by Deere (1982). She notes that the household in the Peruvian Andes yields use values and exchange values; here I note the similar phenomenon in the Huaraz markets, where both exchange values and use values are created.

4. Esculies et al. (1977) point out that 99 percent of retail activities in Peru are in the hands of small sellers.

5. Despite the shared labor process of male and female marketers, there *are* critical differences between the situation of women marginalized in the least-remunerated sales and that of men in capital-intensive commerce. This is discussed further in Babb (1984b).

6. See Mercado (1978) and Bunster (1983) for discussion of Lima market women and street vendors. Their Lima research calls attention to the integrated work activities of women who carry the double load of household responsibility and petty commerce. Figueroa and Anderson (1981) also include women in commerce in their useful overview of Peruvian women.

7. For example, the dual society, or traditional/modern sector, view (Frank 1969), or the informal/formal economy model (Bromley 1978b).

CHAPTER 4. MARKET/PLACES AS GENDERED SPACES

1. In this chapter, all references to "this volume" and "present volume" point to Seligmann (2001), *Women Traders in Cross-cultural Perspective: Mediating Identities, Marketing Wares*. I was invited to comment on this collection of writings on women marketers and to discuss new directions in research.

PART III. GENDERED POLITICS OF WORK, TOURISM, AND CULTURAL IDENTITY

COMMENTARY

1. Another version of the work was presented in 1985 at a political economy conference, "Economic Anthropology: Critiques and Applications," at the University of Utah. I was in the company of other anthropologists, including Scott

Cook and William Roseberry, at that small gathering addressing radical political economy.

2. For an excellent discussion of traveling feminist theories and the challenges of translation across the Americas, see Alvarez et al. 2014.

3. In fact, beginning in the early 1990s in Nicaragua, my research engaged with cultural questions and cultural struggles (Babb 2001a).

4. Feminist analysts based outside Peru have contributed important book-length accounts of gender injustice that took place during the period of violence (Bueno-Hansen 2015; Theidon 2004). Several Peruvian writers have addressed the physical and psychological violence perpetrated against women during that time, something that goes beyond the scope of the present discussion.

5. World March of Women, http://lofcamp.pl/world-march-of-women/, accessed May 14, 2016 (site discontinued).

6. Lydia Simas, "Women of the Americas March in Peru," Grassroots International, November 25, 2015, https://grassrootsonline.org/blog/newsblogwomen-americas-march-peru/.

7. Wide+ website, http://wideplus.org/news/the-13th-encuentro-feminista-latinoamericano-y-del-caribe-in-peru-lima-22–25-november-2014/, May 14, 2016 (page discontinued).

CHAPTER 5. WOMEN'S WORK

My lighthearted title is chosen for its double meaning, calling attention to research on women and women's work and suggesting that it may be "women's work" to engender economic anthropology. Indeed women's research and writing may result in a transformation of the subfield. However, bringing gender analysis to economic anthropology can be the work of men and women alike.

1. Some anthropologists might question whether gender is indeed a unit of analysis; however, those who spend a good deal of time thinking about gender in society describe it as "a category of analysis" (*Feminist Studies,* 1987), and it seems unnecessary to quarrel over the terminology. See also the excellent discussion of gender as a category of historical analysis by Scott (1986).

2. See, however, Stein (1986) for some cautionary remarks about taking units of analysis as static categories. I agree that the real emphasis ought to be placed on social relations, which often cut across several "units," such as community, region, nation.

3. To represent the mainstream, I refer to frequently cited texts as well as to the annual proceedings of the Society for Economic Anthropology and to the research annual *Research in Economic Anthropology.* Plattner (1986: 962) calls these two publication series "the quality edge of economic anthropology."

4. For a model case study of the way historical processes have structured unequal economic opportunity for women and men and an argument for the inclusion of gender as a variable, see Hansen's (1980a) study from Lusaka, Zambia.

5. For a discussion of "economic woman" in African marketing, see Robertson (1974).

6. It should be noted that men and women do not represent homogeneous categories of analysis. Social differentiation is based not only on gender but also on social class, ethnicity, and other phenomena. While it is reductionist to disregard gender differences, so it would be reductionist to take gender relations as the only meaningful social relationship. Here, however, I emphasize the need for gender-conscious analysis in economic anthropology.

7. Since this article was prepared for publication, later volumes of these two series have appeared with an average of one to two articles addressing gender issues.

8. There is wide disagreement over the concept of the "informal sector" and its usefulness relative to other concepts, such as "petty commodity production" and "casual work" (Bromley and Gerry 1979). I do not refer to the "informal" and "formal" sectors in the dualistic, static sense, but rather I refer to interlinking and changing sectors of the economy within which the informal is rendered subordinate to the dominant capitalist, formal, sector (Babb 1985b).

9. See, however, Scott (1979) for a discussion of some hidden forms of dependency among Lima's "self-employed" workers in petty manufacturing and commerce.

10. Although they are British *sociologists*, Long and Roberts and their anthropologist colleagues situate their research in the Mantaro Valley largely within the discourse of economic anthropology.

11. I offer a more extended review of Long and Roberts (1984) in Babb (1987c).

12. Elsewhere, Long (Long and Roberts 1984) introduces an anthology on work and the family in rural societies by noting the central importance of women's work and the changing division of labor within households. Perhaps this recognition will inform his future research.

13. Other well-known studies have discussed women as active economic participants in the Peruvian Andes (e.g., Bourque and Warren 1981b; Deere and León de Leal 1981). Here I draw heavily on Mallon's work because it provides so fine a comparison with Long's and Roberts's research conducted in the same region; moreover, although Mallon did not set out to examine gender, she presents a persuasive argument for the need to do so.

14. For more extensive discussion of my research with Huaraz market women, see Babb (1986, 1987a, [1989] 1998).

15. Nash (1986: 16) makes this point in her review of Latin American research over the last decade, noting that there has been a gradual integration of research

on women into the mainstream of the social sciences. Yet Nash and Safa (1986: ii) state, "It is still all too prevalent to read about the peasantry, migration, or the informal economy in Latin America without recognition of the importance of gender differences."

CONCLUSION

1. Marisol de la Cadena was to be a discussant on this panel but was unfortunately unable to attend that year's American Anthropological Association conference. Another discussant, Linda Seligmann, offered valuable remarks on the papers presented.

2. Radcliffe (2015) offers an excellent critique of urban feminist and gender-and-development perspectives as they shape thinking about rural indigenous women in Ecuador.

3. See Mohanty, Russo, and Torres (1991) for a critical discussion of Western feminism's tendency to collapse "Third World women" into a homogeneous category rather than to recognize either the complexity of lives marked by intersectionality, or the mutual imbrication of gender, race, class, sexuality, and nation.

4. Several participants were unable to attend but circulated papers, mentioned here.

5. See Hale and Stephen (2013) for a collection of collaborative research findings supported by the Otros Saberes Initiative of the Latin American Studies Association.

6. In another conference session I organized along with Andrew Canessa for the 2015 meetings of the American Anthropological Association, "World Anthropologies / Decolonial Feminisms," panelists addressed two areas that are rarely part of the same conversation. Pamela Calla, Aída Hernández, Arturo Escobar, Diana Gomez Correal, Meena Khandelwal, Carolyn Martin Shaw, and Hania Sholkamy offered diverse perspectives on the need for feminists to question the geopolitics of knowledge and for world anthropologies to bring the insights of feminism to its call for understanding anthropologies "otherwise."

7. See Babb (2018) on gender and sexuality in Andean worlds for further discussion of recent scholarship.

8. This is my translation from the Spanish on the Chirapaq website, found at http://chirapaq.org.pe/es/mujeres-indigenas/equidad-de-genero (accessed August 27, 1017).

9. As I note elsewhere in this book, Julieta Paredes has more recently collaborated with Adriana Guzmán, and the two of them have conducted workshops at the Latin American and Caribbean Feminist Encuentro and other venues as communitarian feminists committed to decolonizing feminisms.

10. Despite this seeming shift in perspective, de la Cadena (2015: 111) has still more recently commented that she has not changed her mind regarding women being "más indias," does not idealize Andean lives, and still is concerned about social inequalities; I read this as an effort to deflect critiques of the ontological turn in anthropology as being insufficiently responsive to social injustices. I agree with her point that earlier work in the Andes focused more on the political, assigning a lesser status to ritual and cultural tradition. For further discussion of the cultural politics of indigeneity in Peru and elsewhere, see de la Cadena and Starn (2007).

11. Another TV show, *El Negro Mama,* ridiculed Afro-Peruvians with its lead character, a dim-witted man played in blackface by the same actor who performed the lead in *La Paisana Jacinta.* Both programs drew criticism from the United Nations for their racist representations and have been withdrawn from prime-time television in Peru.

12. See "Manifesto of the First Continental Summit of Indigenous Women," Abya Yala Net, May 27–28, 2009, www.abyayalanet.org/node/22.

13. See "For the Emancipation of Our Bodies," the political manifesto of the thirteenth Encuentro Feminista de Latinoamerica y del Caribe, November 22–25, 2014, www.scribd.com/document/239223102/Political-Manifiesto-For-the-emancipation-of-our-bodies-13-EFLAC.

14. For the thoughtful series "Decolonizing Anthropology," see contributions to the blog *Savage Minds: Notes and Queries in Anthropology* (now renamed *Anthrodendum*),April19,2016,https://savageminds.org/2016/04/19/decolonizing-anthropology/.

References

Aaby, Peter. 1977. "Engels and Women." *Critique of Anthropology* 3 (9–10): 25–53.

Adams, Richard N., and Charles C. Cumberland. 1960. *United States University Cooperation in Latin America*. East Lansing: Michigan State University, Institute of Research on Overseas Programs.

Alberti, Giorgio, and Julio Cotler. 1972. *Aspectos sociales de la educación rural en el Perú*. Lima: Instituto de Estudios Peruanos.

Albó, Xavier. 1991. "El retorno del indio." *Revista Andina* 9 (2): 299–366.

Alcalde, M. Cristina. 2010. *The Woman in the Violence: Gender, Poverty, and Resistance in Peru*. Nashville, TN: Vanderbilt University Press.

Alvarez, Sonia E., Evelina Dagnino, and Arturo Escobar, eds. 1998. *Cultures of Politics, Politics of Cultures: Re-visioning Latin American Social Movements*. Boulder, CO: Westview Press.

Alvarez, Sonia E., Claudia de Lima Costa, Verónica Feliu, Rebecca J. Hester, Norma Klahn, and Millie Thayer, eds. 2014. *Translocalities/Translocalidades: Feminist Politics of Translation in the Latin/a Américas*. Durham, NC: Duke University Press.

Ames, Patricia. 2011. "Discriminación, desigualdad y territorio: Nuevas y viejas jerarquías en definición (Perú)." In *Desarrollo, desigualdades y conflictos sociales: Una perspectiva desde los países andinos*, edited by Marcos Cueto and Adrián Lerner, 15–34. Lima: Instituto de Estudios Peruanos.

Anderson, Jeanine. 2011. "Políticas públicas y mujeres rurales en el Perú." *Mujer rural: Cambios y persistencias en América Latina.* Lima: Centro Peruano de Estudios Sociales.

Anderson de Velasco, Jeanine. 1983. *Congreso de investigación acerca de la mujer en la Región Andina: Informe final.* Lima: Asociación Perú Mujer.

Ardito Vega, Wilfredo. 2005. "Mujeres campesinas y relativismo cultural." *Chacarera* (Centro de la Mujer Flora Tristán, Lima) 31:37–38.

Arguedas, José María. 1978. *Deep Rivers.* Translated by Francis Barraclough. Austin: University of Texas Press.

Arizpe, Lourdes. 1975a. *Indígenas en la Ciudad de México: El caso de las "Marías."* Mexico: Sep/Setentas.

———. 1975b. "Mujer campesina, mujer indígena." *América Indígena* 35 (3): 575–85.

———. 1977. "Women in the Informal Labor Sector: The Case of Mexico City." *Signs* 3 (1): 25–37.

Arizpe, Lourdes, and Josefina Aranda. 1981. "The 'Comparative Advantages' of Women's Disadvantages: Women Workers in the Strawberry Export Agribusiness in Mexico." *Signs* 7 (2): 453–73.

Arnold, Denise Y., ed. 1997. *Más allá del silencio: Las fronteras de género en los andes.* La Paz, Bolivia: CIASE/ILCA.

Babb, Florence E. 1976. *The Development of Sexual Inequality in Vicos, Peru.* Council on International Studies, no. 83. Buffalo: SUNY Buffalo.

———. 1979. "Market Women and Peruvian Underdevelopment." Paper presented at the annual meeting of the American Anthropological Association, Cincinnati, Ohio.

———. 1980a. *Women and Men in Vicos, Peru: A Case of Unequal Development.* University of Michigan Occasional Papers in Women's Studies, paper no. 11. Ann Arbor: University of Michigan.

———. 1980b. "Women in the Service Sector: Petty Commerce in Peru." Paper presented at the annual meeting of the American Anthropological Association, Washington, DC.

———. 1981. "Women and Marketing in Huaraz, Peru: The Political Economy of Petty Commerce." PhD diss., SUNY Buffalo.

———. 1982. "Economic Crisis and the Assault on Marketers in Peru." Women in International Development Working Papers. East Lansing: Michigan State University.

———. 1984a. "The Analysis of Gender in Economic Anthropology." Paper presented in the session "Units of Analysis in Economic Anthropology" at the Annual Meeting of the American Anthropological Association, Denver.

———. 1984b. "Women in the Marketplace: Petty Commerce in Peru." *Review of Radical Political Economics* 16 (1): 45–59.

———. 1985a. "Middlemen and 'Marginal' Women: Marketers and Dependency in Peru's Informal Sector." In *Markets and Marketing*. Monographs in Economic Anthropology, no. 4, edited by Stuart Plattner, 287–308. Lanham, MD: University Press of America.

———. 1985b. "Women and Men in Vicos: A Peruvian Case of Unequal Development." In *Peruvian Contexts of Change*, edited by William W. Stein, 163–210. Revised version of Babb 1976. New Brunswick, NJ: Transaction Press.

———. 1986. "Producers and Reproducers: Andean Marketwomen in the Economy." In *Women and Change in Latin America*, edited by June Nash and Helen I. Safa, 53–64. South Hadley, MA: Bergin and Garvey.

———. 1987a. "From the Field to the Cooking Pot: Economic Crisis and the Threat to Marketers in Peru." *Ethnology* 26 (2): 137–49.

———. 1987b. "Marketers as Producers: The Labor Process and Proletarianization of Peruvian Marketwomen." In *Perspectives in U.S. Marxist Anthropology*, edited by David Hakken and Hanna Lessinger, 166–85. Boulder, CO: Westview Press.

———. 1987c. Review of *Miners, Peasants, and Entrepreneurs: Regional Development in the Central Highlands of Peru*, edited by Norman Long and Bryan Roberts. *American Ethnologist* 14 (4): 787–88.

———. [1989] 1998. *Between Field and Cooking Pot: The Political Economy of Marketwomen in Peru*. Rev. ed. Austin: University of Texas Press.

———. 1990. "Women's Work: Engendering Economic Anthropology." *Urban Anthropology* 19 (3): 277–302.

———. 1999. "Mujeres y hombres en Vicos, Perú: Un caso de desarrollo desigual." In *Género y Desarrollo II*, 95–116. Translation of 1980 working paper. Lima: Pontificia Universidad Católica del Perú.

———. 2001a. *After Revolution: Mapping Gender and Cultural Politics in Neoliberal Nicaragua*. Austin: University of Texas Press.

———. 2001b. "Market/Places as Gendered Spaces: Market/Women's Studies over Two Decades." In *Women Traders in Cross-Cultural Perspective: Mediating Identities, Marketing Wares*, edited by Linda J. Seligmann, 228–239. Stanford, CA: Stanford University Press.

———. 2008a. *Entre la chacra y la olla: Cultura, economía política y las vendedoras de mercado en el Perú*. Translation of [1989] 1998 book, with a new preface. Lima: Instituto de Estudios Peruanos.

———. 2008b. "Gender, Race, and Cultural Tourism in Andean Peru and Chiapas, Mexico." Paper presented in the session "Engagement, Authenticity, and Tourism: Gender, Sexuality, Ethnicity/Race, and Space in the Americas" at the annual meeting of the American Anthropological Association, San Francisco, November.

———. 2011. *The Tourism Encounter: Fashioning Latin American Nations and Histories*. Stanford, CA: Stanford University Press.

———. 2012. "Theorizing Gender, Race, and Cultural Tourism in Latin America: A View from Peru and Mexico." In "Race, Gender, Ethnicity, and Sexuality in Latin American Tourism," special issue, *Latin American Perspectives* 39 (6): 36–50.

———. 2017. "Desigualdades entrelazadas: Repensando la raza, el género y el indigenismo en el Perú andino." In *Racismo y lenguaje en el Perú*, edited by Virginia Zavala and Michele Back. Lima: PUCP Press (Fondo Editorial PUCP).

———. 2018. "Gender and Sexuality." In *The Andean World*, edited by Linda J. Seligmann and Kathleen S. Fine-Dare. Routledge Worlds series. New York: Routledge.

Bailón, Jaime, and Alberto Nicoli. 2010. *Chicha Power: El marketing se reinventa*. Lima, Peru: Universidad de Lima.

Barlow, Kathleen. 1985. "The Role of Women in Intertribal Trade among the Murik of Papua New Guinea." In *Research in Economic Anthropology*, vol. 7, edited by Barry L. Isaac, 95–122. Greenwich, CT: JAI Press.

Barnett, Clifford. 1960. "An Analysis of Social Movements on a Peruvian Hacienda." PhD diss., Cornell University. Ann Arbor, MI: University Microfilms.

Barrig, Maruja. 2001. *El mundo al revés: Imagines de la mujer indígena*. Buenos Aires: CLACSO Consejo Latinoamericano de Ciencias Sociales.

———. 2006. "What Is Justice? Indigenous Women in Andean Development Projects." In *Women and Gender Equity in Development Theory and Practice: Institutions, Resources, and Mobilization*, edited by Jane S. Jaquette and Gale Summerfield, 107–34. Durham, NC: Duke University Press.

———, ed. 2007. *Fronteras interiores: Identidad, diferencia y protagonismo de las mujeres*. Lima: Instituto de Estudios Peruanos.

Baud, Michiel, and Annelou Ypeij, eds. 2009. *Cultural Tourism in Latin America: The Politics of Space and Imagery*. Leiden: Brill.

Behar, Ruth. 1990. "Rage and Redemption: Reading the Life Story of a Mexican Marketing Woman." *Feminist Studies* 16 (2): 223–58.

———. 1993. *Translated Woman: Crossing the Border with Esperanza's Story*. Boston: Beacon Press.

Behar, Ruth, and Deborah Gordon, eds. 1995. *Women Writing Culture*. Berkeley: University of California Press.

Benería, Lourdes. 1979. "Reproduction, Production, and the Sexual Division of Labour." *Cambridge Journal of Economics* 3:203–25.

———. 1981. "Accounting for Women's Work." In *Women in Development*, edited by Lourdes Benería, 119–47. New York: Praeger.

Benería, Lourdes, and Gita Sen. 1981. "Accumulation, Reproduction, and Women's Role in Economic Development: Boserup Revisited." *Signs* 7 (2): 338–60.

Benston, Margaret. 1971. "The Political Economy of Women's Liberation." In *Voices from Women's Liberation*, edited by Leslie B. Tanner. New York: Signet.

Berreman, Gerald D., ed. 1981. *Social Inequality: Comparative and Development Approaches*. New York: Academic Press.

Bloch, Maurice, ed. 1975. *Marxist Analyses and Social Anthropology*. New York: John Wily and Sons.

Boesten, Jelke. 2010. *Intersecting Inequalities: Women and Social Policy in Peru, 1990–2000*. University Park: Pennsylvania State University Press.

Bollinger, William. 1980. "Peru Today—the Roots of Labor Militancy." *North American Congress on the Americas* 14 (6): 2–35.

Bolton, Ralph. 2011. "Chijnaya—the Birth and Evolution of an Andean Community: Memories and Reflections of an Applied Anthropologist." In *Vicos and Beyond: A Half Century of Applying Anthropology in Peru*, edited by Tom Greaves, Ralph Bolton, and Florencia Zapata, 215–63. Lanham, MD: AltaMira Press.

Boserup, Ester. 1970. *Woman's Role in Economic Development*. New York: St. Martin's Press.

Bošković, Aleksandar. 2010. *Other People's Anthropologies: Ethnographic Practice on the Margins*. New York: Berghahn Books.

Bossen, Laurel. 1984. *The Redivision of Labor: Women and Economic Choice in Four Guatemalan Communities*. Albany: SUNY Press.

Bourdieu, Pierre. 1984. *Distinction: A Social Critique of the Judgment of Taste*. London: Routledge and Kegan Paul.

Bourque, Susan C., and Kay B. Warren. 1976. "Campesinas and Comuneras: Subordination in the Sierra." *Journal of Marriage and the Family* 38:781–88.

———. 1980. "Multiple Arenas for State Expansion: Class, Ethnicity and Sex in Rural Peru." *Ethnic and Racial Studies* 3 (3): 264–80.

———. 1981a. "Rural Women and Development Planning in Peru." In *Women and World Change*, edited by Naomi Black and Ann Baker Cottrell, 183–97. Beverly Hills, CA: Sage.

———. 1981b. *Women of the Andes: Patriarchy and Social Change in Two Peruvian Towns*. Ann Arbor: University of Michigan Press.

Bracamonte Allaín, Jorge, ed. 2001. *De amores y luchas: Diversidad sexual, derechos humanos, y ciudadanía*. Lima: Centro de la Mujer Peruana Flora Tristán.

Bridenthal, Renate. 1976. "The Dialectics of Production and Reproduction in History." *Radical America* 10 (2): 3–11.

Bromley, Ray. 1978a. "Organization, Regulation and Exploitation in the So-Called 'Urban Informal Sector': The Street Traders of Cali, Colombia." *World Development* 6 (9–10): 1161–71.

———, ed. 1978b. "The Urban Informal Sector: Critical Perspectives." Special issue, *World Development* 6 (9–10).

Bromley, Ray, and Chris Gerry, eds. 1979. *Casual Work and Poverty in Third World Cities.* New York: John Wiley and Sons.

Brown, Wendy. 2008. "The Impossibility of Women's Studies." In *Women's Studies on the Edge,* edited by Joan Wallach Scott, 17–38. Durham, NC: Duke University Press.

Bruce, Jorge. 2007. *Nos habíamos choleado tanto: Psicoanálisis y racismo.* Lima: Universidad de San Martín de Porres.

Buechler, Judith-Maria. 1972. "Peasant Marketing and Social Revolution in the Province of La Paz, Bolivia." PhD diss., Department of Anthropology, McGill University.

———. 1976. "Las Negociantes-Contratistas en los Mercados Bolivianos." *Estudios Andinos* 12:57–76.

Bueno-Hansen, Pascha. 2015. *Feminist and Human Rights Struggles in Peru: Decolonizing Transitional Justice.* Urbana: University of Illinois Press.

Bujra, Janet M. 1982. "Introductory: Female Solidarity and the Sexual Division of Labour." In *Women United, Women Divided,* edited by Patricia Caplan and Janet M. Bujra, 13–45. Bloomington: Indiana University Press.

Bunster, Ximena. 1983. "Market Sellers in Lima, Peru: Talking about Work." In *Women and Poverty in the Third World.* edited by Mayra Buvinić and Margaret A. Lycette, and William Paul McGreevey, 92–103. Baltimore: Johns Hopkins University Press.

Bunster, Ximena, and Elsa M. Chaney. 1985. *Sellers and Servants: Working Women in Lima.* New York: Praeger.

Burman, Anders. 2011. "*Chachawarmi:* Silence and Rival Voices on Decolonisation and Gender Politics in Andean Bolivia." *Journal of Latin American Studies* 43:65–91.

Burton, Michael L., and Douglas R. White. 1987. "Sexual Division of Labor in Agriculture." In *Household Economies and Their Transformations,* edited by Morgan D. Maclachlan, 107–30. Monographs in Economic Anthropology, no. 3. Lanham, MD: University Press of America.

Canessa, Andrew, ed. 2005. *Natives Making Nation: Gender, Indigeneity, and the State in the Andes.* Tucson: University of Arizona Press.

———. 2012a. "Gender, Indigeneity, and the Performance of Authenticity in Latin American Tourism." *Latin American Perspectives* 39 (6): 109–15.

———. 2012b. *Intimate Indigeneities: Race, Sex, and History in the Small Spaces of Andean Life.* Durham, NC: Duke University Press.

Caplan, Patricia, and Janet M. Bujra, eds. 1982. *Women United, Women Divided*. Bloomington: Indiana University Press.

Carpio, Lourdes. 1975. "The Rural Woman in Peru: An Alarming Contradiction." In *Women in the Struggle for Liberation*. Dayton, OH: Women's Project, World Student Christian Federation.

Caulfield, Mina Davis. 1974. "Imperialism, the Family, and Cultures of Resistance." *Socialist Revolution*, no. 20: 67–85.

Chacarera (Centro de la Mujer Flora Tristán, Lima). 1997. "Un mito que hay que destruir: Conversación con Luis Millones." Pp. 14–16.

Chaney, Elsa M. 1976. "Women at the 'Marginal Pole' of the Economy in Lima, Peru." Paper presented at the conference "Women and Development," Wellesley, MA.

Chiñas, Beverly. 1973. *The Isthmus Zapotecs: Women's Roles in Cultural Context*. New York: Holt, Rinehart and Winston.

———. 1975. *Mujeres de San Juan: La mujer Zapoteca del Istmo*. Mexico City: Sep/Setentas.

———. 1976. "Zapotec *Viajeras*." In *Markets in Oaxaca*, edited by Scott Cook and Martin Diskin, 169–88. Austin: University of Texas Press.

Clammer, John, ed. 1978. *The New Economic Anthropology*. New York: St. Martin's Press.

———. 1985. *Anthropology and Political Economy*. London: Macmillan.

Clark, Gracia, ed. 1988. *Traders vs. the State: Anthropological Approaches to Unofficial Economies*. Boulder, CO: Westview Press.

———. 1994. *Onions Are My Husband: Survival and Accumulation by West African Market Women*. Chicago: University of Chicago Press.

Clifford, James, and George E. Marcus, eds. 1986. *Writing Culture: The Poetics and Politics of Ethnography*. Berkeley: University of California Press.

Cohen, Robin, Peter C. W. Gutkind, and Phyllis Brazier, eds. 1979. *Peasants and Proletarians: The Struggles of Third World Workers*. New York: Monthly Review Press.

Comaroff, John L., and Jean Comaroff. 2009. *Ethnicity, Inc.* Chicago: University of Chicago Press.

Comunidad Campesina de Vicos. 2005. *Memorias de la Comunidad de Vicos: Así nos recordamos con alegría*. Huaraz, Peru: Mountain Institute and Asociación Urpichallay.

Cornwall, Andrea, Sonia Corrêa, and Susie Jolly, eds. 2008. *Development with a Body: Sexuality, Human Rights and Development*. London: Zed Press.

Cotler, Julio, and Ricardo Cuenca, eds. 2011. *Las desigualdades en el Perú: Balances críticos*. Lima: Instituto de Estudios Peruanos.

Crain, Mary M. 1996. "The Gendering of Ethnicity in the Ecuadorian Andes: Native Women's Self-Fashioning in the Urban Marketplace." In *Machos,*

Mistresses, Madonnas: Contesting the Power of Latin American Gender Imagery, edited by Marit Melhuus and Kristi Anne Stolen. London: Verso.

Crenshaw, Kimberle. 1989. "Demarginalizing the Intersection of Race and Sex: A Black Feminist Critique of Antidiscrimination Doctrine, Feminist Theory and Antiracist Politics." *University of Chicago Legal Forum*, no. 1: 139–67.

Critique of Anthropology. 1977. 3 (9–10).

Cuche, Denys. 1975. *Poder blanco y resistencia negra en el Perú*. Lima: Instituto Nacional de Cultura.

Cueto, Marcos, and Adrián Lerner, eds. 2011. *Desarrollo, desigualdades y conflictos sociales: Una perspectiva desde los países andinos*. Lima: Instituto de Estudios Peruanos.

Dahlberg, Frances, ed. 1983. *Woman the Gatherer*. New Haven, CT: Yale University Press.

Dalla Costa, Mariarosa. 1972. "Women and the Subversion of the Community." *Radical America* 6 (1): 67–102.

Dalton, George, ed. 1967. *Tribal and Peasant Economies*. Garden City, NY: Natural History Press.

———, ed. 1978, 1979, 1980, 1981, 1983. *Research in Economic Anthropology: A Research Annual*. Vols. 1–5. Greenwich, CT: JAI Press.

Deere, Carmen Diana. 1977. "Changing Social Relations of Production and Peruvian Peasant Women's Work." *Latin American Perspectives* 4 (1–2): 48–69.

———. 1982. "The Allocation of Familial Labor and the Formation of Peasant Household Income in the Peruvian Sierra." In *Women and Poverty in the Third World*, edited by Mayra Buvinic and Margaret A. Lycette, 104–29. Baltimore: Johns Hopkins University Press.

Deere, Carmen Diana, and Alain de Janvry. 1979. "A Conceptual Framework for the Empirical Analysis of Peasants." *American Journal of Agricultural Economics* 61 (4): 601–11.

Deere, Carmen Diana, and Magdalena León de Leal. 1981. "Peasant Production, Proletarianization, and the Sexual Division of Labor in the Andes." *Signs* 7 (2): 338–60.

de la Cadena, Marisol. 1991. "'Las mujeres son más indias': Etnicidad y género en una comunidad del Cusco." *Revista Andina* 9 (1): 7–47.

———. 1995. "'Women Are More Indian': Ethnicity and Gender in a Community Near Cuzco." *Ethnicity, Markets, and Migration in the Andes: At the Crossroads of History and Anthropology*, edited by Brooke Larson and Olivia Harris, 329–43. Durham, NC: Duke University Press.

———. 2000. *Indigenous Mestizos: The Politics of Race and Culture in Cuzco, Peru, 1919–1991*. Durham, NC: Duke University Press.

———. 2006. "The Production of Other Knowledges and Its Tensions: From Andeanist Anthropology to *Interculturalidad?*" In *World Anthropologies:*

Disciplinary Transformations within Systems of Power, edited by Gustavo Lins Ribeiro and Arturo Escobar, 201–24. New York: Berg.

———. 2008. "Alternative Indigeneities: Conceptual Proposals." *Latin American and Caribbean Ethnic Studies* 3 (3): 341–49.

———. 2010. "Indigenous Cosmopolitics in the Andes: Conceptual Reflections beyond 'Politics.'" *Cultural Anthropology* 25 (2): 334–70.

———. 2015. *Earth Beings: Ecologies of Practice across Andean Worlds*. Durham, NC: Duke University Press.

de la Cadena, Marisol, and Orin Starn, eds. 2007. *Indigenous Experience Today*. New York: Berg.

de la Puente, Roberto, dir. 2011. *Choleando: Racismo en el Perú*. Distributed by Relapso Filmes and IDM. Documentary.

Desacatos: Revista de Antropología Social (Centro de Investigaciones y Estudios Superiores en Antropología Social, Distrito Federal, México). 2009. "Reivindicaciones étnicas, género y justicia." Special issue, no. 31:7–10.

de Soto, Hernando. 1989. *The Other Path: Invisible Revolution in the Third World*. New York: Harper and Row.

DeWind, Adrian. 1975. "From Peasants to Miners: The Background to Strikes in the Mines of Peru." *Science and Society* 39 (1): 44–72.

Diamond, Stanley, ed. 1979. *Toward a Marxist Anthropology: Problems and Perspectives*. New York: Mouton.

Dobyns, Henry F. 1971. "Enlightenment and Skill Foundation of Power." In *Peasants, Power, and Applied Social Change: Vicos as a Model*, edited by Henry F. Dobyns, Paul L. Doughty, and Harold D. Lasswell, 137–66. Beverly Hills, CA: Sage.

———. 1974. "The Cornell-Peru Project: Experimental Intervention in Vicos." In *Contemporary Cultures and Societies of Latin America*, edited by Dwight B. Heath. 2nd ed. New York: Random House.

Dobyns, Henry F., Paul L. Doughty, and Harold D. Lasswell, eds. 1971. *Peasants, Power, and Applied Social Change: Vicos as a Model*. Beverly Hills, CA: Sage.

Doughty, Paul L. 1971. "Human Relations: Affection, Rectitude, and Respect." In *Peasants, Power, and Applied Social Change: Vicos as a Model*, edited by Henry F. Dobyns, Paul L. Doughty, and Harold D. Lasswell, 89–113. Beverly Hills, CA: Sage.

Draper, Patricia. 1975. "!Kung Women: Contrasts in Sexual Egalitarianism in Foraging and Sedentary Contexts." In *Toward an Anthropology of Women*, edited by Rayna Rapp Reiter, 77–109. New York: Monthly Review Press.

Eber, Christine, and Christine Kovic, eds. 2003. *Women of Chiapas: Making History in Times of Struggle and Hope*. New York: Routledge.

Edholm, Felicity, Olivia Harris, and Kate Young. 1977. "Conceptualizing Women." *Critique of Anthropology* 3 (9–10): 101–30.

Elmendorf, Mary Lindsay. 1972. *The Mayan Woman and Change.* Centro Intercultural de Documentación, Cuaderno no. 81. Cuernavaca, Mexico: Centro Intercultural de Documentación.

Engels, Frederick. [1884] 1972. *The Origin of the Family, Private Property and the State.* New York: International Publishers.

Escobar, Arturo. 2008. *Territories of Difference: Place, Movements, Life, Redes.* Durham, NC: Duke University Press.

Esculies Larrabure, Oscar, Marcial Rubio Correa, and Verónica González del Castillo. 1977. *Comercialización de alimentos: Quiénes ganan, quiénes pagan, quiénes pierden.* Lima: Centro de Estudios y Promoción del Desarrollo.

Espinosa Miñoso, Yuderkys, Diana Gómez Correal, and Karina Ochoa Muñoz, eds. 2014. *Tejiendo de otro modo: Feminismo, epistemología y apuestas descoloniales en Abya Yala.* Popoyán, Colombia: Editorial Universidad del Cauca.

Etienne, Mona, and Eleanor Leacock, eds. 1980. *Women and Colonization: Anthropological Perspectives.* New York: Praeger.

Ewig, Christina. 2010. *Second-Wave Neoliberalism: Gender, Race, and Health Sector Reform in Peru.* University Park: Pennsylvania State University Press.

Fanon, Frantz. 1967. *A Dying Colonialism.* New York: Grove Press.

Fee, Terry. 1976. "Domestic Labor: An Analysis of Housework and Its Relation to the Production Process." *Review of Radical Political Economics* 8 (1): 1–8.

Feldman, Heidi Carolyn. 2006. *Black Rhythms of Peru: Reviving African Musical Heritage in the Black Pacific.* Middletown, CT: Wesleyan University Press.

Femenías, Blenda. 2005. *Gender and the Boundaries of Dress in Contemporary Peru.* Austin: University of Texas Press.

Feminist Studies. 1987. "A Word to Prospective Contributors." 13 (2).

———. 2008. "The 1970s Issue." 34 (3).

———. 2016. "Guidelines for Submissions." 42 (3).

Feminist Theory. 2013. "Beauty, Race and Feminist Theory in Latin America and the Caribbean" 14 (2).

Ferber, Marianne A., and Michelle L. Teiman. 1981. "The Oldest, the Most Established, and Most Quantitative of the Social Sciences—and the Most Dominated by Men: The Impact of Feminism on Economics." In *Men's Studies Modified: The Impact of Feminism on the Academic Disciplines,* edited by Dale Spender, 125–40. New York: Pergamon.

Fernandez-Kelly, María Patricia. 1981. "The Sexual Division of Labor, Development, and Women's Status." *Current Anthropology* 22 (4): 414–19.

———. 1983. *For We Are Sold, I and My People: Women and Industry in Mexico's Frontier.* Albany: SUNY Press.

Figueroa, Blanca, and Jeanine Anderson. 1981. *Women in Peru*. International Reports: Women and Society. London: Change International Reports.

Firth, Raymond, ed. 1967. *Themes in Economic Anthropology*. London: Tavistock.

Fitzgerald, E. V. K. 1976. *The State and Economic Development: Peru since 1968*. Cambridge: Cambridge University Press.

———. 1979. *The Political Economy of Peru, 1956–78: Economic Development and the Restructuring of Capital*. New York: Cambridge University Press.

Flores Galindo, Alberto. 1987. *Buscando un Inca: Identidad y utopia en las Andes*. Lima: Instituto de Apoyo Agrario.

Flores Ochoa, Jorge A. 2011. "The Case of Kuyo Chico." In *Vicos and Beyond: A Half Century of Applying Anthropology in Peru*, edited by Tom Greaves, Ralph Bolton, and Florencia Zapata, 265–79. Lanham, MD: AltaMira Press.

Foster-Carter, Aiden. 1978. "Can We Articulate 'Articulation'?" In *The New Economic Anthropology*, edited by J. Clammer, 210–49. New York: St. Martin's Press.

Francke, Marfil. 1990. "Género, clase y etnía: La trenza de la dominación." In *Tiempos de ira y amor: Nuevos actores para viejos problemas*, edited by Carlos Iván Degregori, Nelson Manrique, Gonzalo Portocarrero, and Antonio Zapata. Lima: Centro de Estudios y Promoción del Desarrollo.

Frank, Andre Gunder. 1969. "Dialectic, Not Dual Society." In *Latin America: Underdevelopment or Revolution*, 221–30. New York: Monthly Review Press.

Fraser, Nancy. 1997. *Justice Interruptus*. New York: Routledge.

Friedl, Ernestine. 1967. "The Position of Women: Appearance and Reality." *Anthropological Quarterly* 40 (3): 97–108.

———. 1975. *Women and Men: An Anthropologist's View*. New York: Holt, Rinehart and Winston.

Fuller, Norma, ed. 2004. *Jerarquías en jaque: Estudios de género en el area andina*. Lima: Red para el Desarrollo de las Ciencias Sociales en el Perú.

Galindo, María, and Julieta Paredes. 1992. *Piel, pan y sangre: Éticas y estéticas . . . feministas*. La Paz, Bolivia: Mujeres Creando.

García, María Elena. 2005. *Making Indigenous Citizens: Identity, Development, and Multicultural Activism in Peru*. Stanford, CA: Stanford University Press.

———, ed. 2008. "Indigenous Encounters in Contemporary Peru." Special issue, *Latin American and Caribbean Ethnic Studies* 3 (3).

Gerry, Chris. 1978. "Petty Production and Capitalist Production in Dakar: The Crisis of the Self-Employed." *World Development* 6 (9–10): 1147–60.

Gil Tébar, Pilar R. 1999. *Caminando en un solo corazón: Las mujeres indígenas de Chiapas*. Atenea, Spain: Universidad de Málaga.

Godelier, Maurice. 1977. *Perspectives in Marxist Anthropology*. Cambridge: Cambridge University Press.

Golash-Boza, Tanya Maria. 2011. *Yo Soy Negro: Blackness in Peru*. Gainesville: University Press of Florida.

González, Olga M. 2011. *Unveiling Secrets of War in the Peruvian Andes*. Chicago: University of Chicago Press.

Gotkowitz, Laura, ed. 2011. *Histories of Race and Racism: The Andes and Mesoamerica from Colonial Times to the Present*. Durham, NC: Duke University Press.

Greaves, Tom, and Ralph Bolton. 2011. Introduction to *Vicos and Beyond: A Half Century of Applying Anthropology in Peru*, edited by Tom Greaves, Ralph Bolton, and Florencia Zapata, vii–xiii. Lanham, MD: AltaMira Press.

Greaves, Tom, Ralph Bolton, and Florencia Zapata, eds. 2011. *Vicos and Beyond: A Half Century of Applying Anthropology in Peru*. Lanham, MD: AltaMira Press.

Greene, Shane. 2009. *Customizing Indigeneity: Paths to a Visionary Politics in Peru*. Stanford, CA: Stanford University Press.

Greenfield, Sidney M., and Arnold Strickon, eds. 1986. *Entrepreneurship and Social Change*. Monographs in Economic Anthropology, no. 2. Lanham, MD: University Press of America.

Grompone, Romeo. 1981. "Comercio ambulante: Razónes de una terca presencia." *Quehacer* 13:95–109.

Gudeman, Stephen. 1986. *Economics as Culture: Models and Metaphors of Livelihood*. Boston: Routledge and Kegan Paul.

Hakken, David, and Hanna Lessinger, eds. 1987. *Perspectives in U.S. Marxist Anthropology*. Boulder, CO: Westview Press.

Hale, Charles R., and Lynn Stephen, eds. 2013. *Otros Saberes: Collaborative Research on Indigenous and Afro-Descendant Cultural Politics*. Santa Fe, NM: SAR Press.

Halperin, Rhoda. 1980. "Ecology and Mode of Production: Seasonal Variations and the Division of Labor by Sex among Hunter-Gatherers." *Journal of Anthropological Research* 36 (3): 379–99.

Hansen, Karen Tranberg. 1980a. "The Urban Informal Sector as a Development Issue: Poor Women and Work in Lusaka, Zambia." *Urban Anthropology* 9 (2): 199–225.

———. 1980b . "When Sex Becomes a Critical Variable: Married Women and Extra-domestic Work in Lusaka, Zambia." *African Social Research*, no. 30: 831–49.

Harris, Olivia. 1981. "Households as Natural Units." In *Of Marriage and the Market: Women's Subordination Internationally and Its Lessons*, edited by Kate Young, Carol Wolkowitz, and Roslyn McCullagh, 49–67. London: Routledge and Kegan Paul.

———. 1995. "Ethnic Identity and Market Relations: Indians and Mestizos in the Andes." In *Ethnicity, Markets, and Migration in the Andes: At the*

Crossroads of History and Anthropology, edited by Brooke Larson and Olivia Harris, 351–90. Durham, NC: Duke University Press.

Harris, Olivia, and Kate Young. 1981. "Engendered Structures: Some Problems in the Analysis of Reproduction." In *The Anthropology of Pre-capitalist Societies*, edited by J. S. Kahn and J. R. Llobera, 109–47. London: Macmillan.

Harrison, Faye V., ed. [1991] 1997. *Decolonizing Anthropology: Moving Further toward an Anthropology for Liberation*. Arlington, VA: American Anthropological Association.

Hart, Keith. 1973. "Informal Income Opportunities and Urban Employment in Ghana." *Journal of Modern African Studies* 11 (1): 61–89.

Henrici, Jane. 2002. "Calling to the Money? Gender and Tourism in Peru." In *Gender/Tourism/Fun?* edited by Margaret Swain and Janet Momsen, 118–33. Elmsford, NY: Cognizant Communication Corporation.

Henríquez, Narda, ed. 1996. *Encrucijadas del saber: Los estudios de género en las ciencias sociales*. Lima: Pontificia Universidad Católica del Perú.

Hernández Castillo, R. Aída. 2005. "Between Complementarity and Inequality: Indigenous *Cosmovision* as an Element of Resistance in the Struggle of Indigenous Women." Paper presented at the conference "Indigenous Struggles in the Americas and around the World," Toronto, Canada. www.ucgs .yorku.ca/Indigenous%20 Conference/Aida_Hernandez.pdf.

Hernández Castillo, R. Aída, and Andrew Canessa, eds. 2012. *Género, complementariedades y exclusiones en Mesoamérica y los Andes*. Quito, Ecuador: Editorial Universitaria Abya-Yala; London: British Academy; and Copenhagen: International Work Group for Indigenous Affairs.

Hernández Castillo, R. Aída, and Liliana Suárez Navaz. [2008] 2011. Introduction to *Descolonizando el Feminismo: Teorías y prácticas desde los márgenes*, edited by Liliana Suárez Navaz and R. Aída Hernández Castillo, 11–28. Madrid: Ediciones Cátedra.

Herskovits, Melville J. 1940. *The Economic Life of Primitive Peoples*. New York: Knopf.

Hill, Michael. 2008. "Inca of the Blood, Inca of the Soul: Embodiment, Emotion, and Racialization in the Peruvian Mystical Tourist Industry." *Journal of the American Academy of Religion* 76:251–79.

Holmberg, Allan R. 1967. "Algunas relaciones entre la privación psicobiológica y el cambio cultural en los Andes." *América Indígena* 27:3–24.

———. 1971. "The Role of Power in Changing Values and Institutions of Vicos." In *Peasants, Power, and Applied Social Change: Vicos as a Model*, edited by Henry F. Dobyns, Paul L. Doughty, and Harold D. Lasswell, 33–64. Beverly Hills, CA: Sage.

Illich, Ivan D. 1972. *Deschooling Society*. New York: Harper and Row.

———. 1973. "The Futility of Schooling in Latin America." In *To See Ourselves*, edited by Thomas Weaver, 320–26. Glenview, IL: Scott, Foresman.

———. 1982. *Gender.* New York: Pantheon Books.

Isaac, Barry L., ed. 1984, 1985, 1987. *Research in Economic Anthropology: A Research Annual.* Vols. 6–8. Greenwich, CT: JAI Press.

Isbell, Billie Jean. [1978] 1985. *To Defend Ourselves: Ecology and Ritual in an Andean Village.* Prospect Heights, IL: Waveland.

———. 2011. "Cornell Returns to Vicos, 2005." In *Vicos and Beyond: A Half Century of Applying Anthropology in Peru,* edited by Tom Greaves, Ralph Bolton, and Florencia Zapata, 283–308. Lanham, MD: AltaMira Press.

Jaquette, Jane S., ed. 1974. *Women in Politics.* New York: John Wiley and Sons.

Jelin, Elizabeth. 1977. "Migration and Labor Force Participation of Latin American Women: The Domestic Servants in the Cities." *Signs* 3 (1): 129–41.

———. 1980. "The Bahiana in the Labor Force in Salvador, Brazil." In *Sex and Class in Latin America,* edited by June Nash and Helen I. Safa. New York: J. F. Bergin.

Jellinek, Lea. 1977. "The Life of a Jakarta Street Trader." In *Third World Urbanization,* edited by Richard Hay Jr. and Janet Abu-Lughod, 244–56. Chicago: Maaroufa Press.

Kahn, Joel S., and Josep R. Llobera, eds. 1981. *The Anthropology of Pre-capitalist Societies.* London: Macmillan.

Kalman, Rowenn. 2017. "Environmental Stewardship and the Production of Subjectivities: Indigenous, Scientific, and Economic Rationalities in Ancash, Peru." PhD diss., Michigan State University.

Kapchan, Deborah. 1996. *Gender on the Market: Moroccan Women and the Revoicing of Tradition.* Philadelphia: University of Pennsylvania Press.

Katzin, Margaret F. 1959. "Higglers of Jamaica." PhD diss., Northwestern University.

Kelly, Patty. 2008. *Lydia's Open Door: Inside Mexico's Most Modern Brothel.* Berkeley: University of California Press.

Keren, Donna J. 1987. "The Waiting Proletariat: A New Industrial Labor Force in Rural Maquilas." In *Perspectives in U.S. Marxist Anthropology,* edited by David Hakken and Hanna Lessinger, 140–65. Boulder, CO: Westview Press.

Kurz, Richard B. 1987. "Contributions of Women to Subsistence in Tribal Societies." In *Research in Economic Anthropology,* vol. 8, edited by Barry L. Isaac, 31–59. Greenwich, CT: JAI Press.

Larson, Brooke, and Olivia Harris, with Enrique Tanderer, eds. 1995. *Ethnicity, Markets, and Migration in the Andes: At the Crossroads of History and Anthropology.* Durham, NC: Duke University Press.

Latin American and Caribbean Ethnic Studies. 2008. 3 (3).

Latin American Working Group Newsletter. 1980.

Leacock, Eleanor. 1978. "Women's Status in Egalitarian Society." *Current Anthropology* 19 (2): 247–76.

———. 1979. "Class, Commodity, and Status of Women." In *Toward a Marxist Anthropology: Problems and Perspectives*, edited by Stanley Diamond, 185–99. New York: Mouton.

LeClair, Edward E., and Harold K. Schneider, eds. 1968. *Economic Anthropology*. New York: Holt, Rinehart and Winston.

Lee, Richard B. 1979. *The !Kung San: Men, Women, and Work in a Foraging Society*. New York: Cambridge University Press.

Lee, Richard B., and Irven DeVore, eds. 1968. *Man the Hunter*. Chicago: Aldine.

Leeds, Anthony. 1976. "Women in the Migratory Process: A Reductionist Outlook." *Anthropological Quarterly* 49 (1): 69–76.

Leons, Madeline Barbara, and Frances Rothstein, eds. 1979. *New Directions in Political Economy: An Approach from Anthropology*. Westport, CT: Greenwood Press.

Lewis, Eshe, dir. 2012. *Negro soy: Voces Negras del Pacífico Peruano*. Toronto: University of Toronto. DVD.

Lind, Amy, ed. 2010. *Development, Sexual Rights and Global Governance*. New York: Routledge.

Little, Walter E. 2004. *Mayas in the Marketplace: Tourism, Globalization, and Cultural Identity*. Austin: University of Texas Press.

Long, Norman. 1979. "Multiple Enterprise in the Central Highlands of Peru." In *Entrepreneurs in Cultural Context*, edited by S. M. Greenfield, A. Strickon, and R. T. Aubrey, 123–58. Albuquerque: University of New Mexico Press.

Long, Norman, and Bryan Roberts, eds. 1978. *Peasant Cooperation and Capitalist Expansion in Central Peru*. Austin: University of Texas Press.

———, eds. 1984. *Miners, Peasants and Entrepreneurs: Regional Development in the Central Highlands of Peru*. New York: Cambridge University Press.

Lugones, María. 2010a. "The Coloniality of Gender." In *Globalization and the Decolonial Option*, edited by Walter D. Mignolo and Arturo Escobar, 369–90. New York: Routledge.

———. 2010b. "Toward a Decolonial Feminism." *Hypatia* 25 (4): 742–59.

Lynch, Barbara. 1982. *The Vicos Experiment: A Study of the Impacts of the Cornell-Peru Project in a Highland Community*. AID Evaluation Special Study 7. Washington, DC: USAID.

Mackintosh, Maureen. 1981. "Gender and Economics: The Sexual Division of Labour and the Subordination of Women." In *Of Marriage and the Market*, edited by Kate Young, Carol Wolkowitz, and Roslyn McCullagh, 1–15. London: CSE Books.

Maclachlan, Morgan D., ed. 1987. "Household Economies and Their Transformations." *Monographs in Economic Anthropology*, no. 3. Lanham, MD: University Press of America.

Mahmood, Saba. 2008. "Feminism, Democracy, and Empire: Islam and the War of Terror." In *Women's Studies on the Edge,* edited by Joan Wallach Scott, 39–66. Durham, NC: Duke University Press.

Maldonado-Torres, Nelson. 2011. "Thinking Through the Decolonial Turn: Post-continental Interventions in Theory, Philosophy, and Critique—an Introduction." *Transmodernity* 1 (2).

Mallon, Florencia E. 1983. *The Defense of Community in Peru's Central Highlands.* Princeton, NJ: Princeton University Press.

———. 1987. "Patriarchy in the Transition to Capitalism: Central Peru, 1830–1950." *Feminist Studies* 13 (2): 379–407.

———. 1995. *Peasant and Nation: The Making of Postcolonial Mexico and Peru.* Berkeley: University of California Press.

Mangin, William P. 1954. "The Cultural Significance of the Fiesta Complex in an Indian Hacienda in Peru." PhD diss., Yale University. Ann Arbor, Michigan: University Microfilms.

———. 2011. "Early Years of the Vicos Project from the Perspective of a Sympathetic Participant Observer." In *Vicos and Beyond: A Half Century of Applying Anthropology in Peru,* edited by Tom Greaves, Ralph Bolton, and Florencia Zapata, 19–38. Lanham, MD: AltaMira Press.

Mannarelli, María Emma. 1992. "¿Todo tiempo pasado fue mejor?" *Chacarera* (Centro de la Mujer Flora Tristán, Lima) 9:8–11.

Manrique, Nelson. 1999. *La piel y la pluma: Escritos sobre literatura, etnicidad y racismo.* Lima: Sur.

Marx, Karl. 1967. *Capital,* vol. 1. New York: International Publishers.

Matos Mar, José. [1984] 2010. *Desborde popular y crisis del estado: Veinte años después.* Lima: Fondo Editorial del Congreso del Perú.

Meiksins, Peter. 1981. "Productive and Unproductive Labor and Marx's Theory of Class." *Review of Radical Political Economics* 13 (3): 32–42.

Meillassoux, Claude. 1972. From Reproduction to Production: A Marxist Approach to Economic Anthropology. *Economy and Society* 1 (1): 93–105.

———. 1975. *Femmes, greniers, et capitaux.* Paris: Maspero.

Meisch, Lynn A. 2002. *Andean Entrepreneurs: Otavalo Merchants and Musicians in the Global Arena.* Austin: University of Texas Press.

Mejía Chiang, César. 2011. *Cultura popular limeña y prensa chicha.* Lima: Grupo Editorial Mesa Redonda.

Mendoza, Rosa. 2003. *La dimensión de género en el desarrollo.* DVD presented at the International Workshop on Gender and Andean Culture, Marcará, Peru.

Mendoza, Zoila S. 2008. *Creating Our Own: Folklore, Performance, and Identity in Cuzco, Peru.* Durham, NC: Duke University Press.

Mercado, Hilda. 1978. *La madre trabajadora: El caso de las comerciantes ambulantes.* Series C, no. 2. Lima: Centro de Estudios de Población y Desarrollo.

Mignolo, Walter D. 2010. "Introduction: Coloniality of Power and De-colonial Thinking." In *Globalization and the Decolonial Option,* edited by Walter D. Mignolo and Arturo Escobar, 1–21. New York: Routledge.

Mignolo, Walter D., and Arturo Escobar, eds. 2010. *Globalization and the Decolonial Option.* New York: Routledge.

Mintz, Sidney W. 1971. "Men, Women, and Trade." *Comparative Studies in Society and History* 13:247–68.

Mitchell, Juliet. 1973. *Women's Estate.* New York: Vintage.

Mitchell, William. 2011. "Anthropological Hope and Social Reality: Cornell's Vicos Project Reexamined." In *Vicos and Beyond: A Half Century of Applying Anthropology in Peru,* edited by Tom Greaves, Ralph Bolton, and Florencia Zapata, 81–101. Lanham, MD: AltaMira Press.

Mohanty, Chandra Talpade. [1986] 2003. "Under Western Eyes: Feminist Scholarship and Colonial Discourses." In *Feminism without Borders: Decolonizing Theory, Practicing Solidarity,* edited by Chandra Talpade Mohanty, 17–42. Durham, NC: Duke University Press.

———. 2013. "Transnational Feminist Crossings: On Neoliberalism and Radical Critique." *Signs* 38 (4): 967–91.

Mohanty, Chandra Talpade, Ann Russo, and Lourdes Torres, eds. 1991. *Third World Women and the Politics of Feminism.* Bloomington: Indiana University Press.

Molyneux, Maxine. 1986. "Mobilization without Emancipation? Women's Interests, State, and Revolution." In *Transition and Development: Problems of Third World Socialism,* edited by Richard R. Fagen, Carmen Diana Deere, and José Luis Coraggio, 280–302. New York: Monthly Review Press.

Moser, Caroline O. N. 1978. "Informal Sector or Petty Commodity Production: Dualism or Dependence in Urban Development?" *World Development* 6 (9–10): 1041–64.

———. 1980. "Why the Poor Remain Poor: The Experience of Bogota Market Traders in the 1970s." *Journal of Interamerican Studies and World Affairs* 22 (3): 365–87.

Nash, June. 1986. "A Decade of Research on Women in Latin America." In *Women and Change in Latin America,* edited by June Nash and Helen Safa, 3–21. South Hadley, MA: Bergin and Garvey.

———. 2001. *Mayan Visions: The Quest for Autonomy in an Age of Globalization.* New York: Routledge.

Nash, June, and María Patricia Fernandez-Kelly, eds. 1983. *Women, Men, and the International Division of Labor.* Albany: SUNY Press.

Nash, June, and Helen I. Safa, eds. 1976. *Sex and Class in Latin America.* New York: Praeger.

———, eds. 1986. *Women and Change in Latin America.* South Hadley, MA: Bergin and Garvey.

Nelson, Nici. 1979. "How Women and Men Get By: The Sexual Division of Labour in the Informal Sector of a Nairobi Squatter Settlement." In *Casual Work and Poverty in Third World Cities*, edited by R. Bromley and C. Gerry, 283–302. New York: John Wiley and Sons.

Núñez del Prado, Oscar. 1973. *Kuyo Chico, Applied Anthropology in an Indian Community*. Chicago: University of Chicago Press.

Núñez del Prado Béjar, Daisy Irene. 1975a. "El poder de decisión de la mujer quechua andina." *América Indígena* 35 (3): 623–30.

———. 1975b. "El rol de la mujer campesina quechua." *América Indígena* 35 (2): 391–401.

Ødegaard, Cecilie Vindal. 2010. *Mobility, Markets and Indigenous Socialities: Contemporary Migration in the Peruvian Andes*. Burlington, VT: Ashgate.

Oliart, Patricia. 2008. "Indigenous Women's Organizations and the Political Discourses of Indigenous Rights and Gender Equity in Peru." *Latin American and Caribbean Ethnic Studies* 3 (3): 91–308.

Orlove, Benjamin S. 1993. "Putting Race in Its Place: Order in Colonial and Postcolonial Peruvian Geography." *Social Research* 69:301–36.

———. 1998. "Down to Earth: Race and Substance in the Andes." *Bulletin of Latin American Research* 17 (2): 207–22.

Ortiz, Sutti, ed. 1983. *Economic Anthropology: Topics and Theories*. Monographs in Economic Anthropology, no. 1. Lanham, MD: University Press of America.

Ortiz, Teresa. 2001. *Never Again a World without Us: Voices of Mayan Women in Chiapas, Mexico*. Washington, DC: Epica.

Osterling, Jorge P. N.d. "La reubicación de los vendedores ambulantes de Lima: ¿Un ejemplo de articulación política?" Unpublished manuscript.

Paredes, Julieta, and María Galindo. N.d. *Sexo, placer, y sexualidad*. La Paz, Bolivia: Mujeres Creando.

Peletz, Michael G. 1987. "Female Heirship and the Autonomy of Women in Negeri Sembilan, West Malaysia." In *Research in Economic Anthropology*, vol. 8, edited by Barry L. Isaac, 61–101. Greenwich, CT: JAI Press.

Petras, James, and A. Eugene Havens. 1979. "Peru: Economic Crises and Class Confrontation." *Monthly Review* 30 (9): 25–41.

Phillips, Lynne, and Sally Cole. 2013. *Contesting Publics: Feminism, Activism, Ethnography*. London: Pluto Press.

Plattner, Stuart, ed. 1985. *Markets and Marketing*. Monographs in Economic Anthropology, no. 4. Lanham, MD: University Press of America.

———. 1986. Review of "Research in Economic Anthropology: A Research Annual." *American Anthropologist* 88 (4): 962.

Poole, Deborah, ed. 1994. *Unruly Order: Violence, Power, and Cultural Identity in the High Provinces of Southern Peru*. Boulder, CO: Westview Press.

Portocarrero, Gonzalo. 2009. *Racismo y mestizaje y otros ensayos*. Lima: Fondo Editorial del Congreso del Perú.

Pribilsky, Jason. 2009. "Development and the 'Indian Problem' in the Cold War Andes: *Indigenismo*, Science, and Modernization in the Making of the Cornell-Peru Project at Vicos." *Diplomatic History* 33 (3): 405–26.

———. N.d. "Culture's Laboratory: Scientific Imagination, Applied Anthropology, and the Making of the Cornell-Peru Project at Vicos." Unpublished manuscript.

Price, Richard. 1961. *Watanaki: Courtship and Marriage Institutions in Vicos, Peru*. Columbia-Cornell-Harvard Summer Field Studies. Cambridge, MA: Harvard University. Mimeographed.

———. 1965. "Trial Marriage in the Andes." *Ethnology* 4:310–22.

Quijano, Aníbal. 1980. *Dominación cultura: Lo cholo y el conflicto cultural en el Perú*. Lima: Mosca azul editores.

———. 2000. "Coloniality of Power, Eurocentrism and Latin America." *Nepantla: Views from South* 1 (3): 533–80.

Radcliffe, Sarah A. 2015. *Dilemmas of Difference: Indigenous Women and the Limits of Postcolonial Development Policy*. Durham, NC: Duke University Press.

Rapp, Rayna. 1979. "Review Essay: Anthropology." *Signs: Journal of Women in Culture and Society* 4 (3): 497–513.

Reiter, Rayna Rapp, ed. 1975. *Toward an Anthropology of Women*. New York: Monthly Review Press.

———, ed. 1977. "The Search for Origins." *Critique of Anthropology* 3 (9–10): 5–24.

Remy, Dorothy. 1975. "Underdevelopment and the Experience of Women: A Nigerian Case Study." In *Toward an Anthropology of Women*, edited by Rayna Rapp Reiter, 358–371. New York: Monthly Review Press.

Ribeiro, Gustavo Lins, and Arturo Escobar, eds. 2006. *World Anthropologies: Disciplinary Transformations within Systems of Power*. New York: Berg.

Rivera Cusicanqui, Silvia. 2010. "The Notion of 'Rights' and the Paradoxes of Postcolonial Modernity: Indigenous Peoples and Women in Bolivia." *Qui Parle* 18 (2): 29–54.

———. 2012. "Ch'ixinakax Utxiwa: A Reflection on the Practices and Discourses of Decolonization." *South Atlantic Quarterly* 111 (1): 95–109.

Robertson, Claire. 1974. "Economic Woman in Africa: Profit-Making Techniques of Accra Market Women." *Journal of Modern African Studies* 12 (4): 657–64.

———. 1984. *Sharing the Same Bowl: A Socioeconomic History of Women and Class in Accra, Ghana*. Bloomington: Indiana University Press.

Rohrlich-Leavitt, Ruby, ed. 1975. *Women Cross-culturally: Change and Challenge*. New York: Mouton.

Rohrlich-Leavitt, Ruby, Barbara Sykes, and Elizabeth Weatherford. 1975. "Aboriginal Women: Male and Female Anthropological Perspectives." In

Toward an Anthropology of Women, edited by Rayna Rapp Reiter, 110–26. New York: Monthly Review Press.

Rosaldo, Michelle Zimbalist. 1980. "The Use and Abuse of Anthropology: Reflections on Feminism and Cross-cultural Understanding." *Signs* 5 (3): 389–417.

Rosaldo, Michelle Zimbalist, and Louise Lamphere, eds. 1974. *Woman, Culture, and Society.* Stanford, CA: Stanford University Press.

Rosaldo, Renato. 1989. *Culture and Truth: The Remaking of Social Analysis.* Boston: Beacon Press.

Ross, Eric B. 2008. "Peasants on Our Minds: Anthropology, the Cold War, and the Myth of Peasant Conservatism." In *Anthropology at the Dawn of the Cold War: The Influence of Foundations, McCarthyism, and the CIA,* edited by Dustin M. Wax, 108–32. London: Pluto Press.

Rothstein, Frances. 1979. "Two Different Worlds: Gender and Industrialization in Rural Mexico." In *New Directions in Political Economy: An Approach from Anthropology,* edited by Madeline Barbara Léons and Frances Rothstein, 249–66. Westport, CT: Greenwood Press.

Rousseau, Stéphanie. 2009. *Women's Citizenship in Peru: The Paradoxes of Neopopulism in Latin America.* New York: Palgrave Macmillan.

Rousseau, Stéphanie, and Anahi Morales Hudon. 2017. *Indigenous Women's Movements in Latin America: Gender and Ethnicity in Peru, Mexico, and Bolivia.* New York: Palgrave Macmillan.

Rovira, Guiomar. 1997. *Mujeres de maíz.* Mexico City: Ediciones Era.

Rubin, Gayle: 1975. "The Traffic in Women: Notes on the 'Political Economy' of Sex." In *Toward an Anthropology of Women,* edited by Rayna Rapp Reiter, 157–210. New York: Monthly Review Press.

Ruiz Bravo, Patricia, ed. 1996. *Detrás de la puerta: Hombres y mujeres en el Perú de hoy.* Lima: Pontificia Universidad Católica del Perú.

Sacks, Karen. 1974. "Engels Revisited: Women, the Organization of Production, and Private Property." In *Woman, Culture, and Society,* edited by Michelle Zimbalist Rosaldo and Louise Lamphere, 207–22. Stanford, CA: Stanford University Press.

———. 1982. *Sisters and Wives: The Past and Future of Sexual Equality.* Urbana: University of Illinois Press.

Safa, Helen I., and Eleanor Leacock, eds. 1981. "Development and the Sexual Division of Labor." Special issue, *Signs* 7 (2).

Sahlins, Marshall. 1972. *Stone Age Economics.* Chicago: Aldine.

Said, Edward W. [1978] 2003. *Orientalism.* New York: Vintage.

Sara-Lafosse, Violeta. 1983. *Campesinas y costureras: Dos formas de explotación del trabajo de la mujer.* Lima: Pontificia Universidad Católica del Perú.

———. 1984. *Comedores comunales: La mujer frente a la crisis.* Lima: Grupo de Trabajo, Servicios Urbanos y Mujeres de Bajos Ingresos.

Schildkrout, Enid. 1986. "Children as Entrepreneurs: Case Studies from Kano, Nigeria." In *Entrepreneurship and Social Change*, edited by S. M. Greenfield and A. Strickon, 195–223. Lanham, MD: University Press of America.

Schiwy, Freya. 2010. "Decolonization and the Question of Subjectivity: Gender, Race, and Binary Thinking." In *Globalization and the Decolonial Option*, edited by Walter D. Mignolo and Arturo Escobar. New York: Routledge.

Schmidt, Ella. 2016. "History as Narration: Resistance and Subaltern Subjectivity in Micaela Bastidas' 'Confession.'" *Feminist Review*, no. 113: 34–49.

Schmink, Marianne. 1977. "Dependent Development and the Division of Labor by Sex: Venezuela." *Latin American Perspectives* 12–13:153–79.

Schmitz, Hubert. 1982. "Growth Constraints on Small-Scale Manufacturing in Developing Countries: A Critical Review." *World Development* 10 (6): 429–50.

Schneider, Harold K. 1974. *Economic Man: The Anthropology of Economics.* New York: Free Press.

Scott, Allison MacEwen. 1979. "Who Are the Self-Employed?" In *Casual Work and Poverty in Third World Cities*, edited by Ray Bromley and Chris Gerry, 105–29. New York: John Wiley and Sons.

Scott, Joan W. 1986. "Gender: A Useful Category of Historical Analysis." *American Historical Review* 91 (5): 1053–75.

Seddon, David, ed. 1978. *Relations of Production: Marxist Approaches to Economic Anthropology.* London: Frank Cass.

Seligmann, Linda J. 1989. "To Be In Between: The Cholas as Market Women." *Comparative Studies in Society and History* 31 (4): 694–721.

———. 1993. "Between Worlds of Exchange: Ethnicity among Peruvian Market Women." *Cultural Anthropology* 8 (2): 187–213.

———, ed. 2001. *Women Traders in Cross-cultural Perspective: Mediating Identities, Marketing Wares.* Stanford, CA: Stanford University Press.

———. 2004. *Peruvian Street Lives: Culture, Power, and Economy among Market Women of Cuzco.* Urbana: University of Illinois Press.

Service, Elman R. 1966. *The Hunters.* Englewood Cliffs, NJ: Prentice-Hall.

Shapiro, Judith. 1983. "Anthropology and the Study of Gender." In *A Feminist Perspective in the Academy*, edited by Elizabeth Langland and Walter Gove, 110–29. Chicago: University of Chicago Press.

Sikkink, Lynn. 2001. "Traditional Medicines in the Marketplace: Identity and Ethnicity among Female Vendors." In *Women Traders in Cross-cultural Perspective: Mediating Identities, Marketing Wares*, edited by Linda J. Seligmann, 209–25. Stanford, CA: Stanford University Press.

Silverblatt, Irene. 1987. *Moon, Sun, and Witches: Gender Ideologies and Class in Inca and Colonial Peru.* Princeton, NJ: Princeton University Press.

Simon, Beatrice. 2009. "*Sacamefotos* and *Tejedoras*: Frontstage Performance and Backstage Meaning in a Peruvian Context." In *Cultural Tourism in*

Latin America: The Politics of Space and Imagery, edited by Michiel Baud and Annelou Ypeij, 117–40. Amsterdam: Brill.

Slocum, Sally. 1975. "Woman the Gatherer: Male Bias in Anthropology." In *Toward an Anthropology of Women,* edited by Rayna Rapp Reiter, 36–50. New York: Monthly Review Press.

Southall, Aidan, ed. 1973. *Urban Anthropology.* New York: Oxford University Press.

Spalding, Karen W. 1967. "Indian Rural Society in Colonial Peru: The Example of Huarochirí." PhD diss., University of California, Berkeley. Ann Arbor, Michigan: University Microfilms.

Speed, Shannon. 2008. *Rights in Rebellion: Indigenous Struggle and Human Rights in Chiapas.* Stanford, CA: Stanford University Press.

Speed, Shannon, R. Aída Hernández Castillo, and Lynn M. Stephen, eds. 2006. *Dissident Women: Gender and Cultural Politics in Chiapas.* Austin: University of Texas Press.

Starn, Orin. 1991. "Missing the Revolution: Anthropologists and the War in Peru." *Cultural Anthropology* 6 (1): 63–91.

Stavig, Lucía. 2017. "Who Are the 'Women' of Women's Rights? Feminism, Indigeneity, and Forced Sterilization in Peru." Master's thesis, Lethbridge University, Canada.

Stavig, Ward. 1995. "'Living in Offense of Our Lord': Indigenous Sexual Values and Marital Life in the Colonial Crucible." *Hispanic American Historical Review* 75 (4): 597–622.

Stein, William W. 1961. *Hualcán: Life in the Highlands of Peru.* Ithaca, NY: Cornell University Press.

———. 1974. *Countrymen and Townsmen in the Callejón de Huaylas, Perú: Two Views of Andean Social Structure.* Council on International Studies, no. 51. Buffalo: SUNY Buffalo.

———. 1975a. *Modernization and Inequality in Vicos, Peru: An Examination of the "Ignorance of Women."* Council on International Studies, no. 73. Buffalo: SUNY Buffalo.

———. 1975b. "The Peón Who Wouldn't: A Study of the Hacienda System at Vicos." *Papers in Anthropology* (Norman, OK) 16 (2): 78–135.

———. 1976. "The Struggle for Free Labor in Rural Peru." *Revolutionary World* (Amsterdam) 17–18:119–74.

———. 1978. "A Radical Perspective on Underdevelopment." In *Explorations in Philosophy and Society,* edited by Charles Cunneen, David H. Degrood, Dale Riepe, and William W. Stein, 127–90. Amsterdam: B. R. Gruner.

———. 1986. "The Practice of Economic Anthropology in the Peruvian Andes: Community, Household, and Relations of Production." *Revista Andina* 8:549–606.

————. 2000. *Vicisitudes del discurso del desarrollo en el Perú: Una etnografía de la modernidad del Proyecto de Vicos.* Lima: Casa SUR.

————. 2003. *Deconstructing Development Discourse in Peru: A Meta-Ethnography of the Modernity Project at Vicos.* Lanham, MD: University Press of America.

Stephen, Lynn. 2002. *Zapata Lives! Histories and Cultural Politics in Southern Mexico.* Berkeley: University of California Press.

Sternbach, Nancy Saporta, Marysa Navarro-Aranguren, Patricia Chuchryk, and Sonia E. Alvarez. 1992. "Feminisms in Latin America: From Bogotá to San Bernardo." *Signs* 17 (2): 393–434.

Strasma, John. 1976. "Agrarian Reform." In *Peruvian Nationalism: A Corporatist Revolution,* edited by David Chaplin, 291–326. New Brunswick, NJ: Transaction Books.

Strathern, Andrew. 1982. "The Division of Labor and Processes of Social Change in Mount Hagen." *American Ethnologist* 9 (2): 307–19.

Stronza, Amanda. 2008. "Through a New Mirror: Reflections on Tourism and Identity in the Amazon." *Human Organization* 67:244–57.

Suárez Navaz, Liliana, and R. Aída Hernández Castillo, eds. 2008. *Descolonizando el feminismo: Teorías y prácticas desde los márgenes.* Madrid: Ediciones Cátedra.

Sudarkasa, Niara. 1973. *Where Women Work: A Study of Yoruba Women in the Workplace and in the Home.* Anthropological Paper no. 53, Museum of Anthropology. Ann Arbor: University of Michigan.

Terray, Emmanuel. 1972. *Marxism and "Primitive" Societies.* New York: Monthly Review Press.

Theidon, Kimberly. 2004. *Entre prójimos: El conflict armado interno y la política de la reconciliación en el Perú.* Lima: Instituto de Estudios Peruanos.

Thorp, Rosemary, and Geoffrey Bertram. 1978. *Peru, 1890–1977: Growth and Policy in an Open Economy.* New York: Columbia University Press.

Thorp, Rosemary, and Maritza Paredes. 2010. *Ethnicity and the Persistence of Inequality: The Case of Peru.* New York: Palgrave Macmillan.

Trager, Lillian. 1976–77. "Market Women in the Urban Economy: The Role of Yoruba Intermediaries in a Medium-Sized City." In "Women in Urban Africa, Part 2," special issue, *African Urban Notes* 3:1–9.

van den Berghe, Pierre. 1994. *The Quest for the Other: Ethnic Tourism in San Cristóbal, Mexico.* Seattle: University of Washington Press.

van den Berghe, Pierre, and Jorge Flores Ochoa. 2000. "Tourism and Nativistic Ideology in Cuzco, Peru." *Annals of Tourism Research* 27 (1): 7–26.

Vargas, Virginia. 2008. *Feminismos en América Latina: Su aporte a la política a la democracia.* Lima: Programa Democracia y Transformación Global.

Vasques de Miranda, Glaura. 1977. "Women's Labor Force Participation in a Developing Society: The Case of Brazil." *Signs* 3 (1): 261–74.

Vázquez, Mario C. 1952. "La antropología cultural y nuestro problema del indio: Vicos, un caso de antropología aplicada." *Perú Indígena* 2:7–157.

———. 1961. *Hacienda, peonaje y servidumbre en los Andes peruanos.* Lima: Editorial Estudios Andinos.

———. 1965. *Educación rural en el Callejón de Huaylas: El caso de Vicos: Un punto de vista antropológico.* Lima: Editorial Estudios Andinos.

———. 1971. "The Interplay between Power and Wealth." In *Peasants, Power, and Applied Social Change: Vicos as a Model,* edited by Henry F. Dobyns, Paul L. Doughty, and Harold D. Lasswell, 65–88. Beverly Hills, CA: Sage.

Vich, Víctor, ed. 2005. *El Estado está de vuelta: Desigualdad, diversidad y democracia.* Lima: Instituto de Estudios Peruanos.

———. 2006. "La nación en venta: Bricheros, turísmo y mercado en el Perú contemporáneo." In *La Ruta Andina: Turísmo y desarrollo sostenible en Perú y Bolivia,* edited by Annelou Ypeij and Annelies Zoomers, 187–97. Quito, Ecuador: Ediciones Abya-Yala.

Vogel, Lise. 1973. "The Earthly Family." *Radical America* 7 (4–5): 9–50.

Vogt, Evon Z. 1994. *Fieldwork among the Maya: Reflections on the Harvard Chiapas Project.* Albuquerque: University of New Mexico Press.

Wallerstein, Immanuel. 1974. *The Modern World-System.* New York: Academic Press.

Wallman, Sandra, ed. 1979. *Social Anthropology of Work.* New York: Academic Press.

Weiner, Annette. 1976. *Women of Value, Men of Renown.* Austin: University of Texas Press.

Weinpahl, Jan. 1984. "Women's Roles in Livestock Production among the Turkana of Kenya." In *Research in Economic Anthropology,* vol. 6, edited by Barry L. Isaac, 193–215. Greenwich, CT: JAI Press.

Weismantel, Mary. 1995. "Masculine Women/White Indians: Andean Cholas." Paper presented at the annual meeting of the American Anthropological Association, Washington, DC, November.

———. 2001. *Cholas and Pishtacos: Stories of Race and Sex in the Andes.* Chicago: University of Chicago Press.

Wellesley Editorial Committee. 1977. *Women and National Development: The Complexities of Change.* Chicago: University of Chicago Press.

Wiegman, Robyn. 2008. "Feminism, Institutionalism, and the Idiom of Failure." In *Women's Studies on the Edge,* edited by Joan Wallach Scott, 39–66. Durham, NC: Duke University Press.

———. 2012. *Object Lessons.* Durham, NC: Duke University Press.

Wilson, Tamar Diana, and Annelou Ypeij. 2012. "Introduction: Tourism, Gender, and Ethnicity." *Latin American Perspectives* 39 (6): 5–16.

Wolf, Margery. 1985. *Revolution Postponed: Women in Contemporary China.* Stanford, CA: Stanford University Press.

————. 1992. *A Thrice-Told Tale: Feminism, Postmodernism, and Ethnographic Responsibility.* Stanford, CA: Stanford University Press.

World Development. 1978. "The Urban Informal Sector." Special issue, 6 (9–10).

Young, Kate, Carol Wolkowitz, and Roslyn McCullagh, eds. 1981. *Of Marriage and the Market: Women's Subordination in International Perspective.* London: CSE Books.

Ypeij, Annelou. 2006. *Produciendo contra la pobreza: La microempresa vista desde el genero.* Lima: Instituto de Estudios Peruanos.

Zapata, Florencia. 2011. "Remembering Vicos: Local Memories and Voices." In *Vicos and Beyond: A Half Century of Applying Anthropology in Peru,* edited by Tom Greaves, Ralph Bolton, and Florencia Zapata, 309–43. Lanham, MD: AltaMira Press.

Zimbalist, Andrew, ed. 1979. *Case Studies on the Labor Process.* New York: Monthly Review Press.

Zorn, Elayne. 2004. *Weaving a Future: Tourism, Cloth, and Culture on an Andean Island.* Iowa City: University of Iowa Press.

Index

Page numbers in italics denote photographs.

beliefs resulting from, 206; and tourism, 159; and trial marriage/premarital sex, criminalization of, 206. *See also* hacienda system; male bias; Western bias

coloniality of power, shift to, 47

Comaroff, John and Jean, 184

Congress on Research on Women in the Andean Region (1982), 1–2, 90–91, 200–201

Continental Summit of Indigenous Women (2009), 215–16

Cornell-Peru Project (CPP): overview, 31, 36, 55–57; and contemporary tourism project, 189–90; critics of, 41–42, 226n4, 227n9; literature about, silence on gender in, 38–41, 61, 226–27nn4–7; and male bias in development endeavors, 42–43, 61–62, 82; "PCP" annotation on field-workers' names, 228n3; and politics of care, 53; research, publication, and reception of Babb critique, 35, 36–37, 42–44, 48–49, 52–54, 203, 226nn2–3, 227n14; time period of, 36; unpublished fieldnotes as source, 56, 228nn1–3

—GENDER DISPARITIES IN: overview, 49, 52–53, 83–85; agricultural modernization and, 52, 62–64, 71, 228n6, 229n11; authority of father in the family, 82; cash economy and, 62–63, 71–72, 229nn12,14; children's socialization and, 72–75; community leadership development, 66–67, 81, 82; contemporary awareness within project, of, 42; education and, 67–69, 72, 74–75, 83, 229n16; elimination of women's paid and unpaid positions, 63, 69–70, 71; gleaning rights, loss of, 63–64; inter-relatedness of factors in, 68–69; and men as main targets of change, 36, 46, 52, 61–70; production/reproduction frame-work and, 49, 70–79, 229nn11–14,16–17; public vs. private spheres and, 64, 69–70, 229n10; sexuality and, 78–79; and skills, introduction of new, 64–66, 71, 229nn8–9

—HACIENDA LIFE AND: family solidarity and, 80–83; inequalities kept in check among peasants, 80–81; leases and work exchange requirements, 57, 60, 72; peons (*colonos*), registered, 57, 63; permanent expropria-tion of, 57; pilferage, 64, 80; resistance to, 79–83; rights/privileges of, 63–64, 80; whipping of serfs, 64, 228n7; women and children in fields of, 57, 63, 64; women's institutionalized positions in, 63

—HACIENDA LIFE, GENDER COMPLEMENTA-RITY AND: age and, 58–59; bonds of the family and, 60–61; and cattle, care for, 60, 70; decision-making and, 59–60, 62; economic power of women and, 59, 60, 72; everyday and specialized activities of, 57–58; flexibility of women's roles, 58, 228n4; male bias and perception of, 82; marriage and, 59–60; public vs. private sphere and, 58, 60–61, 70; reciprocal labor (work parties) and, 59, 69; rigidity of, 58, 69; sexuality and, 61, 75–78; unattached adults, difficulties of, 58–59, 228n5; Vicosino voices on, 39–40; women's subordinate role in public, 69

cosmovision, indigenous Andean: feminist activism to support, 163; and gender complementarity, 11–12, 21, 51, 207; and inclusion of "other-than-human" in new ways of knowing, 48, 227n13; principle of dualisms in, 11–12

CPP. *See* Cornell-Peru Project (CPP)

cultural anthropology, postmodern turn of, 157–58

cultural bias, and misreading of gender com-plementarity, 53, 225–26n1

cultural capital, 155, 186, 199; definition of, 184

cultural diversity, 162–63

cultural politics: author's turn to, 156–57; of indigeneity, 185–86, 209, 237n10; market women and, 136–39, 141; Nicaragua and, 103; tourism and, 157–58

cultural relativism, 53

cultural tourism, definition of, 183, 193. *See also* tourism—gender, indigenous identity, and cultural tourism

Cuzco, Peru, tourism in, 187, 198

Dagnino, Evelina, 103

Dalla Costa, Mariarosa, 79

decolonial feminisms: overview, 10–11; ambivalence toward, indigenous activists and, 218–19; and appropriation of ideas from the South, 30; and "arrogant certi-tude," questioning of, 153; attribution of sources and, 30; Congress on Research on Women in the Andean Region as prefig-uring, 200–201; diverse sources of new knowledge of, 47–48; and earlier feminist debates, 6; feminist gatherings in support of, 163–64, 201; and gender as category of analysis, 9, 153, 154; and gender

decolonial feminisms *(continued)*
complementarity, 11–12, 27, 203–4,
207–8, 209, 224n12; and need for
writings from Andean women, 208–9;
and production/reproduction framework,
207–8; as term, 224n7; and tourism, 159;
and women as seen as "more Indian," 209,
237n10; working with indigenous women
activists, 216–17; World March of Women
and, 160–61, 208
decolonial feminist anthropology: overview,
217, 222; collaborative research and, 205–
6, 217, 219–21, 236n6; and internal disagreements among feminists within global
North and within global South, 202–3,
208–9; literature review, 10–11, 26–28,
204–5, 224n11, 224–25nn11–13; as
questioning received wisdom, 202;
questions to address in, 25–26, 28–29
decolonial theory: overview, 9; emphasis on
difference and coloniality of power, 47.
See also decolonial feminisms; decolonial
turn
decolonial turn, 6, 9–12; definition of, 9–10;
vigor of, 12
Deere, Carmen Diana, 23, 83–84, 200,
231n3, 233n3
de Janvry, Alain, 231n3
de la Cadena, Marisol: American Anthropological Association conference session
addressing work of, 202, 230n7, 236n1;
and José María Arguedas, 10; Maruja
Barrig on, 47; critique of gender complementarity, 98–99; on decolonizing effort,
209; on *indigenismo*, 20, 28; on indigenous cosmopolitics, 48, 227n13; on
women as *más indias* (more Indian), 23,
95, 185, 188–89, 190–91, 197, 209, 230n7,
237n10
de la Puente, Roberto, 211
dependent capitalism: gender division of
labor and integration into, 22–23, 111–12,
130–32; inequalities of integration into,
22–23, 130–31; informal sector in, 109–
10, 119
Derrida, Jacques, 38
desigualdad. See inequality *(desigualdad)*
de Soto, Hernando, 230n6
DeWind, Adrian, 229n9
Diamond, Stanley, 170
discrimination: Afro-Peruvians and, 16, 210,
237n11; and ethnic dress, *19*, 20, 210, 212,
214; multiple forms of, faced by Andean

women, 23–24, 202. *See also* indigenous
identity; race and racism
Dobyns, Henry, 42, 64–65
domestic service: as extension of housework,
124–25; as part of informal sector, 110;
and political consciousness, 113–14,
120–21
domestic violence: as current problem, 50;
decolonial feminism and, 12; increases in,
as difficult to measure, 51–52; as posing a
challenge to gender complementarity, 22,
24, 27, 51. *See also* sexual violence
Domínguez, Edmé, 164
Doughty, Paul, 62, 63–64, 73, 74–75,
226–27n7
dress. *See* ethnic dress

economic anthropology: overview, 32;
culturalist perspective, 169; exchange-
distribution emphasis in, 169–70;
formalist-substantivist debate, 168,
174–75; Marxist debates, 170–71, 175;
units of analysis of, 166, 234n2
—AND GENDER AS CATEGORY OF ANALYSIS:
overview, 165–67, 181–82; and center vs.
periphery of discipline, 166, 169–70, 171,
181–82, 234n3, 235–36n15; developments
in research toward, 172–75, 181–82; dis-
missal of/resistance to, 1, 146–48, 151,
167–72; and gender as social construct,
165–66; informal sector and, 168, 174,
175–81, 235nn9–13; research, publication,
and reception of Babb's works, 145–48;
and women's work as "non-economic," 168
economy. *See* dependent capitalism; economic anthropology; formal economy;
informal sector; neoliberalism
Ecuador: Citizen Revolution, 204; cultural
identity and, 138, 204; gender complementarity and, 204; and "return of the
Indian," 20
education: gender disparities of Cornell-Peru
Project and, 67–69, 72, 74–75, 83,
229n16; of girls, 50, 67–68, 83, 190. *See
also* language use
Elmendorf, Mary Lindsay, 229n17
emotional work, recognition of, 93–94
Engels, Frederick, 49, 70, 94, 124, 170
Escobar, Arturo, 9, 42, 103, 224–25n13
Espinosa Miñoso, Yuderkys, 27, 30
ethnic dress: discrimination and, *19*, 20, 210,
212, 214; as form of cultural resistance,
46–47, 82, 102, 138; and tourism, *149*,